STUDIES IN BIBLICAL
AND JEWISH FOLKLORE

THIS MONOGRAPH IS ISSUED AS NO. 13 IN THE INDIANA UNIVERSITY FOLKLORE SERIES AND AS VOL. 51 IN THE MEMOIR SERIES OF THE AMERICAN FOLKLORE SOCIETY.

EDITED BY

Raphael Patai

Francis Lee Utley

Dov Noy

STUDIES IN BIBLICAL
AND JEWISH FOLKLORE

INDIANA UNIVERSITY PRESS · BLOOMINGTON

Indiana University Folklore Series Number 13
Indiana University, Bloomington, Indiana

Publication Committee

E D I T O R : Richard M. Dorson
Assistant Editor: W. Edson Richmond
Assistant Editor: Warren E. Roberts
Consulting Editor: John W. Ashton

The Indiana University Folklore Series was founded in 1939 for the publication of occasional papers and monographs by members of the faculty.

C O N T E N T S

Preface

The editors are proud to make available this rich variety of folk literature and custom from West and East, modernity and antiquity, and they are also humble before the magnitude and complexity of the task. The original gathering of articles was begun in 1954 by Dov Noy (Neumann) while he was teaching and studying at Indiana University. When the initial plan for financing publication broke down, and Dr. Noy returned to Israel, he placed the collection in the hands of Professor Raphael Patai. Professor Patai subsequently arranged for new financing and obtained several additional articles included in this volume. In 1957 Professor Francis Lee Utley was asked to help with the final editing. In some cases this involved rewriting the original with a view to making it more concise and idiomatic; and, in the matter of documentation, an attempt was made to bring the notes and references into conformity with American practice. No excessively precise "consistency" has been sought, but in a work of such diversified scholarly traditions there were inevitably a few divergences. The final stages of editing and financial arrangement were carried out by Thomas Sebeok and Richard Dorson from their vantage point in Bloomington.

For the generous financial assistance that made possible the publication of this monograph the editors wish to express their very deep gratitude to the Max Atran and Lucius N. Littauer foundations and to the Graduate School of Indiana University.

1 | Introduction

The Significance
of Near Eastern
Folklore

STITH THOMPSON   Indiana University

by Stith Thompson

FOR THE FOLK traditions of Orient and Occident the Near East has always been of the highest importance, but except as found in the ancient literary monuments the folklore of this region has never been adequately explored. A whole generation of scholars found the springs of European traditional story in India, with the result that the tales and fables of India and Europe were assiduously collected and studied. But if many identities in plot thus showed themselves in these areas so remote from each other, how were they to be explained? Speculations as to routes of travel from East to West or the reverse were often made with too little regard for the history, the geography, or the folk life of the intervening regions.

For the purely literary monuments the transmission from East to West is clear enough. We can follow such works as the *Panchatantra* through versions with definite dates and places as it passes into Persian, Arabic, Syrian, Hebrew, and Greek to Europe and Mediaeval Latin literary tradition. The *Seven Sages*, the *Jatakas*, and various parts of the *Ocean of Story*—all such classical Indic works appear eventually in the literature of mediaeval Europe, often through the intermediation of learned Jews.

These literary streams that have flowed through the Near East have been charted and their courses ascertained with reasonable certainty. But what of the tales and traditions of everyday folk in Iran, in Mesopotamia, in Turkey, in Syria, and in Palestine? Until our own generation the folklore collections from these lands have been sparse indeed. Now some interest

5

has been aroused and some solid accomplishment achieved, particularly in Turkey, where Professors Eberhard and Boratav have issued their monumental study of Turkish tale types, *Typen Türkischer Märchen* (Wiesbaden, 1953). Some new Persian, Arab, and Iraqi collections are now available, but they are certainly not representative enough of lands where tale-telling continues as one of the great activities of the bazaars.

Of all the lands of the Near East the oral folklore of Palestine is perhaps the least known. There are a few old collections illustrative of the traditions of the nineteenth-century population, principally Syrian and Arabic, but little that suggests the new Jewish state. We are in great ignorance about how much, if any, of the oral tradition of the days of Solomon or the Maccabees survived on Palestinian soil over the past two or three thousand years.

Certainly Jewish folklore cannot be equated with Palestinian. Long before the age of Titus the Jews were carrying their way of life and their sacred and secular traditions to remote parts of the Mediterranean world and setting up through the centuries a commerce not only of merchandise but also of ideas, customs, learning, and folklore. Were the traditions of the Jews of Mediaeval Spain essentially Jewish or essentially Spanish? Or an indistinguishable mixture? If we knew enough about the secular folklore of Jewish groups in Europe and America, would we find a common element setting it off from the lore current among their neighbors? And if so, would this seem to represent something that goes back to ancient Israel?

To attempt an exact answer to these questions with present information would be rash. But as there takes place a vast "ingathering" of Jews—a reversed Diaspora—in modern Israel, an unprecedented opportunity presents itself to the student of Jewish folklore. Here is a great laboratory where he can penetrate the memories of Jews from many parts of the world and see how much they share in common and how much they have left behind them in the long centuries of separation.

Such a study of the folklore of modern Israel demands an extraordinary acquaintance with folk tradition all over the world, for in any enlightened view the multiplicity of origins (whether in ancient Palestine, the Near East, or Europe, whether Polish, German, Spanish, or some other) must be easily recognized. It is of interest in this connection that the Warburg Foundation in London is sponsoring a research program along these lines.

Not all folklore studies in the Near East present so baffling a problem as those having to do with Palestine, but the whole area has had so complicated a history—now with rapid conquests and change and again with a thousand years of stagnation—that a clear reading of the record is as difficult as the deciphering of an ancient palimpsest manuscript. The study of such a folklore is therefore not for the timid, but only for those willing to give labor and devotion to a task calling for erudition, energy, tact, and judgment. May our generation bring this about.

Jewish Folklore and

Jewish Tradition

R A P H A E L P A T A I

Theodor Herzl Institute, New York City

by Raphael Patai

i

FIFTEEN YEARS ago in a programmatic paper, "Problems and Tasks of Jewish Folklore and Ethnology,"[1] I expressed the hope that the study of the folklore of present-day Jewish communities would receive the highest priority within the general field of Jewish learning. The years which have elapsed since then have brought no realization of this hope. While the great ethnic upheavals in the life of the post-Nazi remnant of the Jewish people hastened the oblivion of the living folklore of the Jewish communities, the study of Jewish folklore progressed at a snail's pace. In Israel itself, after five years of struggling for existence in the face of overwhelming odds, the Palestine (later: Israel) Institute of Folklore and Ethnology and its journal *Edoth* became war casualties. Thus the few students of folklore in the new state remained without the stimulus of a scientific forum. Outside Israel, no periodical publication devoted to Jewish folklore has existed since 1925, when Max Grunwald's *Jahrbuch für jüdische Volkskunde* was suspended. In regional and general folklore journals, Jewish folklore has figured very meagerly.

Only two articles dealing with Jewish folklore have appeared in the *Journal of American Folklore* since the publishing of "Problems and Tasks of Jewish Folklore and Ethnology."[2] "Folklore Research in North America" (the "Report of the Committee on Research in Folklore in North America in 1945 and 1946")[3] contained individual reports on studies in American regional, German-American, Spanish-American, Afro-

American, and American-Indian folklore; but there was no report on Jewish folklore, in spite of the fact that a great deal of the activity of the Yiddish Scientific Institute (Yivo) was devoted to these studies. With whomever the fault lies— and it seems that lack of interest on the part of Jewish folklorists is to a great extent responsible—the facts are that Jewish folklore has not figured so prominently in American folklore research as have several other bodies of folklore and that the study of American Jewish folklore has not been so integral a part of American folklore research as the study of the folklore of other nationalities in this country.

ii

The great ethnic upheavals referred to above, including the establishment of the state of Israel and the large-scale "ingathering of the exiles," have brought about in the objective circumstances of the Jewish people a number of significant changes which are not only limiting but also contributing factors in the study of Jewish folklore. These changed circumstances, coupled with the recent advances in the world-wide effort of systematic folkloristic study, call for a re-examination and restatement of the scope of Jewish folklore. Let us begin with a glance at the reasons given in the *Standard Dictionary of Folklore, Mythology, and Legend*[4] for excluding Jewish folklore from its series of excellent survey articles which outline the folklore of several important culture groups in the world.[5] As stated in Theodore Gaster's article on Semitic folklore, "modern Semitic folklore, including especially that of the Arabs and Jews, has been excluded, on the grounds that much of it is due to direct borrowings from other peoples and can therefore not be described as distinctive."[6]

This statement raises two immediate questions concerning Jewish folklore. First, is it justifiable to include the folklore of the Jews under "modern Semitic folklore"? The only legitimate definition of "Semitic folklore" is the one correctly given in Dr. Gaster's article: "the folklores of the peoples who spoke (or speak) Semitic languages." While this definition enables us to include under "modern Semitic folklore" the folklore of those Jewish communities whose colloquial speech belongs to the Semitic language family (such as the Jews of the Arab lands, of Kurdistan, and of Ethiopia), it excludes the folklore of the great majority of the Jews whose speech has until very recently been Yiddish, that is Judaeo-German, and whose folklore by the same token would have to be included in Germanic folklore. The same linguistic classification would commit us to include the folklore of the Persian, Afghan, and Bokharan Jews under Iranian, rather than under Semitic, folklore. It thus becomes evident that contemporary Jewish folklore as a whole cannot be regarded as a subdivision of "modern Semitic folklore."

The second question is whether it was justifiable to omit from the *Dictionary* a survey article on Jewish folklore "on the grounds that so much of it is due to direct borrowings from other peoples and can therefore not be described as distinctive."

No one familiar with Jewish folklore would deny that "much of it is due to direct borrowings from other peoples." This is true, however, of the folklore of practically every people, even of those who have lived until recently in relative isolation. A comparative study of the total folklore inventory of a culture (if such were available) would inevitably lead to the conclusion that only a very small part of it is, beyond any doubt, not "due to direct borrowings." Incidentally, the instrumentality of the Jews in these processes of borrowing, and especially in the transmission of folklore from the East to the West, is being more and more clearly recognized.

It would seem, moreover, that the distinctiveness of a body of folklore is not contingent upon the amount of borrowing characterizing it. Consequently, it does not follow that a folklore much of which "is due to direct borrowing from other peoples"

can on this count "not be described as distinctive." The amount
of borrowing is usually determined with the help of the prevalent methods of folklore research by a study of motifs. But in
addition to the more easily discernible, definable, and classifi-
able motifs contained in a piece of narrative folklore, the latter
is also characterized by such traits as mood, flavor, spirit, and
atmosphere. These traits may account for its distinctiveness
even though its motifs and structure (i.e., its concrete content)
may be borrowed. As Bascom has recently emphasized, "the
problem of stylistic features of a body of folklore is regarded as
of primary importance . . . as well as the analysis of tales in terms
of plot, incident, conflict, climax, motivation, and character development."[7] In fact, much of the specifically Jewish character
of Jewish folklore can be found precisely in these elements to
which the usual classificatory techniques of motif analysis are
not applicable.

iii

In addition to vitiating the argument on which the exclusion
of modern Jewish folklore from the *Dictionary* was based, the
above considerations demonstrate something definite about
Jewish folklore itself. We recognize that the prevalent classification of folklore into subdivisions characterized by a common
language and by residence in contiguous geographical territo-
ries is not applicable to the folklore of the Jews. In this respect,
even the folklore of the Gipsies can be regarded as closer typo-
logically to the folklore of other nations than to Jewish folklore.
When we speak of Gipsy folklore, the reference is to a folklore
characterized by many local variants. Gipsies reflect the influence of several countries and adhere to different religions (there
are Catholic and Protestant as well as Moslem Gipsies), but
they utilize everywhere the same linguistic medium: the common and ancient Gipsy language rooted in Sanskrit and closer
to Hindustani than to any other living tongue.[8] In contrast, the

unifying characteristic of Jewish folklore is not the language it utilizes but the common religious tradition underlying it.

Another people whose culture is occasionally pointed out as manifesting certain analogies to the Jews are the Armenians. Like the Jews, the Armenians live in many different countries and cherish everywhere the traditions of their common origin and history. But the Armenians, unlike the Jews, have preserved until very recently their Armenian language. Again, unlike the Jews, the Armenians are split into two mutually intolerant religions, one represented by the Armenian Orthodox Church and the other by the Armenian Catholic Church.

iv

Since Jewish folklore is obviously the folklore of the Jews, the temporal and spatial extent of its subject matter must be co-extensive with the duration of Jewish history and the spatial dispersion of the Jewish people. This much is evident. But, in addition, the Jews were throughout their long history a literate people who developed at an early date the habit of committing to writing whatever they regarded as important in their oral traditions. As a result, the history of Jewish folklore is characterized, in each epoch, by a continuous process of lifting out considerable bodies of folklore from the stream of oral tradition and freezing them in written form. This process started with the earliest documents incorporated in the Hebrew Bible, in which the narrative element is fascinating both in the uniqueness of its style and spirit and in the incomparable interest of its motifs and content. The process continued through the early post-Biblical literature of the Apocrypha, in which, incidentally, the polyglot character of Jewish folklore—initially indicated in some of the late books of the Biblical canon itself—is first fully manifested; then branched off into the Greek writings of the Jewish Hellenists, of whom Philo of Alexandria and Josephus Flavius are the classical exponents; and culminated—

still in antiquity—in the "great sea" of Talmudic literature which sprang up in Palestine and then flourished simultaneously there and in Babylonia.

With the spatial spread of the Diaspora from ancient times onward, the originally unified Jewish tradition branched out into more and more independent branches. Hebrew and Aramaic remained the principal languages of literary expression, but Arabic, Persian, Ladino, and Yiddish soon appeared. Everywhere, however, the same process continued: oral traditions found their way into writings which, irrespective of their main intent, became repositories of the folklore of their age without detracting from the stream of oral, living, folk tradition, which continued undiminished century after century. The history of Jewish folklore therefore illustrates in detail B. A. Botkin's generalization that "The transference of oral tradition to writing and print does not destroy its validity as folklore but rather, while freezing or fixing its form, helps to keep it alive and to define it among those to whom it is not native or fundamental.[9]

Consider as an example the rich harvest of books of customs, or, better, one of their subvarieties, the collections of magical or religio-magical prescriptions used in obtaining benefits and preventing or curing ills. The earliest example of these within Hebrew tradition is contained in the book of Genesis (in the story of Rachel and the mandrakes). Talmudic literature contains many such examples, but even more are found in Jewish literature of the Middle Ages and in later periods down to the 19th century.

In spite of the many outside influences that it absorbed and the changes that it underwent in many localities and in the course of many centuries, the specifically Jewish component in the folk life of the Jews everywhere is ultimately based on Talmudic or Biblical origins. Single customs cannot in every instance be traced back to the Talmud or the Bible, but in Biblical, and even more so in Talmudic times, a tendency developed among the Jewish people to conduct their entire lives, from the cradle to the grave, and including all daily and periodic activities, in conformity with explicit or implict rules (these latter contained either in the Writ or in oral tradition and known as *Halakha*, a term covering the normative part of all Jewish tradition). This religious oral tradition became the main molding force of Jewish life, with all its customs and usages.

With the passage of centuries in post-Talmudic times the reliance on rules not only continued but became more pronounced, creating the need for repeated recapitulations of the Law in a series of codes once every few generations.[10] Thus a considerable part of Jewish literature in the Middle Ages consisted of collections of rules of conduct, of *do's* and *don't's*, which, although extending into all walks of life, had an essentially religious character and derived their binding force from the Bible and the Talmud as the ultimate sources of authority. The number of these codes increased, and the latest one, the *Shulḥan 'Arukh*, was provided with commentaries. Also, handy compendia, based on the *Shulḥan 'Arukh* and giving its essential rulings in brief form, were prepared. Thus the habit of looking for guidance in a handbook became widespread, and supplemental handbooks containing collections of customs (*minhagim*) and other handbooks containing remedies and prescriptions were compiled both in Europe and in the Orient, first in handwriting, then in print. So many of these collections were prepared that one would expect much or all of the oral traditions to have been absorbed into the written word; but instead the exact opposite seems to have been true. In fact, the more that is committed to writing in any age and place, the richer the oral tradition that continues to flow thereafter. Therefore, much as the student of Jewish folklore may be enthralled by the wealth of manuscript and printed collections of customs, remedies, and prescriptions dating from past centuries, he finds himself in a world of even greater unexplored riches when he turns to the living lore of any Jewish community still anchored in its traditions.

The quasi-religious character of these books of customs and remedies is attested to by the fact that they were compiled, copied, printed, and used by Jews whose entire life was dominated by religious tradition as embodied in the first place in the religious codes. Scrupulous fulfillment of all the most minute rules of the *Shulḥan 'Arukh* went hand in hand with unquestioning belief in the binding force of local custom and in the efficacy of the prescriptions collected in books of remedies. Law and lore were followed together for centuries, until, with the onset of the Enlightenment, they were both questioned and in many places, both discarded.

In certain specific details occasional contradictions can be discovered between the local tradition and, especially, the instructions contained in the remedy books, on the one hand, and the hard and fast rulings of the officially sanctioned codes of conduct, on the other. In most cases these contradictions went unnoticed, but whether noticed or not, the old Talmudic observation that custom is stronger than law was confirmed again and again.

v

While living Jewish custom and its repositories are thus the outgrowth of the *Halakha*, Jewish tales, legends, fables, parables, and other types of folk literature go back to the narrative parts of the Bible and to the second main component of Talmudic literature, the so called *Agada*, which also includes ethical teachings. In one of the varieties of the Talmudic *Agada* a superstructure of legends and tales was built upon the concise Biblical foundations. In post-Talmudic times, the development of Jewish legend and tale shows a close parallel to that of Jewish custom and usage. On the one hand, the legend material was excerpted from the Talmud and the Midrashim and published in separate volumes, such as the *'Ein Ya'qov* (c. 11th century) and the *Yalqut Shim'oni* (13th century). On the other hand, an independent literature grew up consisting of collections of tales and legends which either follow the narrative portions of the Bible (e.g., the *Sepher Hayashar* in the 12th century) or deal with non-Biblical themes and show traces of outside influences to varying degrees. An important variety in this latter category is the collections of fables (e.g. the *Mishle Shu'alim*, or Fox Fables, of Berekhya ben Natronai Hanaqdan in the 13th century) which continue a trend found in the Talmud and even earlier in the Bible itself (e.g., Yotham's fable, Judges 9:8-15).

Like Jewish folk custom, the Jewish folktale also retained its close affiliation with Jewish religion, both being regarded as manifestations of Jewish tradition, which in its totality has always remained inseparable from Jewish religion and its cornerstone, the Five Books of Moses. Again, as in the case of Jewish folk custom, however much of this originally unwritten literature was being put to writing, more of it remained to be orally transmitted down to the time when the Enlightenment began to make its inroads upon Jewish traditional life in Europe. In the Orient, both custom and oral literature remained intact for several additional generations, until in our day the "ingathering" of several Oriental Jewish Diasporas in Israel initiated the process of their assimilation to the secular, Western culture of the modern Jewish state, with its inevitable concomitant—the disappearance of folk traditions.

vi

Legends, myths, tales, and other types of unwritten literature function as sanctions of custom and belief. This general thesis is fully borne out by an examination of Jewish folklore. Indeed, the close interlacing of custom and legend, and their mutual interdependence, are characteristics of Jewish folklore that are found in all Jewish literary sources from the most ancient times down to the present day. The story of Jacob's fight with the angel at the ford of Jabbok (Gen. 32) explains the origin of the name Israel and of the prohibition of eating the sinew of the thigh vein. The story of the levity committed by the men and women in the Temple of Jerusalem (Talmudic sources) explains the custom of separating the sexes during services.[11] The legend of the medieval martyr Rabbi Amnon explains the origin and the significance of the moving prayer *Un'tane Toqef*, recited on the New Year and on the Day of Atonement. The innumerable stories about the piety, the wisdom, and the miracles of Hassidic rabbis from the 18th century on, explain and motivate the veneration of their followers. And the equally colorful tales told to this day by Oriental Jews about their own miracle-working rabbis (*hakhams or moris*) motivate and sanction the custom of visiting the shrines of these holy men and of performing certain rites at their tombs.

As long as the customs and beliefs were part of the reality of the life of Jewish communities in the West or in the East, the survival of legends and tales was assured, for by providing a sanction for customs and beliefs, the legends and tales, too, constituted an integral part of the living religious culture of each community. Once the beliefs crumble under the influences of a modern, Western, secular atmosphere, and once the customs are no longer practiced for the same reason, or cannot be practiced because of the migration of the community into a new country (e.g., from Morocco, Yemen, or Iraq to Israel), the unwritten literature, having lost its function, is bound to be forgotten soon after.

vii

Several conclusions can be drawn from the foregoing remarks on folk custom and folk literature as the two main categories of Jewish folklore.

First, it seems evident that in the study of Jewish folklore it is possible to an even lesser degree than in other folklores to deal separately with folk custom on the one hand and with folk literature on the other. As an anthropologist, one agrees with the anthropological defintion of folklore as "dependent on oral transmission" and thus including "myths, legends, tales, proverbs, riddles, the texts of ballads and other songs, and other forms of lesser importance, but not folk art, folk dance, folk music, folk costume, folk medicine, folk custom or folk belief."[12] But as a student of Jewish culture one knows that Jewish legends and tales can be studied only in the context of Jewish folk custom. If the scholarly consensus is that folk custom is not a legitimate object of study for the folklorist because it belongs to the realm of anthropology, then the Jewish folklorist must be an anthropologist as well in order to be able to study fully the inseparable oral and behavioral components of Jewish tradition.

Second, it has been found that modern Jewish folklore everywhere, as expressed in this two-in-one manifestation of the oral and the behavioral, is merely the surface appearance of an ore that goes deep down into the bedrock of Jewish tradition. No Jewish custom, or belief, or piece of unwritten literature can be fully understood and adequately studied without a thorough search of that vast accumulation of written literature in which so much of the Jewish tradition of past centuries has received a fixed form. A student of Australian folklore may have nothing to build on but the actually existing oral tradition of the tribe he studies. Methods developed for studying such "historyless" human groups are inadequate for the purpose of studying the folklore of the Jews, who have been the "people of the book" for millennia.

Third, a few conclusions can be reached about the outside influences on Jewish folklore, of which there have been many in every age and in every place. The tradition-bound and religion-dominated character of Jewish life everywhere up to the Enlightenment provided it with an extraordinary capacity for absorbing elements of foreign cultures. The life of a Jewish community under the aegis of its own religious tradition was one

and indivisible. Religion was always ready, soon after something new appeared on the horizon, with its decisive reaction:
whether to reject it as *ḥuqqat ḥagoy* (the law or custom of Gen-
tiles) or to accept it, digest it, and make it part of the Jewish
tradition. If the decision fell in the latter direction, a very short
time later the non-Jewish origin of the trait was forgotten, and
it acquired the same binding force, the same traditional sanction, as any traditional Jewish *minhag*. Or, if it was a tale or a
fable or a legend, its acceptance meant that it had come to be
regarded as a legitimate addition to the old Jewish storehouse of
oral literature, and in this case, too, its non-Jewish origin was
soon completely forgotten.

This tendency to incorporate foreign elements constitutes an
additional challenge for the student of Jewish folklore. He must
always be familiar with the results of general folklore studies,
for Jewish folklore always contains non-Jewish elements and
must be studied in its relation to them.

Finally—a warning. Israel the state and Israel the people have
to be made aware of the acute danger of the total submergence
of the folklore of the surviving Jewish communities in the new,
nascent culture of Israel. In 1945 only the folklore of the European Jewish remnant seemed to be threatened with oblivion,
while the folklore of the Oriental Jews, who in those days still
lived in relative peace in their tradition-favoring Moslem environment, seemed to be safe for generations to come. Now, only
fifteen years later, the danger of extinction is greater for the
folk traditions of the Oriental Jews than for those of the European Jews. There are no more Jewish communities left in
Yemen and Iraq; in other Oriental countries their number has
been drastically reduced and their communal life broken down.
In Israel, which in the last ten years has absorbed close to a half
million Oriental Jews, the dominant atmosphere of Western
society and culture is more unfavorable for the continued survival of Oriental Jewish folk traditions than it is for the continued existence of Western Jewish folklore.

Notes

1. Published in Hebrew as the introductory article of the journal *Edoth* (Jerusalem) I (Oct., 1945), No. 1, 1–12; and subsequently in an English translation in the *Journal of American Folklore*, II (1946), 25–39.

2. L. R. C. Yoffie, "Songs of the '12 Numbers' and the Hebrew Chant of Echod Mi Yodea," *JAF*, LXII (1949), 382–411; Ruth Rubin, "19th Century Yiddish Folksongs of Children in Eastern Europe," *JAF*, LXV (1952), 227–54.

3. Cf. *JAF*, LX (1947), 350–416.

4. Maria Leach (ed.), *Standard Dictionary of Folklore, Mythology, and Legend* (2 vols.; New York, 1949–50).

5. Europe and America are most fully covered, the former by survey articles dealing with Basque, Celtic, Estonian, European, Finnish, French, Germanic, Latvian, Lithuanian, Romany, Slavic, Spanish folklore; the latter by articles on African and New-World Negro, American, Mexican and Central American Indian, North American Indian, Pennsylvania Dutch, South American Indian and Spanish folklore (which includes Spanish America). Although even this coverage is far from complete (we miss, e.g., Hungarian and Balkan folklore), it is unquestionably much more adequate than the spotty coverage of the rest of the world. Asia is represented only by articles on Chinese folklore, Indian and Persian folklore and mythology, Japanese folklore and Semitic folklore (the latter confined to a discussion of the ancient Near East). Oceania and Australia are discussed in four articles, while Africa is summarily dealt with in an article which includes also New-World Negro Folklore. The folklore of the contemporary Middle East (which comprises the rich, though insufficiently explored, folklore of Iran, Turkey and the Arab lands) is excluded altogether, as is Jewish folklore.

6. Cf. II, 981.

7. William R. Bascom, "Folklore and Anthropology," *JAF*, LVI (1953), 289.

8. Cf. *Standard Dictionary of Folklore*, II, 953.

9. *Ibid.*, I, 398.

10. The Mishna (c. A.D. 200); the Babylonian Talmud (c. 500); the code of Yitzhaq Alfasi (1013–1103); the code of Maimonides (1135–1204); the code of Jacob ben Asher (c. 1269–1343); the *Shulhan 'Arukh* of Joseph Caro (1488–1575).

11. Cf. Raphael Patai, *Man and Temple in Ancient Jewish Myth and Ritual* (Edinburgh, 1947).

12. Bascom, *op. cit.*, p. 285. Cf. also Bascom's subsequent discussion of the scope of folklore in his paper, "Verbal Art," *JAF*, LXVIII (1955), 245–52.

2 | Biblical Folklore

Remarks on the Origin and History of an "Alphabet of Ben Sira" Fable

BACIL F. KIRTLEY University of Maine

by Bacil F. Kirtley

THE TALE of the fox, the fishes and Leviathan (the topic of this study) is first recorded for Jewish tradition in the Hebrew *Alphabet of Ben Sira.*[1] Briefly, the story is this:

Soon after the Creation, God ordered the Angel of Death to throw a pair of animals of each species into the sea that each creature of the land might have a counterpart living in water. When the Angel of Death came to the fox, he found him howling and crying beside the seashore. Asked the reason for his distress, the fox answered that he was lamenting his friend who had been thrown into the sea, and he pointed to the reflection of himself in the water. The Angel of Death, being deceived, let the fox go. A weasel who learned the trick from the fox also succeeded in escaping. At the end of a year, when Leviathan assembled all the creatures of his sea domain, only the fox and the weasel were missing. Leviathan sent messengers to discover how these animals had escaped God's edict. When he learned of the fox's cunning, he wished to eat his heart and by so doing absorb his intelligence. He sent large fishes to bring him the clever animal. When the fishes found the fox beside the sea, they told him that Leviathan was dying and that he was to be made king. The fox, mounted upon the back of one of the fishes, was carried out to sea, supposedly to his coronation. At length he became worried and asked the fishes to tell him the truth. One of the fishes then said that Leviathan, jealous of his shrewdness, wanted to eat his heart and become as clever as he. To this the fox replied that he should have been told earlier, for foxes, he said, always left their hearts at home. Thereupon the fishes returned him to shore to fetch his heart. Once upon land the fox jeered at the fishes for believing that a creature without a heart could live. Leviathan killed and ate his stupid emissaries.

29

Thus it has remained that although there are creatures in the sea corresponding to those on land, there are none like unto the fox and the weasel.

Two distinguished scholars of Hebrew folklore, Dr. Moses Gaster and Professor Louis Ginzberg, have commented upon the *Alphabet* version of this fable. Gaster[2] indicates the tale's close correspondence to the ruse story of the fourth book of the *Panchatantra*, "The Story of the Monkey and the Crocodile." He also suggests that it has absorbed a part of another tale; the ending, he believes, comes from the story of the lion who kills an ass and entrusts the corpse to a fox. The fox, so the tale continues, secretly eats the ass's heart, then dupes the lion into believing the ass has no heart.

Ginzberg, like Gaster, recognizes that the fable of the *Alphabet* is closely related to the *Panchatantra* frame story. Also, like Gaster, he believes that the mythical Ben Sira fused three distinct tales: the tale about the fox and the Angel of Death; the tale about the fox and the fishes; and, finally, as an ending for the *Alphabet* fable, the tale about the lion, the jackal, and the ass:

Evidently the story of the fox and the Angel of Death has no connection with the story of the fox and the fish. The latter is identical with the Indian fable of the monkey and the crocodile (*Panchatantra*, IV, 1), which corresponds to the fable of the ape and the turtle in the *Kalilah and Dimnah*. The end of the fable, as told in the *Alphabet*, does not belong to this fable, but to the Indian one of the lion, the jackal, and the ass (*Panchatantra*, IV, 3). The author, however, did not draw upon the *Panchatantra*, but upon some version of the *Kalilah and Dimnah*, as is evident from the fact that in the latter the two fables are joined, while in the *Panchatantra* there is no direct connection.[3]

Professor Ginzberg considers a source in Indian-Arabic fable literature more probable than another in older Jewish writings, "since the author [Ben Sira] knows a number of animal fables which are not extant in the older Jewish literature."[4]

Both Gaster and Ginzberg unquestionably are correct when they write that the story of the fox and the Angel of Death has "no connection" with the remainder of the fable. The episode is inorganic and has occurred in no other translation or reworking during the tale's tortuous literary genealogy in Europe and the Near East.[5]

Ginzberg states in the quotation above that in the *Kalilah and Dimnah* the story of the ape and the tortoise is joined to that of the lion, the jackal, and the ass, and that the stories are not at all connected in the *Panchatantra*. This is erroneous. In the *Tantrakhyayika*, the oldest and most authentic text of the *Panchatantra*, as well as in the Somadeva version in the *Ocean of Story* (also in oral versions from Africa) the stories are linked in exactly the same way as in the *Kalilah and Dimnah*. Therefore, even if there are elements of the lion, the jackal, and the ass story in the *Alphabet* fable—and beyond a vague nuance in the fox's taunt, there is almost certainly none—these do not render one source more probable than the other. No other element in the story indicates that it issued *directly* from either the *Panchatantra* or the *Kalilah*. Several elements suggest that Ben Sira's fable may have come from an oral source.

The part of the *Alphabet* fable which has been designated above as "the fox and the fishes" and which henceforth will be called by its oldest title, the "Tale of the Monkey and the Crocodile," has a continuous oral and written history of over two thousand years, a fact which must be reckoned with in a discussion of the origin of its variants.

Though the place of ultimate origin of the "Monkey and the Crocodile" as an oral tale—the place, that is, where it became fixed into a more or less stable tale type—can never be known positively, the early date at which it was incorporated into the two ancient collections of Indian narrative, the *Jatakas* and the *Panchatantra*, makes India the probable home. Almost certainly it antedated these collections. The area over which the tale is distributed supports a hypothesis of Indian origin. To the west of India, oral versions are found distributed (though thinly) from Zanzibar to Moscow; to the east, the tale occurs from Korea and Japan to the Philippines; and to the south, versions have diffused into Malaya and Indonesia.[6]

The literary history of the fable is extensive. Three versions are found in the *Jatakas*, the canon of which, according to Rhys Davids,[7] "forms the most reliable, the most complete, and the most ancient collection of folklore now extant in any literature in the world." The *Jatakas*, it appears, were composed in Northern India before the time of Asoka, who was crowned in 270 B.C., and were taken over bodily from the folklore of that region.[8] With the spread of Buddhism throughout Asia went the *Jatakas*, and with the *Jatakas*, the "Tale of the Monkey and the Crocodile."

Sometime around the beginning of our era—between A.D. 200 and A.D. 500—the *Panchatantra* was formed, possibly in northern, possibly in southwestern India, and this collection also contained "The Monkey and the Crocodile." From a lost Sanskrit recension of this original compilation of the *Panchatantra* a Pahlavi translation, also lost, was made around A.D. 550. From this in turn came the Arabic translation, *Kalilah and Dimnah*, and from the Arabic, the Hebrew translation, which was the fountainhead of the versions known in Europe during the Middle Ages.

The *Kalilah* reached Europe in the eleventh century and before 1600 had been translated into Greek, Latin, Spanish, Italian, German, English, Old Slavonic, and Czech.[9] Indeed, the *Calila e Dimna* bore the distinction of being the first book of prose tales written in Castilian.[10] Probably throughout medieval Europe no other collection enjoyed greater popularity than did this one.

Between the *Tantrakhyayika* version of "The Monkey and the Crocodile" and Hans Sachs's two versions (1547 and 1563)[11] of the same fable—these are poetic reworkings, based upon *Das Buch der Beispiele*—are a good many intermediate translations; yet the tale as told by Sachs retains almost all the characteristic traits of the oldest known version. The most significant alteration is that the role of the crocodile in the *Tantrakhyayika* is given a tortoise in Sachs's poems. This change, however, which had already occurred in the Arabic *Kalilah*, resulted from the ambiguous meaning of the Indic word which designated the water-dwelling animal.[12] In Sachs, as in the *Tantrakhyayika*, the land animal still (in one version) feeds the water animal, wins its friendship, and evokes the jealousy of the latter's wife. The wife still sends the reluctant husband after the land animal's heart, and the duped land animal still escapes, after a water voyage upon his foe's back, by the counter-trick of saying that his heart has been left in a tree.

The plot of Sachs's poems—distant, though legitimate, descendants of the *Tantrakyayika*—differs only triflingly from the ancient versions, while the *Alphabet* plot is reordered drastically—to a degree that it can hardly be based upon any literary prototype. Leviathan, king of the fishes,[13] replaces the wife of the water animal as the being for whom a portion of the land animal's body is desired. The substitution of a royal personage for a wife occurs in no literary variant either in Europe or Asia. On the other hand, this motif is common among oral variants.

In a version from Moscow[14] and one from Korea,[15] the land animal's body-part is wanted specifically for the "king of fishes"; in two Swahili tales and one Vahehe,[16] it is wanted for the sultan of the sea; in a Japanese version[17] it is wanted for a sea princess, and in another[18] for a dragon sea queen, and in yet another Swahili tale[19] for a shark king. In versions where royalty displaces the water animal's wife as the intended recipient of the land animal's body-part, the beginning of the story is reshaped and differs markedly from the beginning of the story in the *Panchatrantra*. Only the African, of the versions which make this change, begin, as does the *Panchatantra*, with the land and water animals striking up a friendship. The others— as well as two Chinese versions[20]—begin in some land beneath the waves where water-dwelling animals originate a scheme to lure an ape, monkey, or fox into their power so that his heart or liver, to which magical powers are ascribed, may be eaten. In this way, too, begins the episode of the fox and fishes in the *Alphabet* fable. With one exception, versions with this beginning derive from the Orient. The exception, the Russian tale, is probably a variant arrived at by verbal retelling of the *Alphabet* tale itself.

The *Alphabet* fable includes another trait which finds no parallel outside the Far East. Leviathan punishes his stupid emissaries for their failure to bring him the fox by killing and eating them. In the Japanese tales the emissary, a jellyfish, is, by the king's order, beaten to a pulp when he lets the monkey trick him (hence, the gelatinous condition of the creature's body nowadays).

Other peculiarities of the *Alphabet* fable have parallels only among the oral versions of the East—quite possibly because as an oral tale it has flourished only there. In the East, particularly in Indonesia, the water-transportation episode of the fable is often a sequel to a previous episode which is an independent narrative unit, as is the *Alphabet* story of the fox and the Angel of Death. Also, only in Japanese, Indonesian, and *Alphabet* versions does the fable end in an "arbitrary etiology." Of themselves, the etiological endings, which differ greatly from tale to tale, do not so much indicate a close relationship between versions as they reflect a characteristic phenomenon of oral tradition.

The *Alphabet* fable, therefore, has its closest affinities not with any version stemming directly from the *Panchatantra* and its translations but with versions found in oral circulation. In the Near Eastern region the African versions—which were probably introduced to the Negroes by Arabian slavers and traders—are in many respects closer to the *Alphabet* fable than are any literary forms. The Russian tale, probably derived from the *Alphabet*, is also quite near it. The Far Eastern variants of the tale, however, reproduce most faithfully the singularities of the Hebrew fable. Several explanations might be offered for this disconcerting correspondence. The Far Eastern tale and the Hebrew fable, it may be conjectured, descend from a common literary source. However, until such a prototype is discovered (which is unlikely), this possibility can be discounted. Again, the explanation may be that the Hebrew fable, along with the Far Eastern tale, is an early oral form of the story, one never included in the ancient compilations, which diffused from India both to the East and West. The authoritative translations from the *Panchatantra* stream may have superseded, in the West, the tradition recorded by Ben Sira. Since the "Tale of the Monkey and the Crocodile" in the Near East and Europe—unlike the tale in the Far East—belongs principally to learned literature, such a displacement is conceivable. Yet, there exists a final possibility: the Oriental version may have been borne directly to the Near East and there transplanted. For centuries caravans through Central Asia and Turkestan linked China with the Near East; and Chinese ships, "vessels manned by a thousand men, with gardens aboard . . ." plied a coastwise trade as far west as East Africa.[21] Therefore, direct connection between the Hebrew and Oriental spheres of culture did exist.

At present, no final explanation for the curious resemblance between the Hebrew and Oriental versions of the fable is possible. Either of the two last conjectures seems equally probable. The Oriental and Hebrew forms may be directly related, or they may have diffused orally from a mutual prototype. Further research, particularly in Central Asian material, will perhaps reveal a definite answer.

Notes

1. The version given here is taken from Moses Gaster's *Rumanian Bird and Beast Stories*, Memoirs of the Folk-Lore Society (London, 1915), pp. 365 ff. Mr. Gaster's text is a translation of the Venice edition of 1544. Of Ben Sira, nothing definite is known; and of the *Alphabet* little more can be said than that it probably had taken its present form by the second half of the twelfth century. See L. Ginzberg, "Ben Sira," *The Jewish Encyclopedia*, 12 vols. (New York and London, 1902), I, 680. The following works include important bibliographies of this tale type: L. Bødker, *De Gamle Vijses Exempler oc Hoffsproch, II: Noter og Register* (København, 1953), Motif K544; K. Campbell, *The Seven Sages of Rome*, (Boston, 1907), p. lxxxiii; V. Chauvin, *Bibliographie des Ouvrages Arabes*, 4 vols. (Liège, 1892), I, 99; Oskar Dähnhardt, *Natursagen*, 4 vols. (Leipzig and Berlin), 1907-12, IV, 1-26; R. B. Dixon, *Oceanic*, in *Mythology of All Races*, ed. Louis H. Gray *et al.*, 13 vols. (Boston, 1916), IX, 344, notes 20-25; D. S. Fansler, *Filipino Popular Tales*, Memoirs of the American Folklore Society, XII (Lancaster and New York, 1921), pp. 374-77; G. H. Tawney and N. M. Penzer, *The Ocean of Story*, 10 vols. (London, 1926), V, 127, n. 1; Stith Thompson, *Motif-Index of Folk-Literature*, 6 vols. (Bloomington, Indiana, 1955-58), Motif K544; Jan de Vries, *Volksverhalen uit Oost-Indië*, 2 vols. (Zutphen, 1925-27), II, list No. 3.

2. Gaster, *Studies and Texts*, 3 vols. (London, 1925-28), II, 1243-48.

3. Ginzberg, "Ben Sira," p. 680.

4. Ginzberg, *The Legends of the Jews*, 7 vols. (Philadelphia, 1913-39), V, 57, n. 190.

5. See the "Genealogical Table of the Panchatantra" in Tawney and Penzer, *The Ocean of Story*, V, 232-42, and chart facing p. 242.

6. Only versions which retain several of the more significant tale traits are meant. Many related, though fragmentary, versions occur in Indonesia, Melanesia, Micronesia and Polynesia.

7. T. W. Rhys Davids, *Buddhist India* (Calcutta, 1950), p. 137.

8. *Ibid.*, p. 135.

9. Tawney and Penzer, V, 207.

10. Pedro Penzol, *Las Traducciones del "Calila e Dimna"* (Madrid, 1931), p. 11.

11. E. Goetze and C. Drescher, *Sämtliche Fabeln und Schwänke von Hans Sachs* (Halle, 1903), Nos. 347, 433.

12. See Dähnardt, *Natursagen*, IV, 14, n. 1.

13. Leviathan is also conceived of as a snake and a crocodile. This ambiguity approximates somewhat that of the Sanskrit *sumsumara* and the Pali *sisumara*, terms which denote the water animal of the Indic tale.

14. E. B. Cowell, *The Jatakas or Stories of the Buddha's Former Births*, 10 vols. (Cambridge, 1895–1901), II, 110 (No. 208).

15. Horace N. Allen, *Korean Tales* (New York, 1889), p. 34. The identical story appears in a number of Russian and German collections from Korea.

16. E. Steere, *Swahili Tales, as Told by Natives of Zanzibar* (London, 1922), pp. 1 ff.; G. W. Bateman, *Zanzibar Tales* (Chicago, 1901), pp. 2 ff.; C. Velten, "Die Sprache der Wahehe," *Mitteilungen des Seminars für Orientalische Sprachen 2*, III (1899), 211.

17. D. A. Brauns, *Japanische Märchen und Sagen* (Leipzig, 1885), pp. 64 ff.

18. Yei Theodora Ozaki, *The Japanese Fairy Book* (New York, 1922), pp. 189 ff.

19. Dähnhardt, IV, 22.

20. E. T. Chalmers, *Myths and Legends of China* (London, 1922), pp. 211 ff.; Sian-tek Lim, *More Folk Tales from China* (New York, 1948), pp. 88 ff.

21. A. J. Villiers, *The Coral Sea* (New York, 1949), p. 56.

Jewish and Moslem
Sources of a Falasha
Creation Myth

HAIM SCHWARZBAUM   Jaffa, Israel

by Haim Schwarzbaum

THE BIRHOR, an aboriginal jungle tribe of Chota Nagpur, in India, relate:[1]

When Singbonga, the supreme deity, intended to fashion the earth, he commanded the tortoise to bring up some clay from the bottom of the primeval waters. The tortoise dived into the waters, took up some clay and placed it on his back. In coming up, the clay was washed off by the water. Thus the tortoise failed. The same fate befell Singbonga's second messenger, the crab. At last Singbonga ordered the leech to fetch some clay. The leech dived down to the bottom of the ocean and devoured its fill of clay. It then came up to Singbonga and vomited out the clay from its stomach into the hand of Singbonga, who fashioned the Earth from it.

This is one of the most widely distributed of all myths accounting for the creation of the earth by a demiurge who orders some of his messengers (usually three birds or animals) to dive into the primordial ocean or, in some cases, into the flood waters, in order to fetch soil from the bottom. Usually the first two messengers fail on their errand, and only the third succeeds in getting the soil, out of which the earth is to be created.[2] In many versions from Central and North Asia the devil tries twice to bring up mud or soil from the bottom of the primordial waters and does not succeed until the third time, when he accomplishes his task by transforming himself into a bird or some aquatic creature. Otherwise the soil is melted or washed off before he manages to deliver it to the creator.[3] The basic pattern of the earth-diver myth in its numerous versions has so far been recorded among many aboriginal tribes of India,[4] Central and North Asia,[5] among North American[6] and South American Indians,[7] in Oceania[8] and Africa.[9] It is also very popular in Eastern Europe—Rumania,[10] Russia,[11] Estonia,[12] and Finland,[13] and elsewhere.[13a]

We do not intend, at present, to examine the numerous variants of this myth, nor to deal with the much-debated problem of its origin.[14] It will be sufficient to note here that, in all probability, the myth was disseminated from India, as the most ancient Hindu records describe a Demiurge (Prajapati, Brahma or Vishnu[15]) in the form of a boar or a tortoise diving into the primeval ocean to raise earth from the bottom.

The main purpose of the present paper is to draw the attention of folklorists and students of this myth to the significant fact that in Jewish, Moslem, and Falasha folk literature the same general pattern of the "Three Messengers" motif is found in numerous versions.[15a]

It should be pointed out, however, that the Semitic versions of this myth account for the creation of man (*Adam Harishon*, "First Man"),[16] in contradistinction to the non-Semitic versions, which deal with the creation of the earth. The basic notion that clay, mud, dust, etc.,[17] have to be fetched by messengers of the demiurge, two of whom are unsuccessful, the third alone being successful, is common to both the Semitic and non-Semitic versions of the myth. The main concern of the mythographer, both Semitic and non-Semitic, was to show how the "material" was procured for the creation of the earth or for the creation of man; no line of distinction was drawn between the original creation of the earth and its creation after a flood. V. Elwin has rightly pointed out[18] that "whether the earth had always been there on the floor of the ocean, or whether it had but recently sunk down, the problem was the same—how to get it up again."

Among the Cheros of India, on the other hand, the myth is recorded that God (Bhagwan), having become annoyed at the fruitless efforts of both the first and the second of his messengers (the tortoise and the rat) asks the third messenger, i.e., his personal servant Garur (ancient Hindu, *Garuda*), "to fly somewhere" and get clay for the creation of the earth. Garur then fetches the clay from heaven, not from the bottom of the primordial ocean.[19]

In the Semitic myths of the creation of man the earth plays a prominent part, as will be seen in a Falasha creation myth which is found at the beginning of the *Teezaza Sanbat* ("The Commandments of the Sabbath"), a sort of Falasha Midrash on the Sabbath personified as a queen.[20] The story is as follows:

When the Lord intended to create Man, he sent down the angel Germael to fetch some dust from the Land of Dudalem. As soon as the angel started to dig in Dudalem, the earth sought refuge in the Ineffable Name of the Lord. Germael had to give up digging and return to his sender empty-handed and terror-stricken. He told the Lord that he could not snatch the dust because the earth had invoked the Ineffable Name. The second messenger, the angel Aksael, was also overawed by the Ineffable Name and failed to carry out the commission. The third messenger, the fiend Bernael,[21] rejoiced greatly in the commission,[22] ran quickly out of his camp, and as soon as he arrived in the Land of Dudalem, the earth began to shudder and shiver; Bernael, however, was not intimidated by the Ineffable Name but tore away some dust from the Land of Dudalem "which turned into a vast abyss." The earth started to lament and shriek, but Bernael turned a deaf ear to its groans. He concealed the dust under his cloak[23] and quickly returned to the Lord. The Lord looked down upon the trembling earth and cursed it to quiver and shake until the end of all generations should come to pass. Then He looked at the wicked Bernael and transformed him into fire. Afterwards the Lord ordered the angel Michael to seize Bernael by his foot, hurl him down to the earth and crush him there. Later Bernael implored the Lord to deliver mankind to his charge.[24] God promised him the wicked people.[25]

That this myth did not originate with the Falashas has already been recognized by Leslau.[26] Its general pattern can be traced to one of the most popular Moslem legends, of which we possess numerous versions in both Moslem chronicles and Arab folk literature.[27] There are also several modern oral versions recorded in Palestine[28] and Turkey.[29] There is even a Rumanian parody modeled on this Moslem legend.[30] In general, Jewish and Moslem parallels add considerably to the content and clarity of the Falasha myth.

The Moslem creation story, accounting for the assignment of functions to Azrael and his appointment as Angel of Death, can be summarized as follows:[31]

Allah orders archangel Gabriel to descend to the earth and fetch a handful of dust for the creation of Adam. As soon as the devil (Iblis) hears about Gabriel's mission, he dashes off to the earth, disguised as a holy ascetic and pious adviser,[32] informing the earth that Allah intends to fashion a creature out of its dust in order to set it above all the other creatures.[33] "But I am afraid," says Iblis, "that this new being will rebel against Allah and that his ultimate resort will thus be hell. . . . Thou shouldst adjure him that he dare not take anything from you." The earth behaves accordingly. When Gabriel hears the earth's warning, he becomes awe-stricken and returns to Allah without any dust. The same fate befalls the second messenger, the archangel Michael. Only the third messenger, Azrael, does not pay any attention to the solemn oath, preferring to obey Allah's command. He fetches a handful of different varieties of dust, and out of them Adam is created. When Azrael returns from his mission, he is so aghast that he remains speechless and motionless for forty years. After hearing Azrael's report, Allah praises him very much and as a reward appoints him Angel of Death in charge of fetching the souls of all mortals.[34]

This legend, showing how instrumental in the creation of man is the Angel of Death, expresses the familiar notion that the cycle of coming to be and passing away is eternal and that death is necessary, for otherwise the earth will become overcrowded.[35] Mirkhond[36] has a most illuminating sequel to the legend:

When Azrael learnt about his appointment he began to weep, saying: "Among the children of men there will be prophets and saints who will undoubtedly hate me on this account." Allah rejoined: "I shall send so many complaints and diseases upon mankind that, on account of their afflictions, they will entertain no enmity for thee."

A parallel to this sequel may be found in the Hindu legend told twice in the Mahabharata:[37]

The Goddess of Death, created by Brahma out of pity for the overcrowded earth, complains bitterly that she will be cursed and hated by mortals. Brahma promises that all kinds of plagues and wasting diseases will cause mortals to welcome her with much pleasure.

M. Winternitz[38] considers this legend to be of considerable antiquity because Brahma appears therein as creator.

In addition to the Moslem myth in which Azrael plays the part of Bernael in the Falasha story, there is another Moslem tale, in which Iblis takes the role of Azrael, that shows an even more striking resemblance to the Falasha myth:[39]

The Almighty sent down Iblis, and the latter took some clay from the surface of the earth, from its sweet and salty parts, and thus was Adam created from the very handful of clay brought up by Iblis. That is the reason why Iblis says in the Quran: "Am I to adore one whom Thou hast created out of clay?" [i.e. that handful of clay fetched by myself].

We should like to emphasize that although the points of resemblance between this Moslem legend and the Falasha myth are too numerous to be accidental (Bernael is condemned and punished, Azrael is praised, etc.), nevertheless a closer study of the Falasha story shows that it has been influenced not only by Moslem patterns but also by the Jewish Apocrypha and Rabbinical sources, mainly by the legend of the Fallen Angel embedded in the apocryphal Ethiopic Book of Enoch. Let us examine the points of affinity between these two stories.

Leslau[40] has overlooked the important point that the "Land of Dudalem," mentioned so frequently in the Falasha myth, is not a "misread form of an Arabic source" but is identical with Dudael of the Ethiopic Book of Enoch,[41] which reads quite significantly: "And the Lord again said to Raphael: 'Bind Azazel hand and foot and cast him unto the darkness and make an opening in the desert which is in Dudael and cast him therein. And place upon him rough and jagged rocks.'" These rough and jagged rocks of Dudael are to be identified with Beth Hadudu mentioned in the Mishnah[42] as the locality near Jerusalem whence the scapegoat for Azazel, laden with the sins of the whole community of Israel, was led forth to be hurled to the ground. Very early Rabbinical sources show that some connection was supposed to exist between the Azazel of Leviticus and the "Fallen Angel" Azazel of the Book of Enoch. Very enlightening is the statement of the School of Rabbi Ishmael that the Azazel of Leviticus is so named because in this way atonement is obtained for the sin of the Fallen Angels Uza and Aza.[43] The Falasha mythographer has undoubtedly drawn on a very ancient Jewish source. Thus the spot from which the fiend Bernael seizes the dust for the creation of man is associated with Beth Hadudu-Dudael, the place where the he-goat and the rebel angel Azazel were flung down and where the rough and jagged rocks (Hadudu) were placed upon Azazel. Dudalem is thus a significant place infected by the presence of demons (he-goats) and their leader Azazel. In this respect the Falasha story closely approaches many Asiatic versions, in which it is often stressed that the bits of soil have to be stolen or extorted from a demon-like being who is in charge of the earth.

Very old Hindu mythological sources (e.g., various statements in the *Vedas* and in *Vishnu Purana*, I, 4) emphasize that the newly blossomed earth was suddenly ravished by the Great

Serpent of the Cosmic Sea. Vishnu, assuming the form of a gigantic boar (the third *avatar* of Vishnu), plunges to the bottom of the Cosmic Abyss. With gleaming tusk and four sharp hoofs he tears and tramples upon the Cosmic Serpent and thus rescues the earth from the clutches of this demon, called Hiranyāksha.[44] G. Hatt[45] quite mistakenly maintains that dualism is absent from the old and modern versions of the earth-diver tales. Vishnu overcomes Hiranyāksha, just as in ancient Babylonian mythology Marduk overcomes the Sea Dragon Tiamat. This dualistic trend in ancient India is correctly emphasized by H. Zimmer.[46] Similar notions are also frequently encountered in relatively modern Indian mythology.

According to a Gadaba creation myth[47] the demiurge Mahaprabhu dives to the bottom of the ocean, where Larang, the great *Dano ogre* lives, gets hold of him and squeezes him so hard "that he excretes the earth he had devoured." From the excreted earth the world is formed. In a Bondo creation myth[48] the wild boar, Mahaprabhu's messenger, goes down to the underworld to Kermo Deota and steals from him soil out of which the earth is formed. In a Baiga creation myth[49] the bits of soil have to be secured from the Lower Region (Utra Khand), which constitutes the Kingdom of Burha Nang, the Ancient Serpent. The *Dano* (demon) plays an important part in many Indic creation myths, and often he is forced by the demiurge or by his messenger to vomit the earth which he has swallowed.[50]

In many Rabbinical sources[51] the dust for the formation of Adam is supposed to have been taken from the site of the Temple altar that was to be built later in Jerusalem. It is quite possible that the Falasha mythographer has chosen Dudalem as a symbolic "place of atonement" for the iniquities of the children of Israel, in spite of the basic difference between the holy spot of the altar and the demon-imbued land of Dudalem.

According to another Talmudic tradition[52] the torso of Adam's body came from Babylon, his head from Palestine, his limbs from other lands, but his private parts from Akra de Agma (a town near Pumbedita, notorious according to Ginzberg "on account of the loose morals of its inhabitants"). In this respect the tradition seems to have been influenced by Zoroastrian dualistic ideas, which have left their imprint on many Jewish legends[53] emphasizing the "low" descent of mortals, but even more on Hindu creation stories, where the idea that man has been fashioned from the dirt of the creator's body is quite common.[54] Parallel accounts emphasizing the filthiness of the material out of which man is formed can also be found in other parts of the world.[55] It is of additional interest that in Mandaean mythology the human soul is conducted on its journey through the realms of purification by Pthahil[56] (taking the part of Bernael) and that in many Asiatic creation myths this role is assumed by the devil.[57]

There are further points of resemblance between the Falasha myth and that of the Fallen Angels. In the Falasha story Michael is ordered to hurl down Bernael, just as in the Book of Enoch, Raphael is commanded to cast down Azazel. Both will finally be condemned to fire. Raphael is ordered "to make an opening in the desert which is in Dudael." In the same way Dudalem "turns into a vast abyss" as soon as Bernael snatches the dust from it.

This association of the creation of man with the story of the Fallen Angels is also apparent in an old Jewish legend, perpetuated in the Talmud:[58]

When the Lord intended to create man, He first created a company of ministering angels and said to them: "Is it your desire that We make man in Our image?" They answered: "Sovereign of the world! What will be man's deeds?" The Lord replied: "Such and such will be his deeds." Thereupon they exclaimed: "Sovereign of the Universe, what is man that Thou art mindful of him?" Thereupon the Lord stretched out His little finger among them and consumed them with fire. The same fate befell the second company of opposing angels. The third company of angels, taught by the sad fate of their predecessors, when consulted by the Lord gave their assent to the creation of man.

In this early legend the first two bands of angels, opposing the creation of man, correspond to the two individual angels in the Falasha and Moslem stories, who fail to secure the dust for the creation of man. The third group of angels, endorsing the creation of man, corresponds to the third messenger, who succeeds in procuring the dust needed for the creation of man. It is worth while noticing, in this connection, that the punishment of the opposing angels is that which will be finally inflicted on Azazel, according to the Book of Enoch, and on Bernael, according to the Falasha myth.

This association of the creation story with that of the "Fallen Angels" is even more pronounced in later Midrashic legends: [59]

Rabbi Joseph was asked by his pupils, "What is Azazel?" He said: "When the generation of the Deluge arose and served idols, the Lord was very grieved. Immediately two angels arose and said to the Almighty: 'Lord of the Universe, have not we said before Thou didst create the world, what is man that Thou art mindful of him?' Then the Lord told them that if they inhabited the earth, the evil inclination would overpower them, too, and they would become even more iniquitous than men. The angels asked for permission to descend to the earth and to dwell among men for a test. God yielded to their wish. The angels could not restrain their passions and sinned very much. . . ."

Thus we have here two individual angels opposing the creation of man and as a result becoming "Fallen Angels."

There is a late Midrash which in all probability represents an attempt to reconcile the discrepancies between the older Talmudic traditions of three companies of angels and the Moslem legend of three individual angels: [60]

When God summoned the first group of angels under the leadership of Michael and asked their opinion on the creation of man, they answered scornfully: "What is man that Thou art mindful of

Him?" God immediately consigned them to the big flames, sparing only their leader, Michael. Afterward he called upon the group of Gabriel, and when their answer was the same, He burned them, too, leaving only their leader Gabriel. At last He summoned the third group of Labbiel. Instructed by the fate of their predecessors, they agreed to the creation of man. God was so pleased that he changed the leader's name to Raphael, appointed him Angel of Leechcraft, and handed over to him all kinds of drugs and remedies.

We should bear in mind that, according to the First Book of Enoch,[61] Raphael is the prince of Hades. We have thus a very nice point of affinity with the Moslem creation story. Just as the third messenger Azrael is praised by Allah for procuring the dust and as a reward becomes the Angel of Death, so Labbiel, whose group of angels gives assent to the creation of man, is named Raphael and becomes the Angel of Leechcraft (and of Hades!).[62] The late Midrash anxiously emphasizes that in conformity with the old Talmudic legend only the opposing angels were annihilated, whereas their leaders, Michael and Gabriel, have been spared by the Lord. This, too, corresponds to the Moslem legend.

Another Jewish legend of Moslem origin is the creation story preserved in the Hebrew Chronicles of Yerahmeel:[63]

When Gabriel descended as the Lord's messenger to fetch dust for the creation of man, the earth refused it and drove him away. Gabriel remonstrated: "Why, O earth, dost thou not hearken unto the voice of the Lord?" The earth replied: "I am destined to become a curse, and to be cursed through man."

Recapitulating the main points of the Falasha creation myth, we see that the Falasha mythographer has obviously drawn on Jewish legends, both Apocryphal and Rabbinical, and on Moslem folklore.

All the early Gnostic, Zoroastrian, Zervanist, Mandaean, Manichaean, and Bogomile religious and mythological texts and traditions may, when properly studied by folklorists (and not only by orientalists), throw much fresh light on our earth-diver mythological motif (A812). The dualistic concepts extant in these writings, as well as in the recently discovered Dead Sea Scrolls, are of vast importance in connection with the origin and formation of our motif. This, however, calls for a separate study.

Notes

1. S. C. Roy, *The Birhors* (Ranchi, India, 1925), p. 397; cf. also W. J. Culshaw, *Tribal Heritage, a Study of the Santals* (London, 1949) p. 65.

2. Cf. Stith Thompson, *Motif-Index of Folk-Literature* (Bloomington, Indiana, 1955–58, I, Motif A812 f. See also note 15a, below.

3. See Uno Harva, *Die religiösen Vorstellungen der altaischen Völker* (Helsinki, FFC No. 125, 1938), pp. 96 ff; W. Koppers, "Bhaghwan, the Supreme Deity of the Bhil," *Anthropos*, XXXV–XXXVI (1941), 276; U. Harva, *Die religiösen Vorstellungen der Mordwinen* (Helsinki, FFC No. 142, 1952), p. 135.

4. V. Elwin, *Myths of Middle India* (Madras, 1949), pp. 3–51; S. Fuchs, "Another Version of the Baiga Creation Myth," *Anthropos*, XLVII (1952), 607 ff.; S. Thompson and J. Balys, *The Oral Tales of India* (Bloomington, Indiana, 1958), Motif A812.

5. U. Harva, *op. cit.*, pp. 89–109; O. Dähnhardt, *Natursagen* (Leipzig and Berlin, 1907), I, 2–89; cf. also T. Lehtisalo's admirable *Entwurf einer Mythologie der Jurak-Samojeden* (Helsinki, 1924), pp. 8 f.

6. Stith Thompson, *The Folktale* (New York, 1946), pp. 307 ff.; E. W. Voegelin, "Creation," and "Earth-diver," *Standard Dictionary of Folklore, Mythology, and Legend* (New York, 1950), I, 259, 334; K. Birket-Smith, *Geschichte der Kultur* (Zurich, 1948), pp. 442 f.; R. H. Lowie, *Primitive Religion* (New York, 1948), p. 28; F. Boas, *Race, Language and Culture* (New York, 1949), p. 460; M. C. Boatright, ed., *Texas Folk and Folklore* (Dallas, 1954), p. 12.

7. U. Harva, *op. cit.*, p. 107.

8. Thompson, *Motif-Index*, Motif A811.

9. W. Ruben, *Die Philosophen der Upanishaden* (Bern, 1947), pp. 22 and 309, n. 45, quoting Baumann's *Schöpfung und Urzeit des Menschen in Mythen der afrikanischen Völker* (Berlin, 1936), p. 190.

10. A. Schullerus, *Verzeichnis der Rumänischen Märchen und Mar-chenvarianten* (Helsinki, FFC No. 78, 1928), p. 84.

11. W. R. S. Ralston, *Russian Folktales* (London, 1873), pp. 329 f.

12. O. Loorits in *Folk-Lore* (London, 1934), XLV, 49–73; see also A. Aarne, *Estnische Märchen-und Sagen-varianten* (Hamina, Finland, FFC No. 25, 1918), p. 139.

13. M. Haavio, *Väinämöinen Eternal Sage* (Helsinki, FFC No. 144, 1952), pp. 51 f.; K. Krohn, *Kalevala-Studien*, I, 70; V. 16; A. Aarne, *Verzeichnis der Finnischen Ursprungs-Sagen und Ihrer Varianten* (Hamina, Finland, FFC No. 8, 1912), p. 3.

13a. See *JAF*, LXX (1957), p. 362.

14. Cf. L. Walk, "Die Verbreitung des Tauchmotivs in der Urmeer-schöpfungs und Sintflutsagen," *Mitteilungen der anthropologischen Gesellschaft in Wien*, LXIII (1933), 60 ff.; G. Hatt, *Asiatic Influ-ences in American Folklore* (Copenhagen, 1949), pp. 12 ff. More mate-rial is to be found in H. Schwarzbaum, *The Angel of Death: Studies in Jewish and Moslem Folk-Literature* (in manuscript); cf. also E. W. Count, "The Earth Diver and the Rival Twins: A Clue to Time Corre-lation in North-Eurasiatic and North American Mythology," *Proceed-ings of the 29th International Congress of Americanists*, III (1952), 55–62. Count (p. 61) is rather mistaken when he thinks that only some of the American Indians incorporated the tale into the recitative side of the rituals and that "never . . . in Eurasia is the Earth Diver called upon to perform such a heavy cultural duty." As a matter of fact, our myth con-stitutes an integral part of the ritual and ceremonial of many an Indian tribe. For the Baiga of India see, e.g., Fuchs, *Anthropos*, XLVII (1952), 618; for some North Asiatic tribes, see B. Munkacsi, "Die Weltgott-heiten der Wogulischen Mythologie," *Keleti Szemle* (Budapest, 1908), IX, 206.

15. J. Hertel, *Indische Märchen* (Jena, 1925), No. 1, p. 15; M. Kern, ed., *Das Licht des Ostens, die Weltanschauungen des mittleren und fernen Asiens, Indien, China, Japan* (Stuttgart, n.d.), p. 64; H. Zimmer, *Myths and Symbols in Indian Art and Civilization* (New York, 1946), p. 17 and esp. pp. 77 f.; G. Hatt, *Asiatic Influences in American Folk-lore*, pp. 30 f.; H. V. Glasenapp, *Der Hinduismus* (München, 1922), No. 3, p. 121; M. Leach, *The Beginning, Creation Myths Around the World* (New York, 1956), pp. 22 f.; *Standard Dictionary of Folklore, Mythol-ogy, and Legend*, s.v. "Vishnu."

15a. Noah's Three Messengers (Genesis 8, 6 ff.) are also significant in this connection.

16. Cf. Dov Noy (Neuman), *Motif-Index to Talmudic-Midrashic*

Folk-Literature (Ph. D. dissertation, Bloomington, Indiana, 1954), Motif A1241.

17. *Ibid.*, Motif A1241-A1245.

18. Verrier Elwin, *Myths of Middle India* (Madras, 1949), p. 23; cf. also H. Zimmer, *op. cit.*, pp. 77 f.

19. See D. D. Agarwal, "Ethnographic Notes on the Cheros," *Man in India* (1929), IX, 205.

20. Joseph Halévy, ed., *Teezaza Sanbat* (Paris, 1902), pp. 113 ff.; W. Leslau, *Falasha Anthology* (New Haven, 1951), pp. 11 ff.; A. Z. Aeshcoly, *Sepher Ha-Falashim* (Jerusalem, 1943), p. 141. Aeshcoly's work is in Hebrew.

21. See W. Leslau, *Falasha Anthology*, Index, s.v. "Beliar" and "Bernael." Cf. also A. M. Habermann, *Edah ve-Eduth* (Jerusalem, 1952), p. 129, s.v. "Belial." Habermann's work is in Hebrew. See also Aeshcoly, *op. cit.*, pp. 77 ff.; and 126.

22. In the Midrashic legend of Moses' death [L. Ginzberg, *Legends of the Jews* (Philadelphia, 1911), III, 466 ff.], God commissions the angels Gabriel, Michael, and Zagzagel to fetch Moses' soul, but all of them refuse. Samael, the Angel of Death, as soon as he received permission from God, "went forth in great glee," rejoicing in the commission entrusted to him.

23. The original text is corrupted here. My conjecture is based on the well-known motif appearing in many Asiatic and European versions of our myth (A812.1) stating that the devil delivers only part of the dust to God, hiding the other part in his mouth with a view to creating his own earth later. Cf. U. Harva, *op. cit.*, pp. 89-109. Only in this way can God's wrath in the Falasha myth be accounted for.

24. Iblis (derived from Greek "diabolos") in the Quran also asks for the same boon. He gets the same reply from Allah. Cf. Surah, VII, 14 ff.; XV, 36 f. Cf. also *Motif-Index*, A1145 (Cause of earthquakes).

25. Our summary is based on D'Abbadie Ms. No. 107 (*Cat. Conti Rossini*, 219), fol. 105a–107a. The Ethiopic text is partly corrupted.

26. W. Leslau, *op. cit.*, pp. 9 and 144, n. 34.

27. Tabari, *Annales*, M. J. de Goeje, ed. (Leiden, 1879–1901), I, 87; Kisai, *Kisas al-Anbiyā*, Eisenberg, ed. (Leiden 1922), pp. 22 f.; Thalabi, *Arais al Majalis* (Cairo, 1325), p. 15; Masudi, *Muruj ad-Dahab*, I, 51; Ibn al-Athir, *Chronicon*, Tornberg, ed., I, 19 ff.; Ad-Diyarbakri, *Tarikh al-Khamis*, I, 36, 37; Majlisi, *Bihar al-Anwar*, V, 30; Abd al-Karim al Gilani, *Al-Insan al-Kamil* (Cairo, 1328), II, 19; Al-Buni, *Shams al-Maarif al-Kubra* (Cairo, 1347), III, 13 f.; IV, 54; Mirkhond, *The Rauzat-us-Safa*, Rehatsek, tr., I, 41; J. Morgan, *Mahometism Fully Explained* (London,

1723), pp. 20–23; Edwin Arnold, *Pearls of the Faith or Islam's Rosary* (Boston, 1883), pp. 42–45.

28. J. E. Hanauer, *Folk-Lore of the Holy Land* (London, 1935), pp. 130 f.

29. P. N. Boratov, "Notes sur'Azrail dans le folklore turc," *Oriens* (Leiden, 1951), IV, 71.

30. Petre Ispirescu, *Povetile uncheasului statos cu o precuvantarede Al. I. Odobescu* (Bucharest, 1916), 2nd edition, pp. 307–12.

31. A detailed analysis of the numerous Arab versions is given in H. Schwarzbaum, *Angel of Death*. The present summary is based on Kisai, *Kisas al Anbiyā*, pp. 22 f.

32. Iblis appears as "pious adviser" very frequently in Moslem folk literature. Cf. also II Cor. XI, 14; Quran, VII, 20.

33. The same idea is expressed in the Slavonic Enoch (see Hebrew translation by Cahana, XI, 73 f.). Cf. also B. J. Bamberger, *Fallen Angels* (Philadelphia, 1952), p. 34; I. Enoch 7:6; 87:1; M. R. James, *The Apocryphal New Testament* (1924), pp. 527 ff.

34. In just the same way Labbiel in Midrash Kohen (Yellinek's *Beth Hamidrash*, II, 27) is praised by God and appointed as Angel of Leech-craft assuming the name of Raphael. In a Buryat creation myth quoted by U. Harva, *op. cit.*, p. 104, God blesses the water fowl for bringing up clay and earth from the bottom of the sea. Cf. also *Anthropos*, XLVII, 613.

35. See H. Schwarzbaum, "The Overcrowded Earth," *Numen, International Review for the History of Religions* (1957), IV, 59–74; H. Abrahamsson, *The Origin of Death; Studies in African Mythology* (Uppsala, Sweden, 1951), pp. 76 ff.

36. *The Rauzat-us-Safa*, I, 41.

37. *Mahābharata*, VII, 52 ff.; XII, 256 ff. See also the Assamese legend published by R. G. Lewison in the *Journal of the Royal Asiatic Society of Bengal*, V, 352 f.; A. Essigmann, *Sagen und Märchen Altindiens* (Berlin, 1915), pp. 3 ff.; P. N. Boratov, *op. cit.*, p. 60; *Yalkut Shimeoni* (Frankfurt, Germany, 13th cent.), I, 105; H. Hayes, *Yivo Filologische Shriften* (Vilna, 1928), II, 286; H. Abrahamsson, *op. cit.*, pp. 80 f.

38. M. Winternitz, *Geschichte der indischen Literatur* (Leipzig, 1908), I, 339.

39. Tabari, *Tarikh al-Umam wal-Muluk* (Cairo, 1939), I, 61, lines 12 ff.; the Quran quotation refers to Surah, XVII, 63; while according to Tabari, Iblis is the sole earth-bringer, in Thalabi's account, *loc. cit.*, Iblis does not appear at all; the earth itself accuses man and refuses to grant him any dust.

40. Leslau, *op. cit.*, pp. 25 and 144, n. 22.

41. Ethiopic Book of Enoch. 10:4; cf. I En. 54:5; Bk Jub. 5:6, 7, 10, 48:15; Slavonic Enoch (Cahana), ch. VII; Testament of Levi 18:12; Rev. 12:9, 20:2 ff.

42. Mishnah, Yoma 6:8; see *Enc. Judaica*, s.v. "Bet Charudun" for the various readings of that locality. The Jerusalem Talmud has "Beth Horon," which symbolizes an unclean demon-ridden spot; cf. Babylonian Talmud, tr. Niddah, 61a. See also T. H. Gaster in *Forgotten Religions*, ed. V. Ferm (New York, 1950), p. 123; W. F. Albright, *Archeology and the Religion of Israel* (Baltimore, 1953), pp. 80 f.

43. Bab. Talmud, Yoma, fol. 67b.

44. Cf. *Standard Dictionary of Folklore*, II, p. 1154, s.v. "Varāha."

45. G. Hatt, *op. cit.*, p. 24.

46. H. Zimmer, *op. cit.*, p. 78.

47. V. Elwin, *op. cit.*, p. 37.

48. *Ibid.*, pp. 32 f. No. 8.

49. S. Fuchs, *Anthropos*, XLVII (1952), pp. 607 ff.; Elwin, *op. cit.*, p. 7.

50. Cf. Elwin, *op. cit.*, pp. 5 f.; 27; 39, No. 17; 47, No. 30.

51. L. Ginzberg, *op. cit.*, I, 55; V, 73; Dov Noy, *op. cit.*, A1241; Yellinek, *Bet Hamidrash*, II, 27.

52. Bab. Talmud Sanhedrin, fol. 38b; L. Ginzberg, *op. cit.*, V, 72.

53. Cf. Sanhedrin, fol. 39a, where Zoroastrian dualism is combated and refuted.

54. Cf. S. Fuchs, *loc. cit.*, p. 608; Elwin, *op. cit.*, pp. 47 and 50; see also *Motif-Index*, A1211.1. According to a Bogomil legend "the devil made man, and God set a soul in him." Cf. N. K. Gudzy, *History of Early Russian Literature* (New York, 1949), p. 36. In Mandaean mythology, Pthahil creates man but is unable to furnish him with a soul; see E. S. Drower, *The Mandaeans of Iraq and Iran* (Oxford, 1937), pp. 73 and 257. In the most ancient records of Sumerian mythology, Enki, the water god, decides to do some creating of his own, but he fails. See S. N. Kramer, *Sumerian Mythology* (Philadelphia, 1944), pp. 70 f.

55. The Rabbinic sources stating that Adam's descent was from the dust of the altar involve *eo ipso* the idea of defilement, because the dust itself is considered impure. Cf. Y. Kaufmann, *History of the Religion of Israel* (Tel-Aviv, 1952), I, 543. Written in Hebrew.

56. E. S. Drower, *op. cit.*, p. 95, n. 5. All the variants of our myth (A812.1) should be compared with the rich Mandaean creation accounts.

57. U. Harva, *op. cit.*, pp. 89 ff. and 114 ff.

58. Sanhedrin, folio 38b, based on Gen. 1:26; Pesikta Rabbati 97a; Gen. Rabbah 8:4; Midrash Teh. 8:2; Num. Rabbah 19. Cf. also Quran 2:28 ff.

59. Midrash Abkir in *Yalkut Shimeoni* 1:44; L. Ginzberg, *op. cit.*, I, 148; V, 169 f.

60. Midrash Konen in Yellinek's *Beth Hamidrash*, II, 26 f.; L. Ginzberg, *op. cit.*, I, 53 f.; III, 110; M. Gaster, *The Chronicles of Jerahmeel* (London, 1899), pp. 14 ff.

61. En. 22:1–6; 20:2f.; cf. L. Ginzberg, *op. cit.*, V, 71.

62. In an African myth from the Ewe tribes God commissions men to perform a certain task for Him. They refuse, however, so God instructs the moon to carry out the same task. The latter executes the errand punctually, is much praised by God, and as a reward becomes immortal, whereas man is destined to die; cf. J. Spieth, *Die Ewe Stämme* (Berlin, 1906), pp. 557 and 874.

63. L. Ginzberg, *op. cit.*, I, 54 f.; M. Gaster, *op. cit.*, p. 15.

Noah, His Wife,

and the Devil

FRANCIS LEE UTLEY

The Ohio State University

by Francis Lee Utley

THE SUBJECT of "Noah, His Wife, and the Devil," in view of its Hebraic derivation, may not be inappropriate in a volume of studies of Biblical and Jewish folklore; but this theme can, in addition, give order and focus to what is in essence the history of civilization—of man's attempt, from primitive beginnings to the uncharted present, to turn error into truth, to convert earlier fancies into knowledge and imagination significant for each successive present day. For convenience, this large subject will be treated under five topics: (1) Noah and Science, (2) Noah and the History of Ideas, (3) Noah and the Fine Arts, (4) Noah and Folklore, and (5) Noah—Poetry and Myth. Categories like these are, of course, mere assumptions of discourse; the spiritual, anthropological, or psychological artifact known as the Noah legend is a totality which in reality cannot be broken into parts except for the purposes of discussion.

I. NOAH AND SCIENCE

The categories crisscross at the very beginning, as we turn to Noah's place in the history of science, for here at once we must begin with myth and folklore.

In their earliest form the deluge tales impinge on the sphere of cosmogony. Hans Kelsen[1] and others have shown us how inseparable from the deluge myths are the earliest creation myths, the deluge being often merely a new creation, and only at times an ethical purification. Paul Radin[2] has told us how brilliant was

59

the work of the early philosophers and poets, whose primitive cosmologies are miracles of imagination and perceptive analysis, however disturbing they may be to those of us who prefer the myth of the wasteland or its positivistic and monolithic contemporary, the world viewed as a well-ordered brick house. Some of these tales are rather lengthy, and it is impossible to catch their full imaginative sweep without plenty of leisure of a kind that folklorists lack today—and envy in the old storytellers. We may, however, give a short excerpt from one that was recorded in 1914 by Paul Radin from the Ojibwa of Southeastern Ontario: [3]

Nenebojo, the culture-hero, painted the kingfisher's feathers with their present colors, and the grateful bird revealed to him that the water-lions had killed his brother. In revenge Nenebojo, disguised as an old stump, ambushed the water-lions and beat their brains out. The waters rose as a consequence, and Nenebojo built a raft on which he put two animals of all the kinds that existed, and with them floated about. When they had drifted for a while, Nenebojo said, "I believe that the water will never subside, so I had better make land again." Accordingly, he sent an otter to dive to the bottom of the water and fetch up some earth; but the otter came back without any. Next he sent the beaver on the same errand, but again in vain. Finally he sent a muskrat, and the muskrat returned to the surface of the water with his paws tightly closed. On opening them, Nenebojo found some little grains of sand, and then he discovered other grains in the mouth of the muskrat. So he put all the grains together, dried them, and blew them into the lake with the horn which he used for calling the animals. In the lake the grains of sand formed an island. Nenebojo enlarged the island and sent out a raven to find out how large it was. But the raven never returned. So Nenebojo decided to send out the hawk, the fleetest of all birds on the wing. After a while the hawk returned, and being asked whether he had seen the raven anywhere, he said he had seen him eating dead bodies by the shore of the lake. Nenebojo said, "Henceforth the raven will have nothing to eat but what he steals." Then Nenebojo sent out the caribou to find out the size of the island. The animal soon returned, saying that the island was not large enough. So Nenebojo blew more sand into the water, and when he had done so, he ceased to make the earth.

The story contains many details of primitive science. Earlier folklorists would have jibbed at the Biblical borrowings—the deluge as a kind of punishment, the pairs of animals of every kind on Nenebojo's raft, the failure of the raven to return. But the central motif of the tale, the earth-diver animal who re-creates the earth with the help of the culture-hero, or demi-urge, is indigenous to Canada, as are the "water-lions," the hawk, the caribou, and Nenebojo's horn. Not only does the tale contain the primitive etiological, or just-so, stories of how the kingfisher got his gaudy colors and the raven his thieving nature, but the ultimate etiology of how the earth was created a second time. Successive creations of this kind, it should be noted, circumvent what Aristotle would call the infinite regress in mechanistic or scientific explanation. Consider, for example, the Hindu theory that the earth is supported by a turtle who rests on a dragon who lies on an elephant. One doesn't bother to explain how the elephant is supported—something, as Robert Frost would say, has to be left to God. We may smile at the sudden interruption of the infinite regress, but most of us, as philosophers or scientists, can get no farther except by closing our systems, as physics is sometimes charged with doing, and structural linguistics wants very much to do.

It would be pleasant to go on with a number of these etio-logical tales associated with the flood, such as the Kathlamet version of the Nenebojo story,[4] which shows how bears lost their tails by jumping out of the ark too quickly and breaking them off, or the Eskimo story (a venture in evolution theory) which explains that mammoths found in the ice were skeptical beasts who refused to board Noah's Ark.[5] But it is more perti-nent here to show how this earth-diver story, which I have called indigenous because its origin in America is probably

pre-Columbian, circumnavigates the North Pole all the way
from Ontario to European Russia. Afanasiev relates a long tale
(which will be reconsidered further on in this paper) about
Noah, his wife, and the devil, as told by Great Russian peasants. Embedded in the tale is the following episode:[6]

> After the flood God came and said: "Is everybody alive?"
> "Thank you, Lord, everybody is alive."
> "Come out, then, all of you."
> All came out. The devil jumped out last, and said, "See, God, you
> wanted to drown me, but here I am, and I am your great enemy."
> "If you are my great enemy, take my hand."
> The devil tried to take His hand, but could not catch it and let
> his arm down.
> "Let me take your hand now," said God. He took the devil's
> hand, and the devil, who always tries to be God's brother, said:
> "Oh, Oh! I shall be rather a younger brother."
> "Get you then, my younger brother, into the sea, grasp a hand-
> ful of earth, let us plant earth."
> They came to a hill around which was the sea. The devil went
> into the sea, picked up a handful of earth but could not pull it out,
> for water washed it out of his hand. He went in three times, and
> on the fourth try, God said, "Brother, use the words, 'My Lord
> Jesus Christ.'"
> The devil said "My Lord Jesus Christ," dove into the sea, and
> pulled out some earth in his hands, no more than two poppy seeds.
> "Go in again, this is not enough earth."
> And so the devil tried to deceive God by putting some earth into
> his mouth, but God circumvented him, and created the meadows,
> woods and groves.

This dualistic tale, which, according to Dähnhardt,[7] was borrowed by the heretical Christian sect of Bogomiles from Iranian dualism, is many times paralleled in Siberia, as in a tale
told by the Yakuts.

Here, unassociated with the flood tale but having some affinity with it, is another story of Satan as a demiurge and earth-
diver:[8]

Twice the devil dived without succeeding, but the third time he changed himself into a swallow and managed to bring up a little mud in his beak. Christ blessed the morsel of mud, which then became the earth, at first flat and smooth as a plate. Intending to create for himself a world of his own, Satan deceitfully hid a part of the mud in his throat. But Christ understood the wiles of the devil and struck him on the back of the neck so that the mud squirted out of his mouth and formed the mountains on the originally smooth surface of the earth.

This slightly more lucid version shows us that, despite the Christian coloration, we are still dealing with a tale close to that of the Ojibwa, the tale of an earth-diver who is Satan but who is also a swallow, like the animal- and bird-divers of the American Indian.

So much for primitive science and the flood. Were one to trace in detail the Semitic flood tale, through its inception in Sumeria and Babylonia, through its Hebrew development in the Bible and in the Talmud and Midrash, and through its Christian and Mohammedan exegesis, one could cite countless just-so stories of the same kind. But we must leap over centuries in time and culture to the seventeenth century, when the flood tale becomes a center of the disputes about faith and reason, in the closed systems of theology and also in those of the new physical sciences. The Renaissance version, which is best told in Don Cameron Allen's *The Legend of Noah*,[9] cannot be detailed here; but we might note, in this connection, the curious paradox that once the pious scientists sought to find an explanation according to mechanistic principles, they raised more doubts and complexities than they could answer with their new battery of abstractions. The climactic debate began with Thomas Burnet's *The [Sacred] Theory of the Earth*,[10] in which the earth, originally smooth, a perfect *a priori* creation (as it was in the Yakut tale which has been cited) was said to have derived its mountains and sea valleys from the deluge. The debate continued with John Woodward,[11] who applied the physical concept of specific gravity to the deposit of fossils and geological strata laid down by the deluge, and with Edmond Halley,[12] who thought his famous comet might have been the catastrophic cause which shattered the earth's crust and released the fountains of the deep—the subterranean waters of the abyss—upon the world. That these scientific simplicities brought less light than heat to the subject is clear from a series of questions asked by John Arbuthnot, an eighteenth-century satirist who assailed Woodward:[13]

What brought the Water of the Abyss upon the surface of the Globe? What succeeded in its room? What dissolv'd the Fossils? and at the same time spared the Animal and Vegetable Substances? What stopt the precipitated Matter in the Descent so that it did not fill up the Cavity of the great Abyss? By what means . . . [did the Strata attain] their Solidity so soon as the Matter whereof they consisted, was arriv'd at the Bottom? What effected the Disruption of the Strata? All these the Doctor has tickt for; putting us off at this time only with the Reason why the Strata ranged themselves in their present order: viz., the different Gravity of the Matter whereof they consist.

We need not trace this geological and physical controversy through succeeding centuries, except to cite the dramatic reversal of Dean William Buckland, who after a brilliant defense of the Mosaic Deluge[14] finally became convinced that geology could not be strictly reconciled with Genesis.[15] Since his time, diluvial geology has receded like the deluge itself in its tenth month.

The usual moral drawn from this chapter in science is that people were rather stupid the day before yesterday. One might counter this modern assurance by observing that the deluge debates were productive of many sciences and branches of learning: physics, astronomy, and geology; comparative religion and folklore; genetics and anthropology; textual criticism, linguistics, and chronology; zoology and paleontology. We have seen physics, astronomy, and geology in process. Comparative religion and folklore have sought to explain the far-flung stories of a deluge which were taken as evidence of the migration of Noah's sons; and these migrations formed the basis for the first speculations about the races of man, with their implications for genetics and anthropology. Textual criticism grew up largely as the application of the eye to the variable words of Noah's story in the Bible; linguistics long revolved around the question of what language was spoken by Noah (Hebrew? Latin? Mayan? High Dutch?); chronology developed around the attempts to synchronize the Mosaic with the Greek accounts of history; zoology and paleontology began to raise the question of the origin of fossils and to wonder how the American animals on the ark got to Palestine and then back from Ararat to America. This is a veritable display of the axiom "out of error, truth," though it provides no assurance that we have yet found ultimate truth, or achieved closed systems—social, physical, or anthropological—which can remain safely closed.

2. NOAH AND THE HISTORY OF IDEAS

Science is closely related to our second topic, Noah and the history of ideas. Perhaps the only difference is that intellectual history must concern itself with faith and metaphysics as well as with the axioms of scientific reason, or that climates of opinion come closer at times to folklore than they do to the heady logic of physics, which seems occasionally, for the layman enjoying the climate, to be more mystical than real to his own common-sense view. Perhaps the subject most germane to our discussion is that of Biblical exegesis, the question of how literal was the sacred text. The basic problem was whether to choose a miraculous or a mechanistic explanation of the wonders of the flood. The clash of opinion is best seen briefly in a related story, that of Joshua's arrested sun when he "fit the Battle of Jericho." Faced by this interruption of natural law, the Renaissance Catholic usually abandoned physics and fell back wholly on miracle; the Protestant might attribute the darkening of the sky to a snow flurry; and Spinoza threw the whole phenomenon back on the psychology of Joshua himself, who thought the universe was geocentric. Normally we contrast Protestant literalness with Catholic imagination, but it should be remembered that the medieval scholastics wrote interminable accounts (which owed much to Aristotle, except for gaps which could not have been filled until the time of Copernicus or Newton) of the structure, sanitation, and mechanics of the ark.

At times, like Lovejoy's disciples, seeking high points in the shift of attitude towards the flood, one settles upon a few figures who are genuine originators of exegesis: St. Augustine, Luther, Pierre Bayle, and Voltaire. These are not necessarily the world's soundest thinkers, but they are great men—originators, men of dramatic influence, pioneers in the history of ideas, even when their ideas seem, from hindsight, to be wrong. The first is St. Augustine, who generously offers numerous conflicting explanations of the dark places in the Bible, because he is fortified by his view that faith comes before understanding, that there is nothing ultimate in this kind of thinking, nothing which will destroy the City of God, of which the Ark is a prefigurative symbol.[16] Luther, insisting on the literal text, opposes the Church's diverse allegories, but he creates a new allegory of his own. Noah is a prophet who, like Luther, enjoys a glass of wine, or rather beer, now and then and who is mocked and scorned by Ham and by the arrogant generation destroyed by the flood, as Luther was mocked and scorned by his three enemies, Turk, Papist, and Jew.[17] Pierre Bayle, in his enticing late-seventeenth-century encyclopedia (a supplement to Moreri), leaves the physical facts about Noah to Moreri and confines himself to an entry on "Cham," in which he displays a double vision much like that of some of our modern poets. Making pious comments about the absurdities and obscenities of Rabbinical fables, among them the suggestion that Noah's wife was incestuous with her son Cham, Bayle manages to "deluge" the whole story with mud.[18] Voltaire is quite as concerned and twice as sly, and he never tires, in his extensive writings, of discrediting the flood tale, as in his celebrated remark that the fossils found in the Alps were probably left there not by the flood but by pilgrims returning from Jerusalem.[19]

In the nineteenth century these encyclopedic minds disappeared and the more modest task of discrediting the Bible by fragmented scientific study was scattered among a host of students, such as Buckland and Lyell,[20] who gave the *coup de grâce* to the geological flood, or Andree[21] and Frazer,[22] who showed that the widespread flood tales, long used to prove that eyewitnesses of the flood had populated every land on earth, really demonstrate just the opposite. There are also plenty of the others, the too-late-born. One could cite a Catholic of a decade ago[23] and a Lutheran of more recent years[24] who again defended the literal truth of the tale against all geological evidence. We still hear of scientific expeditions to scale the heights of Ararat in order to find the relics of the ark, though the early Syriac Christians tried to circumvent that form of curiosity by explaining that the mountain had angels on it to prevent men from going too high.[25] We need say little about other recent manifestations of the old interest, except to point out that Immanuel Velikovsky,[26] who has explained creation and the Joshua story by a strange mixture of synchronized folklore and selective observation which so far simulates science as to cause some scientists to try to have his books hindered in their distribution, has promised a book on the flood. Thus it remains part of the climate (perhaps the Patagonian part) of opinion.

3. NOAH AND THE FINE ARTS

With his usual persistence, Noah also invades the history of art. The field is vast, but there is room for a few generalizations based on the examination of several hundred pictures. As Allen[27] has shown especially with regard to the Renaissance, the arts follow and illuminate the history of ideas. The first evidences are on Phrygian coins[28] and Roman catacomb frescoes, where Noah and sometimes his wife are pictured as *orantes*, or praying figures, in a rude box-like ark not much larger than the figures themselves and accompanied by a dove with an olive branch, all of it demonstrating the human and religious truths of salvation and baptism. The contribution of the active artists of the Middle Ages was to break the story into its parts, into such dramatic episodes as God's Command to Noah, the Building of the Ark, the Entry of the Animals, the Exit and Sacrifice, and the Drunkenness of Noah. Most of these episodes keep close to the literal Bible text, though in a fourteenth-century manuscript (*Queen Mary's Psalter,*[29] in the British Museum) we encounter one version (presumably Slavic*) that does not. Noah's wife is seduced by the devil to give Noah a potion that is to make him reveal the secret of what he is building; the devil enters the ark in the shadow of Noah's wife and makes a hole in the ark; and the serpent plugs the hole with his tail. (This rare iconographical motif is illustrated in the accompanying picture, from a Russian manuscript once in the possession of the nineteenth-century Count Uvarov.[30] Most of the other manuscripts tediously repeat pictures of an anatomized three-story ark.)

In the notable twelfth-century frescoes of Saint Savin,[31] one panel is almost completely filled by an ark with a crescent-shaped hull and a monstrous figurehead. Eight human souls are in the top story; the birds, except for the extrapolated raven, are in the middle; and the animals are in the bottom. A few corpses float casually about, and two giants of Rabbinical origin try to save themselves by climbing on the boat, which is clearly more important than the people whom it shelters or rejects. In a famous series in the *Loggie* of the Vatican,[32] Raphael began the Renaissance practice of pushing the ark to the rear of the

* The origins of this tale are discussed in Sec. iv, following.

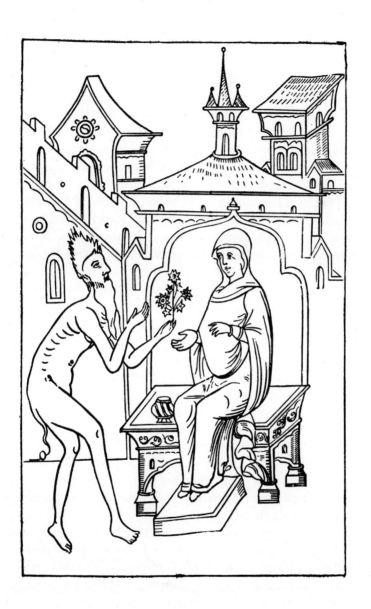

stage. In one picture—of the building of the ark—this is only partly so, since we see a commanding framework filling the picture, with a heroic Noah and his workmen in the foreground. But in another the ark is surrounded by flashes of lightning in the rear, while drowning humanity tries to save itself in the foreground. This interest in the human aspects of the flood is anticipated in the fifteenth-century Bennozo Gozzoli,[33] whose "Drunkenness of Noah" becomes a lively rustic scene of wine-making; the traditional half-naked Noah, who is being covered by his pious sons, is shoved to one side, where the eye is distracted by a fascinating study of the columns above. Michaelangelo's three frescoes in the Sistine Chapel[34] are among the high points of the Renaissance: the drunkenness of Noah, humanized by a digging agriculturalist, a huge wine vat, and the powerful limbs of Noah and his three sons; the sacrifice after the flood, in which the altar is subordinated to the complex design of interweaving human arms of the eight survivors; and above all, the highly detailed flood scene, with its cubic ark in the middle distance and its countless studies of the doomed mortals in the foreground, seeking escape in trees and heights, in a half-careening boat, and in poorly constructed shelters. Humane and moving as this story is, its naturalism and humanitarianism fall short of Nicolas Poussin's seventeenth-century "L'Hiver ou Le Déluge,"[35] where striving humanity swims, clambers on rocks, and tries to preserve itself in struggling rowboats, with the ark now in the far distance and the human beings themselves partly obscured by the landscape details with which Poussin was obsessed. One religious symbol remains, the serpent clambering up the rocks. This touch of diabolism is perhaps repeated in a rather lurid painting by William Bell Scott (1811–90),[36] in which the center of interest is no longer the ark and its eight survivors, nor the landscape, nor the suffering victims of the flood, but the luxurious and vicious orgies of a doomed generation. More architecture than art is displayed in one of the numerous eighteenth-century *Kupferbibels*,[37] which gives detailed plans for the three stories of the ark and many other details of the carpentry. The old theme has not lost its savor today. In several of Bernard Reder's fanciful woodblocks in the Museum of Modern Art[38] we see a concentration on ancillary scenes and more design than narrative. The "Meal on the Ark" is dominated by pillars and suggests a medievalistic attempt to divide the scene between rather too festive human beings and some hungry animals that are being fed. In the "Giant Escaping the Flood" there seems to be a miniature ark in the background, but the center of the composition shows a massive use of horizontal cloud and vertical giant.

Art demonstrates immediately because it counts primarily upon vision, and what it demonstrates (for the purposes of this essay) is the constant readaptation of the old parable to the dominant emotions of the time—the early Christian desire for salvation, the speculative curiosity of the Middle Ages and the Enlightenment, the humanitarian sympathies of the Renaissance, the undisciplined, nineteenth-century love of the exotic, and the religion of art and the search for novelty in the twentieth century.

4. NOAH AND FOLKLORE

The most significant story of Noah, his wife, and the devil is the one in *Queen Mary's Psalter*. This story (tale-type 825 in the Aarne-Thompson classification[39]) will serve to introduce our discussion of "Noah and Folklore."

The origins of AT 825 are complex. It is a folktale based on a written source, of course, for somewhere in its center lies the Biblical version. But it also owes much to Jewish and Moslem commentary, to concepts borrowed either from the Persian struggle between good and evil or from the basic primitive dualism of all mankind, to Greek Christian commentators like Epiphanius,[40] who records a Gnostic tale of how Noah's Wife Pyrrha burned up the ark when she sat on it, and perhaps to the shamanistic rites and myths of primitive tribes in Northern Europe and Asia. Possibly the tale was put together and disseminated by the Bogomiles, a Bulgarian dualistic sect who had a great influence on the Albigensians of southern France in the Middle Ages; but there are difficulties in this interpretation, as conceived by Veselovskij[41] and developed by Oskar Dähnhardt.[42] (I have been able to supplement Dähnhardt's extensive collectanea in his four-volume *Natursagen* with a mass of new material from Slavic and Arabic printed sources, and with freshly recorded variants from the folklore archives of Finland, Lithuania, Estonia, Rumania, Latvia, Turkey, and Ireland.)

The proper approach to such material is to order and compare it, using the techniques of the Finnish geographical-historical school. Here it will suffice to present some excerpts from typical versions from Russia, Estonia, and Ireland. The Russian earth-diver fragment from the *Legendy* of Afanasiev, who records a nineteenth-century version of a tale which is at least three centuries older in its original form, has already been mentioned. Let us follow the rest of the tale:[43]

Noah [taking the place of Adam] ate the apple on the instigation of his wife Evga, and God immediately decided to have a flood. He told Noah to build the ark but to keep it secret. Noah built it for several years in the forest. The devil asked him what he was doing, but Noah refused to answer. The devil asked Evga to inquire, but Noah the righteous told his wife that he simply had been walking in the forest—looking at the trees and amusing himself. So the devil directed Evga to make some beer with hops in it. Noah meanwhile had completed his work and was congratulating himself that he had finished half a year ahead of schedule. He came home and started eating.

"Evga," he said, "is there anything to drink after the meal?" [She gave him the brew, which, other versions say, was made with the froth from the mouth of a boar or a horse.] Then Noah told all, and the devil destroyed the ark. In six months Noah built it again [often in other versions with the help of an angel and by means of miraculously collected or miraculously fitted timbers].

When the animals were brought together, the devil told Evga, "Take the shoe off your left foot and look at me through the toes, and don't go into the ark until the terrible flood comes, until the water spreads all over, and until Noah says to you, 'Come to me, you cursed one, or you will drown.' "

Evga obeyed and Noah called out the evocative words. As soon as he heard them, the devil jumped into the ark, turned into a mouse, and gnawed a hole in the bottom. The snake plugged the hole with his head. [According to other versions, Noah promised the snake the blood of one man per day in return for his services, and then destroyed the snake by fire to avoid the bargain; but since the ashes became fleas or mosquitos, the snake still got the blood of one man per day. Then follows the curse on the raven, who has forgotten to return to the ark because he was lured by the bodies of the dead—henceforth he must live on carrion, look like a burnt stump (that is, have a black color), and die as soon as his children are born.]

This elaborate folktale type seems to have spread from Bulgarian and Russian centers to the North, East, and West. In Estonia, for instance, we have many such tales, a collection of which was generously provided by the former director of the archives, Oskar Loorits. Here is one of them:[44]

God showed Noah an island where fir wood was growing and told him to build an ark and have it ready in three years, but not to speak about it to anyone. . . . There were six stones on which Noah started to build the ark. Although he hewed and cut every day, the stones did not dull the edge of the axe. The Old Wicked One [also called the Judas] then came to Noah's wife and asked:

"Where does your husband go every day?"

"I don't know," the woman said.

So the Judas made some wine and gave it to Noah, and Noah's only comment was: "This is very good."

"Wait, wait, then we shall make something better still," said the devil and the wife, and they made a sweeter drink. [In another version the drink is made with "the foam from a boar's snout."]

Noah looked and saw that it was good and sweet and drank

abundantly and became drunk. Then he told his wife that he had
been building an ark and that it would be finished in three days,
and that he would then call aboard whomever he wished and the
flood would come. He went to work again, but when he struck
with his ax it was blunted by the stones, and he could not finish the
work until he called on God to help him. The devil-Judas came
again to Noah's wife, and told her:

"Don't go aboard until he names me, too. Let the water rise
even to the edge, for he won't have the heart to leave you behind."
[The story here follows the other versions, until Noah says: "You
old wicked one, you fiend, come aboard!"] Thus the devil got
aboard. Again he gnawed a hole, and the serpent slipped his tail
into the hole, telling the devil that he had once made the serpent
mislead Eve, but that this time the serpent was on the side of man.

For a long time, despite careful search, I discovered few versions of this legend in the West. Though there are some fourteenth-century Swedish wall-paintings in Scania that illustrate
this motif,[45] nothing more has been found in Sweden, in spite of
the fact that the Swedish archives are unusually complete. So
also in Germany. The thirteenth-century Viennese poet, Jansen Enikel,[46] who was perhaps in direct contact with the Slavic
world, has a version which includes the Devil's ruse (i.e., the
curse) for getting aboard the ark and the helpful animal which
stops the leak. In some way, perhaps through Baltic and North
Sea routes, the tale slipped over to the British Isles. It appears in
a strange fifteenth-century Biblical play from Newcastle,[47] and
also (as noted) in Queen Mary's Psalter. In view of this scarcity
of intervening material, I was indeed astonished when I began
to receive (from James Delargy, the generous director of the
Irish Folklore Commission) a body of tales collected in recent
times in Ireland. I was, admittedly, suspicious of the first tale
that I received, fearing that some collector had primed a storyteller with the Dähnhardt tale or that the Irish storyteller knew
German; but there are so many well-attested Irish versions that
I am content to accept the "miraculous leap" or diffusion to the

West. Here is one of the fullest of the Irish tales, taken down in 1951 by Ciarán Bairéad from Michael Silke of Oran, County Galway:[48]

The ark took twenty-one years to build . . . it was destroyed every seven years. God tells Noah that He is going to send the deluge to destroy the earth and commands Noah to build the ark, and nobody is to know where it is being built or that it *is* being built. . . . On the seventh day a gentleman comes to Noah's wife and asks her where her husband is working; she says she does not know. He then asks for a drink and is given a mug of ale; he spits into it and immediately it forms a froth which spills on to the floor. Previously ale had not frothed, and the result of the stranger's action is that ale has since been the source of temptation and evil. The stranger tells the wife to ask Noah on his return where he is working, and goes away. The wife does so, and on Noah's refusal to reveal the secret, they quarrel [which they had never done previously]. The next day the stranger tells her to repeat the dose of ale, and Noah gets drunk and reveals his secret. The stranger waits for seven years and then, when the ark is almost completed, Noah finds it reduced to matchwood. Noah builds the ark a second time, and after careful instructions, the stranger tells the wife to tempt Noah again with drink. This is difficult, because Noah has been a teetotaller since the last bad experience, but the wife tells him that she will leave him unless he accepts a drink of peace. So he reveals the secret, and the second ark also is destroyed. He is ready to give up, but a voice tells him to go to a certain glen and build the ark there, where the sound of the hammering can be heard over the entire earth so that his adversary will not know the source of the noise. [This hammering motif, which appears also in some Eastern versions, is said to be the origin of the echo.] The stranger comes the third time, but Noah resists all temptation, and the ark is successfully completed. [In other Irish versions the devil gets into the ark by having Noah curse his wife.] On the ark Noah makes seven pegs for the animals which must be tied up, such as horses and cattle, and these animals are the last to go on the ark. The water rises, and Noah discovers that one of the pegs is missing from its hole. He searches everywhere, and when he returns, the seventh peg seems to be there—it is the devil disguised as a peg. To this peg Noah ties the sire-horse, who remains quiet until the deluge has reached its peak and then becomes so violent that Noah has to kill him lest he rend the ark asunder. Thus the mare is without a mate, and Noah is advised by Heaven to take a rib out of himself and place it in the horse, and that is why there is a human rib in the horse and why the horse is so docile. [At this point Mr. Bairéad asked Mr. Silke if he had ever heard any other version of the incident and was told: "That is not what occurred at all, but that is how the tale is usually told. When the sire-horse was killed, Noah received divine permission to perform his functions on the mare, and that is the reason that ever since the horse is so docile, and the old people believed that no animal was closer akin to the human than the horse." There are other versions of] this mating of Noah with the mare.[49] Now Noah realizes that the substitute peg is his adversary and finds the right one in his pocket and stops the water which is pouring in. There follows the curse on the belated raven, who is to be coal-black and to live on carrion. The good dove, however, is blessed by never henceforth being subject to "feather-disease" or moulting.

The similarities between these three tales, Russian, Estonian, and Irish, are sufficient to demonstrate that this lively story has traveled far. That the direction of the borrowing is from the east is clear because of the age of the Russian tales, the presence of Russian culture traits, and other features of the whole legendary complex. The extraordinary closeness of the three versions at first arouses the suspicion that some printed version has intervened. But actually, in view of the sparseness of intervening versions in Western Europe (which seems clearly not to be the fault of scanty collecting), the similarities may help us to understand what has happened. First of all, there is a structural element in the associated Biblical tale which keeps the main outline of the story in its logical form. Secondly, the tale is probably one of those which demonstrate transmission by a long sea-jump rather than by wavelike transmission over land. Stith Thompson says: "As for actual routes of travel, tales follow the paths of the most important cultural intercourse. They will do this over huge stretches of water even with more ease than they will invade a neighboring country of alien culture. ... Many tales have thus gone from Germany immediately to Sweden without touching Denmark."[50] We need not here demonstrate what needs no demonstration, that there has been plenty of merchant trade between the Baltic countries, including Russia, and the British Isles, including Ireland. But it is worthy of note that two places where the legend has reached the West are on the sea—the port of Newcastle and the southern tip of Sweden. One jump by sea presupposes fewer stages than slow diffusion by land and better explains the close similarities among the variants.

A few additional folktales which have grown up around the Biblical flood theme will be briefly referred to here. These include the Arabic story in which the hesitant donkey substitutes for Noah's wife in getting the Devil aboard the ark;[51] the Polish story in which the Blessed Virgin creates a cat out of her glove to pursue the demon mouse;[52] the Arabic tales of how the elephant on the ark sneezed out a pig, and the lion, a cat;[53] the Lithuanian[54] and Finnish tales of how the disproportionate members of donkey and camel are due to a faulty checking system on the ark; the Jewish and German[55] tales of how the blackness of Ham's skin came from his incontinence with his wife, and the other tales of how the phoenix and the unicorn[56] and the Giant Og[57] were towed along by the ark and how the wild animals chased away the sinners who tried to board the vessel and how Noah's vine[58] was fertilized by the blood of the sheep, lion, ape, and pig, accounting for the various stages of drunkenness. The sum of all these is a vivid folk poetry that constantly re-creates the oral myth around a written center.

5. NOAH—POETRY AND MYTH

Our final topic, the Noah legend in written poetry and myth, has a curious timeliness because of the vigorous attempts made by modern critics to equate poetry and myth. Up to a point the critics have been successful in doing so, and in demonstrating how poetry, a private creation and expression, sometimes communicates its meaning so well to an alert reader. But to ignore the distinction between poetry and myth is also dangerous, though the difference may be a matter of degree, or polarity. Leaving aside the always vexed question of origins, the major difference seems to be that written poetry is relatively more consciously formed than ancient or even modern myth. What is common to both is the act of unconscious creation that occurs in the writing of the best poetry; but, though recognizing the need for demonstrating this mutuality, one must acknowledge that the processes of written poetry in a civilization like ours cannot fully reproduce the processes of ancient myth. (Also, we had better remember that consciously to re-create in ourselves the myth-making spirit would be to follow directly the lead of certain special-pleading politicians whose purposes are at least questionable.) William Butler Yeats is a celebrated example of a poet said to create his own myths, but in spite of the elaborate system expressed in *The Vision*, Yeats's really stirring poems revivify old myths rather than create new ones. "Leda and the Swan," "The Second Coming," and "Sailing to Byzantium," for instance, draw heavily on Greek mythology, Christian revelation, the phoenix myth, and the visual myths represented in the mosaics in Saint Sophia in Constantinople.

Myth and poetry are always created in a mysterious fashion, and one of the vexed problems of modern poets is how to evoke whatever unconsciousness remains to us, now that we know so much about the unconscious mind. Whatever complexes exist in Hamlet or the Noah tale, their power owes something to the fact that Shakespeare and the early Semites did not know the theories of Freud and Jung.

Myth suffers a good deal from the mythographers, and no tale has suffered more than that of Noah. The lunar mythologists have had their day with it. Ignoring the boxlike nature of the Biblical ark, and perhaps remembering such medieval representations as those of Saint Savin,[59] Hermann Usener,[60] and others,[61] they have equated the journey of the ark with the journey across the horizon of the crescent moon. The euhemerists, who find history in every folktale, have energetically searched for traces of the exact local catastrophe corresponding to the deluge and have written the history of the migrations of Noah's sons in the light of subsequent events.[62] The vegetarian theorists have made much of Noah in his culture-hero role as the planter of the grape.[63] (In modern Greek folktales[64] Dionysus replaces Noah in the story of Noah and the vine.) The ritualists hint darkly of Canaanite castration ceremonies lying behind what the Bible calls Ham's mockery of his father's nakedness.[65] A psychoanalytical theorist like Geza Roheim[66] finds in the flood some kind of regression to the amniotic fluid where we were happy for the last time, before birth from the sea-like womb. He has never gone so far as to say that the animals on the ark, specifically the male and female, are symbolic evidences of the recurrent evolution of the ebryo, though one may suppose that Noah's ontogeny will recapitulate phylogeny one of these days. Perhaps all these theories are a kind of poetry themselves, but if modern poets use this kind of thinking too freely, their poetry may never attain the universality in time, or immediate popularity, that they really desire. They would do better to turn to the Noah story, as poets have in the past, with a fresh eye not too much distracted by the work of speculative scholars.

I want to concentrate upon a few of the most recent poetic versions, and so I shall do no more than hint at some of their predecessors. The archetypical Gilgamesh epic,[67] which is probably closer to the source of the Semitic flood myth than the Biblical accounts, is poetry itself. The fifth- and sixth-century Christian poet Avitus[68] puts an epic Virgilian sweep into his seascapes and giants before the flood. The eighth-century Caedmonian Genesis[69] has the hammer-like verse of Germanic epic, with its vigorous natural description, its love of violence, and its complete lack of any humanitarian feeling for the sinful doomed ones. Biblical poems of the later Middle Ages, like the Middle-English *Cursor Mundi*[70] the Latin *Aurora* of Peter of Riga,[71] and the French poem of Herman of Valenciennes,[72] cover some of this epic magnitude with the fascination of added apocryphal detail. The sixteenth- and seventeenth-century poets Guillaume du Bartas[73] and Michael Drayton[74] cram the story with Biblical and scientific exegesis, and Vondel's *Noah* (1667)[75] is a highly imaginative dramatic poem which concentrates on the world before the flood and on the conflict (engineered by the devil Apollyon) between Noah and his sinning fellows. In Milton's *Paradise Lost,*[76] the Archangel Michael, after the fall, prefigures Old Testament history to Adam as a prelude to the coming of Christ, a good sign of Milton's unwillingness to cast overboard the traditions of medieval Catholicism, despite his own commitments. Though inevitably influenced by the age in which he lived, Milton provided Adam with certain lines which ring immensely true to an age like our own, which begins to despair of the blessings of knowledge, or at least of "prediction." Speaking of the destruction of his children in the flood, Adam says:[77]

> O Visions ill foreseen! Better had I
> Liv'd ignorant of future, so had borne
> My part of evil onely, each dayes lot
> Anough to beare; those now, that were dispenst
> The burd'n of many Ages on me light
> At once, by my foreknowledge gaining Birth
> Abortive, to torment me ere their being,
> With thought that they must be.

We may remember how the prophecies of Huxley in *Brave New World* and of Orwell in *1984* have disturbed our recent rest—the more so in that we have not, like Milton's Adam, the assurance that an archangel is revealing God's plan to us or that an atoning Christ is prefigured by the rainbow.

In the latter years of the seventeenth century Edward Ecclestone[78] wrote a verse-drama on the flood, using the epic machinery of Milton—councils of the devils, a Moloch who tries to board the ark as in the folktales, and Milton's personified Death and Sin. In the eighteenth century Johann Jakob Bodmer's *Noachide*, which includes a romance between Japheth and Kerenhappuch, was translated into English by Joseph Collyer.[79] According to Collyer, Kerenhappuch (a daughter of Job) was descended from a race that looked very much like the American Indian. Ten of the books in Bodmer's epic follow the now common practice of centering on the world before the flood, and Ham combines the prejudices of a hero of the German and English sentimental drama with the polish of a Lord Chesterfield: [80]

We all know what woes the sons of Adam have suffer'd for listening to female sentiments: yet I hope to view this creature so fair, so lovely, and still preserve my native dignity. . . . [I] persuade myself that all the lustre of female charms, can never allure us to quit the path of wisdom and of duty; for should they make an ignoble use of their attractions, I'll combat them with rigid virtue.

In the nineteenth century Jean Ingelow also concentrated on the world before the flood, without actually getting to the flood in her story. She retells the usual romance of Japheth, a character invariably chosen for love stories, apparently because he, among the sons of Noah, was considered to be the ancestor of the white ("the master") race.[81] Noah's wife, Niloiya, prepares her slave Amarant for marriage with Japheth, and Amarant's response is described in melting tones: [82]

> . . . all the damsel's soul
> Was full of yearning wonder, and her robe
> Slipped from her hand, and her right innocent face
> Was seen betwixt her locks of tawny hair
> That dropped about her knees, and her two eyes,
> Blue as the much-loved flower that rims the beck,
> Looked sweetly on Niloiya.

The most interesting feature of the poem is its attempt to blend the Noah story with the truths of evolution by moralizing the latter. The miscegenation of the giants before the flood, who have tainted their own kind and that of their pygmy slaves (whom they have bred small for the sake of obedience, somewhat in the manner of the rulers of Huxley's *Brave New World*) demonstrates that "evolution" must not be tampered with. Good eugenics leaves evolution to God.

From this nineteenth-century sentimentality we move quickly to the present, when the old parable once more becomes reinvigorated with the imagination of genuine poets. Four recent treatments deserve comment: C. Day Lewis's *Noah and the Waters*, Rumer Godden's *In Noah's Ark*, Roy Campbell's *The Flaming Terrapin*, and André Obey's *Noah*.

Lewis,[83] like many leftist poets, derives his symbolic center from Madame de Pompadour's "Après nous le déluge." The epigraph is from the *Communist Manifesto*, describing how certain members of the ruling class will turn at the crucial moment to the side of the proletariat. The "Flood" is a fantastic ballet dancer, who is opposed by the burgesses with all the weapons in their armory—abuse, compromise, appeals to the spirit of Old England, and finally war—while Noah, one of their own class, becomes "A needle midway between two fields of force" which finally swings toward the left. He says:[84]

> ... see me also as Noah, a man of substance,
> Father of his family, contented simply
> By the intimate circle of the leisured seasons:
> A man of peace, one who responded always
> To the time-honoured charities of hearth and home,
> Preferring death to change. ...
> Well may you look askance when such an one,
> Leaving the lode and gear of his proved fortune,
> Should ask concessions from a savage flood
> And upon rack and ruin build his hopes.

This is the protest of the nineteen-thirties against the bourgeois world, with the poet himself as the deflected compass needle.

We are not brought much farther by the strange mixture of flippancy and seriousness, of bright comment and flabby verse, which is Rumer Godden's *In Noah's Ark*.[85] The conflict is between Ham, the materialist, and Pegasus, the vehicle of poets. Pegasus is thrown into a cell, and his wings are clipped, but he has his revenge when Ham himself turns into a poet at the end of the play. Here we have, as in the woodblocks of Bernard Reder, an appeal to the religion of art, a solution to the world's dilemma which counters that of Day Lewis. But we are not quite sure why all this takes place on Noah's Ark.

Roy Campbell, the South African poet, evokes in *The Flaming Terrapin*[86] a gigantesque vision of the flood, somewhat in the style of Robinson Jeffers, and expresses a tribute to man's indomitable and persistent individualism which is quite unlike Jeffers. The Flaming Terrapin is a prehistoric reptile, a symbol which places the flood in its right geological epoch and draws the ark on to its violent victory. Noah, who bends the terrapin to his task, is conceived in massive and heroic terms:[87]

> ... Upon the snows
> Of Ararat gigantic Noah rose,
> Stiffened for fierce exertion, like the thong
> That strings a bow before its arrow strong
> Sings on the wind; and from his great fists hurled
> Red thunderbolts to purify the world.

In the poem the enemy is, as usual, Satan:[88]

> Now he comes prowling on the ravaged earth,
> He whores with Nature, and she brings to birth
> Monsters perverse, and fosters feeble minds,
> Nourishing them on stenches such as winds
> Lift up from rotting whales.

One supposes that these rotting whales are the brothers of the dead hippopotamus which taints the air in Conrad's story of that liberal gone wrong, Kurtz in *Heart of Darkness*. At any rate, Satan's monstrous offspring are the usual enemies of the poets: mediocrity, plutocracy, "patriotism, Satan's angry son," priests, corruption, and the shadow of death. But individualism wins out, through Noah, the ark, and the terrapin and we end with the silent chanting of the soul: [89]

> Though times shall change and stormy ages roll,
> I am that ancient hunter of the plains
> That raked the shaggy flitches of the Bison:
> Pass, world; I am that dreamer that remains
> The Man, clear-cut against the last horizon.

This man against the sky will remind us slightly more of Edwin Arlington Robinson than of the dehumanized Robinson Jeffers.

Perhaps we blow a little cold at these three Noahs—the flood hero as a revolutionary, as a follower of Pegasus, or as a rampant individualist—but we must admit that the authors have found plenty of wood in the old Babylonian vessel for their youthful, somewhat uncontrolled fire.

André Obey's highly successful play, *Noah*,[90] provides a kind of reconciliation of their fragmented views. It is a skilled psychological drama which, for all the fantasy of its personified beasts, has a breadth of human awareness that lifts it above the other three modern treatments of the legend. The play oscillates between the joy of Noah as he builds the ark and stands before the flood, on the threshold of a new life, and the melancholy which comes to him when the voyage is over. As Francis Fergusson has said in his *The Idea of a Theater*,[91] the play moves in a circle from the cradle to the grave but, by its spiral movement, provides renewed faith in the life-cycle. The ark swarms with tensions, between the animals and the human beings, among the sons of Noah themselves, between the conservative wife and the pragmatic husband, between men and the elements, between youth and age. The realities of life in this floating remnant of the world are not skirted, and there is no overemphasis, either, on the lustful world before the flood or the brave new world to come, for the scenes divide skillfully between the old world, three specimen days on the waters, and the day of landing with the rainbow. Throughout the play the children are full of spit and vinegar and malice, and they show their lack of balance, their youthful *hubris*, in the final scene, where they march to opposite corners of the world yelling bad names at one another—Ham is called nigger, Shem a chink, and Japheth a paleface. They very much recall some of the dangers of our regressive and adolescent epoch in history. Mama, who has never quite been able to understand or endure the whole affair, begins at the end to lose her mind and reverts to the days before the flood, wondering why her old friends do not come to visit her in her loneliness. All this Noah must bear, but he stolidly picks up his axe, the axe with which he had built the protecting ark, and begins to build a new house for the new life. Only in God's rainbow does he find promise, and the implication is that only he can see its meaning.

Obey is too polite a playwright to have put the other poets referred to into his own play, but in a sense they are there—the lonely artist, the unrestrained revolutionary, the breast-thumping individualist, not as the hero Noah in his wisdom, but as the children full of arrogance and mad indirection. The fault of the others is that they have closed their systems, as poets should never do. They fashion their myths too consciously, on the model of the mythographers, whereas Obey lets the myth grow naturally from a ripe human center from which all the best myths gain their life and their significance.[92]

A good friend, an economist, once asked me what *significance* this long study on Noah might possibly have. After all, the subject was ancient history, an irrational legend, and it appears, of all places, in the Old Testament. There was very little time, so I gave him a feeble answer, that it had something to do with the slavery problem (Ham) and with the "labor movement." I should have said, with more force, that the story has manifold significance, if we know how to tap it, as parable, folktale, poetic symbol, or myth, or as plain psychological truth. It has, among other things, the significance of learning for its own sake, a significance too much scanted by the hordes within and without our universities who are tending to reject the books that they would be ignoramuses without. Archimedes helped us a little with our bathtubs, and another writer, Copernicus, helped us to abandon our geocentric universe. There was also a writer named Hegel who helped us to still another writer named Marx. Admittedly, knowledge for its own sake is not enough; one must let one's mind grow through seeing the minds of men at work through recurrent time. In this Noah story we surely see that very thing—the genuinely working minds of highly primitive and highly sophisticated men—vivid and eager, full of *hubris* and full of persistence, imaginative, solid, fanciful, reasoning, breaking closed systems, full of error and of truth.

The Noah story, used sensibly, can bring the man who wants to know something of culture change, and of the permanence of culture, to a number of contrasting cultures: the despotic and canalized (canal-bound) polytheism of Babylonia, the ruder but more consistent monotheism which the Hebrews learned in the Wilderness and the Promised Land, the dedicated devotion of the early Christians who still had some hope for a millennium, the feudalism and formalism of their medieval followers, the humanism of the early Renaissance and the humanitarianism of more recent centuries, the agricultural life of Palestine and the challenging urban life of our own time. We can witness the change of supernatural sanctions from the mad gods of Babylonia to the wrathful God of the Old Testament to the gentle God of André Obey, the change of idea and direction from the cosmologies of Genesis to those of the Siberian, Russian, and Irish peoples who gained part of their etiology from that book, the change from the physicist's paradise of the seventeenth century to the biologist's purgatory of the nineteenth century and the anthropologist's inferno of the twentieth century, the change from the hierarchic world of the past to the present world of social change and protest.

If this theme, which can bind together and give life to all our various specialties, has no significance, one scarcely knows the meaning of the word. It seems to me that, despite storms, the ark still floats and preserves its saving remnant.

Try...to feel
How high and weary it was, on the waters where
He rocked his only world, and everyone's.
Forgive the hero, you who would have died
Gladly with all you knew; he rode that tide
To Ararat: all men are Noah's sons.[93]

Notes

1. Hans Kelsen, *Society and Nature* (Chicago, 1943), pp. 169–85.
2. Paul Radin, *Primitive Man as Philosopher* (New York, 1927).
3. Abridged from the account in Sir James George Frazer, *Folk-Lore in the Old Testament* (London, 1919), I, 305–6.
4. Frazer, *ibid.*, I, 326.
5. Frazer, *ibid.*, I, 328.
6. A. N. Afanasiev, *Narodnyja russkija legendy* (Moscow, 1859), pp. 48 ff. Translated for the writer by Mrs. Tatiana Moseley.
7. Oskar Dähnhardt, *Natursagen* (Leipzig and Berlin, 1907), I, 261 and *passim*.
8. Ugo Holmberg, *Finno-Ugric, Siberian*, in *The Mythology of All Races* (Boston, 1927), IV, 314.
9. Don Cameron Allen, *The Legend of Noah* (Urbana, Ill., 1949).
10. Thomas Burnet, *The [Sacred] Theory of the Earth* (London, 1684). The Latin version, *Telluris Theoria Sacra*, appeared in 1681.
11. John Woodward, *An Essay toward a Natural History of the Earth* (London, 1695).
12. "Some Considerations about the Cause of the Universal Deluge," *Philosophical Transactions*, XXXIII (London, 1726, for 1724–25), 118–23.
13. *An Examination of Dr. Woodward's Account of the Deluge* (London, 1697), as quoted in Lester M. Beattie, *John Arbuthnot: Mathematician and Satirist* (Cambridge, Mass., 1935), p. 196.
14. Dean William Buckland, *Reliquiae Diluvianae* (London, 1823).

15. Buckland, *Geology and Mineralogy Considered with Reference to Natural Theology*, (Bridgewater Treatise VI), 2 vols. (Philadelphia, 1837).

16. See, for instance, *De Civitate Dei*, xv. 26–27.

17. "Vorlesungen über 1. Mose," *D. Martin Luthers Werke* (Weimar, 1883 ff.), XLI, 299, 389–90.

18. *Dictionnaire historique et critique* (Paris, 1820), V, 54.

19. *Oeuvres complètes de Voltaire* (nouvelle édition; Paris, 1877–85), XIX, 475; Andrew D. White, *A History of the Warfare of Science with Theology in Christendom* (New York, 1897), I, 229.

20. See notes 14 and 15 on Buckland; see also Sir Charles Lyell, *Principles of Geology*, 2 vols. (Pittsburg, 1837).

21. Richard Andree, *Die Flutsagen* (Braunschweig, 1891).

22. *Folk-Lore in the Old Testament*, I, 338–61.

23. Donat Poulet, *Tous les hommes sont-ils fils de Noé?* (Ottawa, 1941).

24. Alfred M. Rehwinkel, *The Flood* (Saint Louis, Mo., 1951).

25. *Mandeville's Travels*, ed. P. Hamelius (Early English Text Society, Original Series 153–154; London, 1923–29), II, 92.

26. Immanuel Velikovsky, *Worlds in Collision* (New York, 1950), p. viii.

27. *Legend of Noah*, pp. 155 ff.

28. E. Babelon, "La Tradition Phrygienne du Déluge," *Revue de l'Histoire des Religions*, XXIII (1891), 174–83.

29. Sir George Warner, ed., *Queen Mary's Psalter* (London, 1912), Plates 9–12.

30. Moncure D. Conway, *Demonology and Devil–Lore* (New York, 1879), II, 413. I do not know the present location of the manuscript, once owned by Count Uvarov. Conway reproduced the picture from F. I. Buslaev (*Istoricheskie ocherki russkoĭ narodnoĭ slovesnosti i iskustva*, St. Petersburg, 1861), I, 441.

31. *Romanesque Painting, The Frescoes of Saint Savin: The Nave*, Introduction by Georges Guillard (New York, 1944), Plates II–VII.

32. Oskar Fischel, *Raphael*, Bernard Rackham, tr. (London, 1948), I, 99–100; II, Plate 100.

33. Pietto Bargellini, *La fiaba pittorica de Benozzo Gozzoli* (Florence, 1947).

34. Charles de Tolnay, *The Sistine Ceiling* (Princeton, N. J., 1949), pp. 131–33, Plates 32–39.

35. Theodor Ehrenstein, *Das Alte Testament in der Graphik* (Wien, 1936 ff.), p. 54.

36. W. Shaw Sparrow, *The Old Testament in Art* (London, 1905-6), p. 57.

37. Johann Jakob Scheuchzer, *Kupfer-Bibel* (Augsburg and Ulm, 1731-33), Tafeln XXXV-LXVIII.

38. Exhibited in 1952. The Museum has kindly supplied photographs of three of the prints.

39. Antti Aarne and Stith Thompson, *The Types of the Folk-Tale* (Helsinki, FFC No. 74, 1928), p. 125.

40. Panaria 17, Franciscus Oehler, tr., *Corpus Haereseologici* (Berlin, 1856-60), II, 1, 170-71; Montague R. James, *The Lost Apocrypha of the Old Testament* (London, 1920), pp. 12-13.

41. A. N. Veselovskij, *Razyskanija v oblasti dukhovnago sticha* (St. Petersburg, 1889), V, 11 and *passim*.

42. See n. 7.

43. See n. 6.

44. Hurt Collection II, 52, 758/62 (63), collected in Räpina, Estonia, in 1895.

45. Andreas Lindblom, "Den apokryfa Noahsagen i Medeltidens Konst och Litteratur," *Nordisk Tidskrift för Vetanskap, Konst och Industri* (1917), pp. 358-68. Some parallels collected for me at Lund have recently been discovered and are discussed in "Some Noah Tales From Sweden," which will be published in a homage volume in 1960.

46. Philipp Strauch, ed., *Jansen Enikels Werke* (Monumenta Germaniae Historica: Deutsche Chroniken III, Hannover and Leipzig, 1900), pp. 36-50; see Francis L. Utley, "Noah's Ham and Jansen Enikel," *Germanic Review*, XVI (1941), 241-49.

47. Osborn Waterhouse, ed., *The Non-Cycle Mystery Plays* (Early English Text Society, Extra Series 104; London, 1909), pp. 19-25.

48. From the collections of the Irish Folklore Commission, sent to me by Professor James Delargy.

49. Dr. Dov Noy has reminded me of Adam's mating with the animals before the creation of Eve. See Louis Ginzberg, *The Legends of the Jews* (Philadelphia, 1912-38), V, 87.

50. *The Folktale* (New York, 1946), p. 438.

51. René Basset, *Mille et un contes, récits et légendes Arabes*, 3 vols. (Paris, 1924-26), III, 28.

52. *Zbiór Wiadomości*, VII (1881-82), 110.

53. René Basset, *Contest populaires berbères* (Paris, 1887), pp. 25-26.

54. Utley, "Noah's Ham and Jansen Enikel," p. 243.

55. Utley, pp. 242-44.

56. Dähnhardt, I, 287-89.

57. Dähnhardt, I, 283.

58. Dähnhardt, I, 298-314.

59. See note 31.

60. *Die Sintfluthsagen* (Bonn, 1899).

61. Ernst Böklen, "Die Sintflutsage, Versuch einer neuer Erklärung," *Archiv für Religionswissenschaft*, VIII (1903), 1-61, 97-150.

62. See, for instance, Franz von Schwarz, *Sintfluth und Volkerwanderungen* (Stuttgart, 1894).

63. John Skinner, *A Critical and Exegetical Commentary on Genesis* (New York, 1910), p. 183.

64. John C. Lawson, *Modern Greek Folktales and Ancient Greek Religion* (New York, 1910), p. 43.

65. Eleanor Follansbee, "The Story of the Flood in the Light of Comparative Semitic Mythology," *Religions* (Oct., 1939), pp. 11-21.

66. *Social Anthropology* (New York, 1926), p. 46.

67. See Alexander Heidel, *The Gilgamesh Epic and Old Testament Parallels* (2nd ed.; Chicago, 1949).

68. Rudolfus Peiper, ed., *Alcimi Ecdicii Aviti Viennensis Episcopi Opera Qvae Svpersvnt* (Monumenta Germaniae Historica: Auctorum Antiquissimorum VI. 2; Berlin, 1883), pp. 236-54.

69. George Philip Krapp, ed., *The Junius Manuscript* in *The Anglo-Saxon Poetic Records* (New York, 1931), I, 39-48.

70. Rev. Richard Morris, ed., *Cursor Mundi* (Early English Text Society, Original Series 57; London, 1874-93), I, 96-127.

71. Rotograph of MS Bodleian 822, Library of Congress, Modern Language Deposit 21.

72. I have photostats of Bibliothèque Nationale, MS Fr. 20039.

73. Urban T. Holmes, ed., *The Works of Guillaume de Salluste Sieur du Bartas* (Chapel Hill, N. C., 1935-40), III, 99-118.

74. J. W. Hebel, ed., *The Works of Michael Drayton* (Oxford, 1931-41), IV, 331-54.

75. Joost von [den] Vondel, *Treuerspelen: Tweede Deel*, ed. in *Klassiek Letterkundig Pantheon* (Schiedam, 1853).

76. *The Works of John Milton* (New York, 1931-38), II, 2, 367-77.

77. *Ibid.*, p. 373 (Book xi, 763-70).

78. Edward Ecclestone, *Noahs Flood: An Opera* (London, 1679).

79. Joseph Collyer, tr., *Noah: Attempted from the German of Mr. Bodmer in Twelve Books* (London, 1767).

80. *Ibid.*, pp. 115-16.

81. *The Poetical Works of Jean Ingelow* (New York [1863]), pp. 271-347.

82. *Ibid.*, pp. 315–16.

83. "Noah and the Waters," in *A Time to Dance* (New York, 1936), pp. 97–145.

84. *Ibid.*, p. 136.

85. Rumer Godden, *In Noah's Ark* (New York, 1949).

86. *The Collected Poems of Roy Campbell* (London, 1949), pp. 59–93. *The Flaming Terrapin* was first published in 1924.

87. *Collected Poems*, p. 63.

88. *Ibid.*, p. 74.

89. *Ibid.*, p. 93.

90. Arthur Wilmurt, tr., *Noah* (New York, 1935). Another recent drama, too complex for analysis here, is Ernst Barlach's *Die Sündflut* (Emsdetten, Germany, 1954), first published in 1924.

91. Fergusson, *op. cit.*, p. 220.

92. The text of Clifford Odets' play, *The Flowering Peach*, which puts the Noah story in modern setting, was not available for consideration at the time of writing. Since then Mr. Odets has kindly lent me a script for future study.

93. This quotation is from Richard Wilbur's "Still, Citizen Sparrow," *The Penguin Book of Modern American Verse*, Geoffrey Moore, ed. (London, 1954), p. 302.

3 | Jewish Folktales

The Three Teachings
of the Bird

MARIE CAMPBELL   Glassboro

State College, Glassboro, New Jersey

by Marie Campbell

A FOLKTALE living today in oral tradition or current in folklore collections of the present may have a distinguished life history that can be traced back for centuries through literary sources. This holds true with regard to the sources of a tale listed in *The Types of the Folk-Tale*[1] as MT 150, "Advice of the Fox (Bird)," and in the *Motif-Index*[2] as K604, "The Three Teachings of the Bird."[3]

This tale is so simple that it has only a single narrative motif. For purposes of reference a brief version is provided, the wording exactly as found in one of the numerous editions of the oldest known source of the tale. This version is chosen as representative because it contains all the essential details of the story without descriptive matter and without the lengthy moralizing which frequently accompanies the tale, especially in Christianized accounts. The title is from the source of the tale as quoted below.

A man caught a nightingale, which promised him three precious pieces of advice if he would let her go free. He agreed; whereupon the nightingale said, "Do not attempt the impossible. Regret nothing that is past. Believe no improbable tale." The man then let the bird go free. She, desiring to test him, cried, "Fool, you little know what treasure you have lost. I have within me a pearl as large as an eagle's egg." The man, full of greed, tried to entice the nightingale within his door again, promising to let her go free. The nightingale said, "Now I see what use you will make of my three pieces of advice. I told you never to regret what was past, and yet you are sorry that you let me go free. I advised you not to try the impossible, and yet you are attempting to get me again within your power. I told you never to trust the improbable, and yet you believed me when I said I had within me a pearl greater than my whole body."[4]

The story of "The Three Teachings of the Bird"[5] lives in present-day collections of folktales, both from oral tradition and from literary sources. One such present-day oral version in *The Talking Thrush*[6] was told to the collector by a wandering religious beggar, Rameswar-Puri, of Kharwa, a district in India. A later (twentieth-century) collector heard the tale from children in a village school of Ceylon, specifically on MacCarthy Island, Gambia, and included the tale in his book, *Village Folk-Tales of Ceylon*.[7] The collectors and translators of both books say that the tale as they found it is indigenous and little affected by Aryan influence. The editors of *The Talking Thrush* acknowledge that they have made changes in their "The Quail and the Fowler" because their book is intended for children. "The Three Truths" from the Ceylon collection is said to be translated directly as recorded from school children.

There are also two recent collections of Jewish folklore that contain versions (taken from literary sources) of "The Three Teachings of the Bird." The editor of *A Treasury of Jewish Folklore*[8] gives the German translation of *Der Born Judas* as his source for "The Wise Bird and Foolish Man." In *The Folklore of the Jews*[9] seven sources, most of them German, are listed for "The Three Precepts." The use of these references and others listed in Aarne and Thompson's *The Types of the Folk-Tale* and Thompson's *Motif-Index* and elsewhere has made it possible to trace the tale from its earliest known source in the Buddhistic birth stories[10] to its present form in twentieth-century folklore collections.

The earliest known text is embodied in the Barlaam and Joasaph romance, written in Greek, supposedly by John of Damascus around the beginning of the 7th century A.D. The title in the original Greek text reads: "A profitable story brought to the Holy City from the further part of Ethiopia called India, by John, the Monk, an honorable and virtuous man of the monastery of St. Sabas, containing the life of Barlaam and Joasaph, famous and blessed men."[11]

Later versions of the Barlaam text mention the name of the author but lose sight of the place of origin of this religious romance, which tells of a king ruling India who persecuted those of the faith. (In Christianized versions, it was the Christians who were persecuted.) At the birth of the king's child, five wise men were called in to make predictions for the son. Four of them made predictions pleasing to the king; the fifth predicted that the son would become a Christian. (In the Christian versions of the text the prediction is that the son will become a Christian; in non-Christian versions, a religious hermit.)

To prevent the fulfillment of this prediction, the king had a special palace built in which the child was kept in seclusion, totally ignorant of the world and of the existence of poverty, sorrow, disease, or death. The story tells in detail the circumstances by which the prince caused this life of solitude to be ended. After his emergence from seclusion and his awakening to the ills of the world, the most important person in his life was a hermit named Barlaam, who had spent thirty years praying in the wilderness. Having disguised himself as a merchant to get past the king, Barlaam gained access to the prince and began to teach him about religion. In the course of his teachings he made use of many parables and apologues. When he spoke against the folly of idolatry, he told a story, "The Three Teachings of the Bird," an old Indian tale certainly never intended to be used as a sermon against idol worship. Through the teachings and example of Barlaam the young prince was converted and renounced his royal inheritance to follow Barlaam and give himself completely to the religious life.

The full account of the lives of Barlaam and Joasaph, the prince, along with the text of our tale and other parables, is found in the editions by Budge,[12] Jacobs,[13] and MacDonald.[14]

The parables of Barlaam and an abridged form of the framing tale are given in the manuscript texts of Type 150 considered in this study.[15] The various translations and editions of the *Legenda Aurea*[16] also present an abridgement of the Barlaam story with parables, including Type 150.

It is supposed that the Barlaam text in its earliest form is a Christianized version[17] of a very ancient spiritual romance composed in India by Buddhist propagandists. The supposed writer, John of Damascus, was a most able and learned man, not only in language and matters of religion and philosophy but also in science. He is mentioned in Chaucer's *Prologue* to the *Canterbury Tales* as a "Doctour of Phisick."

Stories from India passed, with Buddhism, into China, Tibet, and other Oriental countries, and also westward, after the departure of Alexander from India. For centuries the book of Barlaam has had extensive circulation and wide popularity in both East and West. Translations abound in Indian, Chinese, Persian, Arabic, Hebrew, and other Oriental languages. More than sixty translations or paraphrases in most of the European languages testify to the esteem in which the story has been held in Europe, especially during the Middle Ages.[18] Manuscript texts are to be found in many of the great libraries and museums the world over.

Although in the earliest known text the author acknowledges that the story came out of India, in the Christianized versions all doctrines and expressions contrary to Christian belief were discarded. So the Buddhistic origin was lost sight of, and it was not until the nineteenth century that it was rediscovered, along with the fact that Prince Joasaph was the Buddha himself. Through the centuries no one seems to have troubled to find out who Barlaam and Joasaph were and where they lived. Their names had the sound of old Hebrew names, and it seems that they were taken to be natives of Palestine carrying on the evangelization of India begun by St. Thomas, the Apostle, a legend accepted as historical fact by medieval Christians. Both

Barlaam and Joasaph were taken over as saints by the Roman Catholic and Greek churchès and were fully canonized in the time of Gregory XIII.

They are treated as saints in the *Legenda Aurea* of Jacobus de Voragine, a Dominican friar of the thirteenth century. He modestly entitled his work *Legends of the Saints*, but his followers glorified the legends as golden and considered them as almost a supplement to the Scriptures of divine revelation. "The welcome with which it was received by the clergy and by the lettered world is attested by the great number of manuscripts of it still extant, and its ready reception by the people generally is evidenced by the fact that within a short time of its first appearance it was translated into the vulgar tongue of most of the nations of Europe."[19] No other book was more generally printed in various languages between the years of 1470 and 1520.

The universal popularity of the Barlaam romance seems to have been due largely to the series of tales, fables, or apologues that Barlaam used in his conversations with Joasaph. In the Middle Ages these episodes came to be used, apart from the romance as a whole, in storybooks, poems, and dramas and as subjects for sermons. The earliest of the European collections was the *Disciplina Clericalis*,[20] a collection compiled by Petrus Alphonsi about A.D. 1106. "His *Disciplina*, in its earliest surviving version, is not written in Spanish but in Medieval Latin, though the author stated that he first composed it in another language— this, it is assumed, was either Hebrew or Arabic—and then rendered it into the language of Western learning."[21] The stories are mostly Oriental, an indication of the role that Alphonsi and other Spanish Jews played in the cultural exchanges of the Middle Ages between East and West. Most of the Spanish compilers of moralized tales utilized ancient motifs, fitting them into the patterns of their own age. From *Barlaam* or perhaps from Jewish oral sources, the tale of "The Three Teachings of the Bird" found its way into Alphonsi's *Disciplina*.

His collection became the foundation for all *exempla* compilations of medieval Europe. Gaster's notes to the Hebrew tale of "The Bird's Three Advices"[22] contain more than thirty entries. Concerning the purpose of the stories, Gaster says, "The tale is no more told or listened to for the mere pleasure of listening. . . . In the new collections they are made to serve a purpose; they are told as an exemplum in order to teach a lesson . . . as the basis for sermons"[23]—exactly what Barlaam had in mind when he told the original tale to Joasaph.

Jacques de Vitry was a Catholic bishop of the 13th century who attained great fame as a preacher. His book of *Exempla*[24] is a collection of sermons which he actually preached, though it is not intended for the exclusive use of the clergy but also for the general edification of the laity. "The Nightingale's Advice" is a part of Sermon XVIII. This tale also appears in the *Gesta Romanorum*,[25] a secular collection based probably on pre-Christian sources. The *Gesta*, most popular of the European secular storybooks of the Middle Ages, was first printed in Latin about 1472. Presumably compiled near the end of the 13th century, its authorship has never been settled. It contains, in addition to a prose version of Type 150, entitled "Of Hearing Good Counsel," a lengthy reworking of the tale in poetry, credited to a Mr. Way and entitled "The Lay of the Little Bird."[26]

Jacobs' edition of *The Fables of Aesop*[27] contains our tale, though it does not appear in all editions of Aesop. According to Jacobs, the Aesopic fable was largely used for political purposes when free speech was dangerous.[28] Another example of fables intended for political use is the *Panchatantra*, an ancient collection of fables written in Sanskrit and used to teach princes the art of politics. Here the fables, usually beast fables, are stories within stories. The present collection, both in manuscript and print, contains Type 150,[29] but the original Sanskrit manuscript, dating probably from the third or fourth century A.D., is lost, and there is no record as to which fables it included. Translations now in existence are based on translations by Jewish scholars into Hebrew, Latin, and Arabic. The earlier translations were made in the centuries before the Crusades and spread widely over Europe. Stories and motifs from the Arabian Nights which traveled to Europe may also have been transmitted by Jews who knew them in the Orient. Burton's *Supplemental Nights*,[30] stories with *Arabian Nights* motifs, includes our tale among the collection.

In some instances a creative writer, usually a poet, has taken this simple tale of the wise bird and greatly expanded it with narrative and descriptive detail. An example is the fourteenth-century Lydgate's "The Churl and the Bird,"[31] which the author attributes to the version in *Disciplina Clericalis*. He elaborately embroiders the single incident into a metrical romance several pages in length. Way's "Lay of the Little Bird," included (as noted) in *Gesta Romanorum* is close to Lydgate's rendering, the difference being largely in dialectal change and in verse form. The bird's preaching in Way's version is somewhat shorter and the description less expansive than in Lydgate's.

MacDonald's three English manuscript texts,[32] of the late 14th and early 15th centuries, are also in verse and are embedded in an abridged form of the Barlaam story. All three texts follow closely the abridgement in the *Legenda Aurea* and vary only in verse and dialect. All of them include the detail about the pearl as large as an ostrich egg.

Among prose versions of the tale there is no great variation except between two versions which are directly from Oriental oral tradition. "The Quail and the Fowler," from *The Talking Thrush*,[33] is a standard version resembling Barlaam, except that it is briefer and does not contain the moralizing epilogue. These changes may be due to the editors' adaptation for children. "The Three Truths," from *Village Folk Tales of Ceylon*,[34] concerns a "Hyaena" and a goat who meet on the road. It is the only version among those considered in this study which is not of a man and a bird. The "three truths" are not pieces of advice at all, but devices to prevent the goat from being eaten by the hyena, and it takes but little wit to outthink the latter. The other prose versions, all of them literary, vary little; all concern a man and a bird who gives advice in exchange for freedom, only to have the man immediately disregard the wise counsel. The wise bird is always female and always has the last word! Though no prose version is long, some are shorter because of abridgement of detail or because the bird does not repeat her three counsels in full. In *The Talking Thrush* and *The Fables of Aesop* the editors admit that they have shortened and simplified the tales because they are intended for children.

The names of the two chief actors change. Usually the bird is a nightingale, sometimes a quail, occasionally simply a "wise bird." The man may be a hunter, a fowler, a laborer, or merely a "foolish man" in contrast to the "wise bird." The jewel which the bird lies about is most often a pearl, but occasionally another precious stone. It is as large as an ostrich egg, an eagle egg, or a goose egg. In versions directly from Jewish sources the talking bird is said to know the seventy languages of mankind, a common Jewish motif.

Through the centuries Jewish scholars, collectors, translators, and editors have had a most important part in the transmission of the tale. They were especially instrumental as intermediaries between Oriental and Occidental cultures, and of recent years they have been responsible for a large proportion of the published versions of Type 150. From a Jewish editor has recently come evidence of the use of the tale as a device for teaching a moral lesson to the very young. *World Over*,[35] a Jewish magazine for young people, made use of the tale in a regular feature called "Legend Land," which tells the story pictorially with a moral purpose. Thus, by a different method, the tale again serves the didactic purpose that it had in the Barlaam romance.

Notes

1. A. Aarne and Stith Thompson, *The Types of the Folk-Tale* (Helsinki, F.F.C. No. 74, 1928), Type 150, p. 34.

2. Stith Thompson, *Motif-Index of Folk-Literature* (6 vols.; Bloomington, Indiana, 1955–58), IV, Motif K604, 322–23.

3. See also Motifs J21.12, 21.13, 21.14.

4. Joseph Jacobs, ed., "Man and Bird," *Barlaam and Josaphat, English Lives of Buddha* (London, 1896), Appendix II, p. cxxi. Commentary in Introduction, pp. lxxx–lxxxi.

5. The title used in the *Motif-Index* for K604, "The Three Teachings of the Bird," is used in this paper to indicate the story generally when the specific title of a given version is not indicated.

6. William Crooke and W. H. D. Rouse, "The Quail and the Fowler," *The Talking Thrush, Stories of Birds and Beasts* (London and New York, 1899), pp. 36–38. The stories, here retold by W. H. D. Rouse, are part of a large collection of Indian folktales made by William Crooke in the course of the ethnological survey of the North-Western Provinces and Andal.

7. Henry Parker, ed., "The Three Truths," *Village Folk Tales of Ceylon* (3 vols.; London, 1914), III, No. 256, p. 354. Mr. Parker collected these tales while with the Ceylon Irrigation Department of the British India Office.

8. Nathan Ausubel, ed., "The Wise Bird and the Foolish Man," *A Treasury of Jewish Folklore* (New York, 1948), p. 628.

9. Angelo S. Rappoport, ed., "Three Precepts," *The Folklore of the Jews* (London, 1937), pp. 175–76.

10. The following references were especially useful to me in tracing the tale from its earliest known sources and in discovering versions of the texts in collections of the Buddhistic Birth Stories: T. W. Rhys Davids, trans., *Buddhistic Birth Stories or Jataka Tales* (London, 1880), Introduction, pp. xxxiii–xxxix; xlviii–l; E. B. Cowell, ed., and H. T. Francis, trans., *The Jataka or Stories of the Buddha's Former Births* (Cambridge, 1905), p. 80; N. M. Penzer, ed., and C. H. Tawney, trans., *Ocean of Story* (10 vols.; London, 1924–28). See also Jacobs, *op. cit.*, pp. lxx, 80, 290.

11. K. S. MacDonald, ed., *The Story of Barlaam and Joasaph* (Calcutta, 1895). Five versions of the Barlaam and the Joasaph story appear in this volume, each containing Tale Type 150, "The Three Teachings of the Bird." Two of the versions are from eighteenth- and nineteenth-century printed sources, and three are from manuscripts of the fourteenth, fifteenth and sixteenth centuries, as indicated below:

(1) "Story of the Nightingale's Three Advices," *The History of the Five Wise Philosophers or The Wonderful Relation of the Life of Jehosaphat, Son of Avenario, King of Berma in India* (London, 1711), pp. 29–31.

(2) "Story of the Nightingale's Three Advices," *The Hystorie of the Hermyte Balaam, from the Golden Legend of Master William Caxton, Don Anew* (London, 1892), pp. 97–98. This book was printed by William Morris at the Kelmscott Press.

(3) "The Archer and the Nightingale," *Barlaam and Josaphat* (Oxford Univ., c. 1376–80), lines 421–28. Written in iambic tetrameter couplets. From the Vernon MS, fol. 100 in Bodleian Library.

(4) "The Forester and the Bird," Barlaam and Hosaphat (beginning of 15th century), lines 500–556. From the Harleian MS, 4196, fol. 199b. Written in iambic tetrameter couplets.

(5) "Bow Man and the Bird," *Barlaam and Hosaphat*, lines 385–430. From the Bodleian MS, 779.

12. Sir. E. A. Wallis Budge, trans., *Baralam and Yewasef or Barlaam and Josaphat* (Cambridge, 1923). References are to "The Nightingale and the Fowler," No. 5, pp. xxii–xxiii, and to "The Parable of the Hunter and the Bird," pp. 63–67.

13. See n. 4.

14. See n. 11.

15. Versions in McDonald, *op. cit.*, from the Vernon MS, fol. 100; Harleian MS, 4196, fol. 199b; and Bodleian MS, 779.

16. Jacobus de Voragine, *Legenda Aurea*, Theodor Grasse, ed. (Dresden and Leipzig, 1846), p. 815; trans. Richard Benz (Jena, 1925), pp. 480–81 (simply a standard version). MacDonald, *op. cit.*, pp. 97–98, gives a version from the *Legenda Aurea*.

17. Perhaps through the Arabic.

18. Specific references here are MacDonald, p. 55, and Budge, pp. xi ff.

19. K. S. MacDonald, ed., *Caxton's Golden Legend*, p. 89.

20. F. W. Schmidt, ed., "Man and Bird," Petrus Alphonse's *Disciplina Clericalis* (Berlin, 1827), No. XXIII, p. 150.

21. J. E. Keller, *Motif-Index of Medieval Spanish Exempla* (Knoxville, 1949), pp. ix ff. References also to the *Disciplina, Exemplum* No. 22, the Barlaam story, p. 345.

22. Moses Gaster, "The Bird's Three Advices," *The Exempla of the Rabbis* (London, 1924), No. 39, pp. 149–50. A collection of *exempla*, apologues, and tales culled from Hebrew manuscripts and rare books in Hebrew.

23. *Ibid.*, p. 6.

24. Thomas F. Crane, ed., "Nightingale's Advice," *The Exempla or Illustrative Stories from the Sermones Vulgares of Jacques De Vitry* (London, 1890), pp. 144–45. Introduction, analysis, and notes. Lines quoted in this study, pp. 144 ff.

25. C. Swan, trans., and Wynnard Hooper, ed., "Of Hearing Good Counsel," *Gesta Romanorum* (London, 1905), Tale 166, pp. 318–19.

26. *Ibid.*, pp. 415–18.

27. Joseph Jacobs, ed., "Labourer and Nightingale," *The Fables of Aesop* (London and New York, 1894), No. LVIII, pp. 138–39; notes, pp. 213–14.

28. *Ibid.*, pp. xv–xxii.

29. Th. Benfey, "Three Wisdoms (Wise Councils of the Bird)," *The Panchatantra* (2 vols.; Leipzig, 1859), I, 380.

30. R. F. Burton, "The Three Teachings of the Bird," *Supplemental Nights to the Book of a Thousand Nights and a Night* (6 vols.; London, 1888), VI, 169.

31. John Lydgate, "The Churl and the Bird," in Eleanor Prescott Hammond, *English Verse between Chaucer and Surrey* (Durham, N. C., 1927), pp. 102–10.

32. See n. 15.

33. See n. 6.

34. See n. 7.

35. November, 1953.

Jewish-American

Dialect Stories

on Tape

RICHARD M. DORSON   Indiana University

by Richard M. Dorson

A BULGING shelf of collections, treasuries, and anthologies of Jewish folk humor, published in the United States within recent years, testifies to a vigorous comic tradition in American life today.* None of these books satisfies the requirements of the professional folklorist. They fail to indicate sources, they mix oral and printed, translated and English texts; they admittedly make stylistic improvements; and they offer few suggestions for any meaningful typology of Jewish jokelore. Some stories recur so regularly that one wonders whether they come from a verbal or literary tradition. Nevertheless, these compilations should stir collectors to investigate the jocular lore of American Jews, and they provide valuable comparative material to check against findings in the field.

One major omission may strike the reader of the omnibuses assembled by S. Felix Mendelsohn, Jacob Richman, and Nathan Ausubel. They contain a considerable variety of humorous taletypes: witty sayings of rabbis, jests about the *schnorrer* (beggar), the *shadchan* (marriage broker), and the cantor, newer cycles dealing with East Side immigrants and Israeli citizens, a spate of Hitler and Nazi gibes—a vast repertoire ranging from Czarist Russia to modern America. Among the thousands of printed tales, however, a mere grudging handful of dialect stories are given. Nathan Ausubel states categorically, in his *A Treasury of Jewish Folklore*, that "A large body of so-called 'Jewish dialect jokes' are not Jewish at all, but the confections

* See bibliography, p. 119.

of anti-Semites who delight in ridiculing and slandering the Jews."[1] This strange assertion eliminates from consideration a major element in American Jewish humor, the mimicry of Yiddish intonation and pronunciation by American-born Jewish storytellers, whose mimetic talent delights responsive audiences. Reading endless Jewish jokes robbed of their dialect sauce soon palls, and even an attempt at dialect transcription presents only a pale copy of the spoken tale. Some creative humorists have, of course, skillfully caught the accents and malapropisms of Jewish-American speech, notably Arthur Kober and Milt Gross. In my boyhood the reading aloud of *Nize Baby* by a clever-tongued counselor to New York Jewish boys proved a hilarious feature of our summer-camp entertainment. Oral Jewish jokelore in this country relies heavily on dialect for good-natured laughs.

An ethnocentric folklorist like Mr. Ausubel fails to appreciate general patterns of folklore that transcend ethnic or cultural boundaries. The telling of dialect stories in the United States develops logically and inevitably from the circumstances of American civilization. American-born youngsters reproduce in fun the linguistic mistakes of their European-born parents or neighbors; such mistakes grow into twice-told jests, or standard jokes are transmuted into the dialect. Jewish dialect humor observes the same conventions which I reported for Finnish, French-Canadian, Cornish, Swedish, and Italian dialect stories from the Upper Peninsula of Michigan, and which evidently apply to many other sections and groups around the country.[2] The dialectician must possess American education and speech, to furnish the frame of a familiar culture pattern for his tale, and know the Old World tongue and folkways well enough to reproduce the immigrant. The resulting contrast between two accents and two cultures offers a winning formula for vocal comedy.

My four main informants, whose tape-recorded tales are transcribed below, all bear out the pattern of American dialect storytelling. They are American-born sons of European Jewish parents, educated in American universities, conversant in varying degrees with the Yiddish language and Jewish culture. Two were summer-school students at Indiana University, Barry Spacks and Herschel Stroyman, and two were colleagues of mine on the Michigan State University faculty, Leo Lapidus and Maurice Crane. Each qualifies as a stellar narrator and entertainer in his own circle. Spacks, a tall and slender young man with poetic talents, used an extraordinary range of inflection in his opening anecdote where little Ikie and his father converse animatedly about an imaginary carriage. Where Spacks underplayed his climaxes effectively, softly hissing the punch word "Anti-Semite" in one tale and producing the sound between gritted teeth to convey the effect of bottled-up rage, Herschel Stroyman, a sturdily built wag, bellowed the final imprecation with a deafening blast when he was telling the same story. Leo Lapidus, short, gentle, and friendly, introduced considerable background commentary with his jests, drawn from his close knowledge of the Yiddish language and orthodox Jewish worship. Morrie Crane, an explosive dynamo reeling off jokes in a torrent, relied least of the four on dialect. He knew only a few words of Yiddish and had picked up his store of stories in good part from night-club entertainers, when he played a clarinet in a jazz band.

On the other hand, Rabbi Alfred Friedman, of Lansing, Michigan, a noted raconteur whose stories had already found their way into my folklore archives through a student collector, employed no dialect in his narration. When I recorded the youthful, handsome rabbi, who had just been called to a large congregation in Brooklyn, he spoke in the cultured tones of an elocution teacher. No one could seem less like the stereotyped rabbi. He owned several collections of Jewish jokes and kept a regular file of usable stories for his public addresses. Obviously his repertoire drew from printed tradition, and rejected dialect trappings. He related only one dialect joke, and that from actual experience, in which a Jewish lady speaking with a heavy accent spurned the traditional orthodox service for the reformed service of up-to-date American Jews. As an important civic figure constantly in the public eye, the rabbi needed an ample fund of clever Jewish anecdotes, but for the very same reason he had to eliminate dialect, which might offend or disturb some of his listeners.

By chance, a fine example of the contrast between dialect and non-dialect storytelling developed in my recording of undergraduate Herschel Stroyman jointly with his father Bernard, an Indianapolis lawyer born in Russia and educated in Israel and at Harvard. The senior Stroyman told traditional Jewish jests, but possessing some accent to begin with, he could not, and made no attempt to, flavor them with dialect (and so I have not included them here). But his son Herschel, speaking flawlessly when introducing his situations, would then break into a highly exaggerated nasal speech, far beyond his father's natural accent, to caricature the Jewish immigrant.

The dialect of the storytellers challenges systematic description or transcription, since it varies between different raconteurs. Further, some vocal eccentricities cannot be caught with alphabetical symbols, such as the nasalized rhythm, the rising inflection of questions, or the throaty *h* and *ch*. Some characteristics of Yiddish English that can be simply indicated are the substitution of *v* for *w* ("My father always said Lvov for the city of Lwow in Poland," Leo Lapidus explained, "not that he couldn't pronounce *w* but because that was the regular pronunciation, and he carried the habit into English"); a *k* sound for *g* in *ing* endings; *e* for *a* before *n*, for instance in *Yenkee*; a soft *s* instead of the harsh *z* that ends *was* or *is*; the short *i* for the long *e*, as *pliz* for *please*. Substituting the present participle for the regular verb form marks the dialect: "Maybe you're not minding I'm borrowing your towel?" Expressive gestures vanish, of course, from the printed page. In one delicious little scene, Lapidus depicts a conversation between two immigrants, who ask the state of each other's health, and that of their families, reply with shrugs, grimaces, and expressive noises, and then congratulate each other on their heart to heart talk. The printed versions capture only part of the oral and none of the visual humor involved.[3]

Rehearing the recorded tales brings out subtleties in the dialect style that are easily missed on the first narration. One persistent comic figure emerges in lifelike dimensions, an eager, apologetic, anxious-to-please, feverishly intense personality, wheedling, remonstrating, and exploding in high-pitched whining accents. He commits all kinds of foibles in "goniff" America, like offering to buy Mr. Macy's store, or asking for a stranger's toothbrush in the washroom, or striding through the deep South in orthodox Hasidic garb, but he never relinquishes his invincible self-possession. His detractors must be anti-Semites, or hillbillies. In the tightest predicament, he can still extricate himself with composure. "Why do you always answer a question with a question?" asks the irritated judge. "Vy not?" comes back the reply.

Style and not content determines what can be called a Jewish dialect story. The same story can be told straight, or in dialect form, or with a varying amount of dialect, and by Jewish or non-Jewish persons. Frequently what seems like a thoroughly Jewish tale turns up far outside Jewish culture. A few examples will illustrate these shifting outlines of an apparently stable and homogeneous lore. A college student, son of a rabbi, told me the following story. An orthodox Jew buys a monkey for a pet, who imitates the religious practices of his master so successfully that his owner takes him to the synagogue and explains that the monkey can follow the service and *daven*. But the animal fails to perform. On the way home his master berates him, until the monkey replies, "Wait till Yom Kippur, and you'll see the odds, you *schlemiel*." This highly Judaized jest reached me on the heels of a non-Jewish analogue: a parrot keeps silent when his master wagers he can talk, but later explains that next day the odds will be twenty to one. J. Frank Dobie once yarned about the minister who refused a meal before preaching his sermon. His host the farmer later privately remarked to his wife, "He mought as well have et." Rabbi Friedman knew this as a Jewish anecdote about a rabbi who ate only one mouthful from the elaborate kosher dishes prepared by his hostess before the Friday evening service. Even Yankee tricks and tall tales appear in Jewish dress. The familiar exchange of brags between two fishermen, one of whom has landed an enormous fish, while the other has caught a lighted candle (you take off ten pounds, and I'll put out the light) finds its counterpart in the Jewish braggarts vaunting the feats of their *rebbis*, one of whom produces five fish in a pot, and the other five kings in his poker hand (you take one fish from the pot, and I'll take away one king).[4] A Cornish joke I heard in northern Michigan describes a conversation between two Cousin Jacks, one of them hurrying to the doctor because he doesn't like his wife's looks, the other deciding to accompany him because he hates the sight of his own wife. Mendelsohn sets this down as a Jewish dialogue.[5] A jest often told me by Negroes concerns the sly Jew who puts a check in the coffin of his deceased friend and takes out the cash left by other friends; and this too comes from Jewish humorists.[6] Other episodes popular among American Negroes are paralleled in Jewish lore, such as Brer Rabbit's mock plea that he not be thrown into the briar bushes and left to die, or the frightened guest made to believe that the host wants to cut off his limbs.[7] These instances from my own collecting experience could be extended to show further overlappings between Jewish and non-Jewish jokelore.

All the stories told below by the four main informants are directly transcribed from tape recordings. A final section of dictated jokes from non-Jewish informants indicates the penetration of Jewish humor into the broad stream of American life. Usually some attempt at dialect rendition accompanies tales in this group, although the relative unfamiliarity with Yiddish speech yields astonishing results. A Southern belle using Jewish dialect brings forth an unclassifiable blend of accents!

Jokes that ridicule and lampoon Jews in the eyes of other peoples cannot easily be separated from jests which, circulating among Jews, contain all the ammunition necessary for anti-Semitic raillery. The same gibe can be told gently or harshly. A current cycle of dialect stories, revolving around the undue readiness of the immigrant Jew in the United States to sniff out anti-Semitism, finds a wide audience among the younger generation of American Jews.

These contemporary, urban, dialect folktales about Jewish acculturation form a fresh and lively addition to the varied strands of American humorous lore.

Texts similar to those presented here are to be found in the Indiana University Folklore Archives, which includes the diversified collections handed in by students in my American Folklore course at Michigan State University and contains, in the folders of Jewish humor, over a hundred stories contributed by Jewish students from Detroit and other cities in Michigan. One fine collection deals entirely with Jewish dialect jokes, that of Mrs. Martha Bernstein of New York City, who was enrolled in a summer-school course which I taught at Harvard University in 1952.

The italicized comments preceding some of the stories include references to other versions of the texts supplied in this paper. In these headnotes I have mentioned variants which appear in the Archives—along with the names of the student collectors and their informants—and variants which have been published in anthologies or journals.

Stories 1, 2, 3, 4A, 5A, 6, and 7 were told by BARRY SPACKS on July 31, 1954, at Bloomington, Indiana, at which time he was attending the School of Letters at Indiana University's Summer School. He was born in Philadelphia in 1931 and, in 1954, was an undergraduate at the University of Pennsylvania.

Stories 5B and 8A were told by HERSCHEL STROYMAN on August 1st, 1954, at Bloomington, Indiana. Born in Indianapolis in 1929, he was graduated from Indiana University in 1954 and is presently a commercial artist in New York.

Stories 9-26, 27A, and 28-35 were told by LEO LAPIDUS in East Lansing, Michigan, on September 15, 1954. He was born in Boston in 1919, was graduated from Harvard in 1931, and was teaching mathematics at Michigan State University at the time he was interviewed. His parents emigrated from Russia in the 1890's.

Story 36 was told by RABBI ALFRED L. FRIEDMAN, of the Congregation Shaarey Zedek in Lansing, Michigan, on September 16, 1954. He was born in New York, moved to Lansing in 1947, and, when I met him, had just been called to Union Temple in Brooklyn.

Stories 4B, 8B, 27B, and 37–64 were told by MAURICE A. CRANE on September 19, 1954, in East Lansing. He was born in Atlantic City, New Jersey, in 1926, and later attended Princeton and Villanova and the Universities of Chicago and Illinois. He has taught in the Basic College at Michigan State University since 1953. His father was born in Poland and his mother in Russia.

Stories 65 to 76, told by non-Jews, were collected in August and September, 1954. No. 65 was told by BRUCE BUCKLEY, a graduate student at Indiana University, who knew several Jewish dialect tales from his high school and college days in Portsmouth and Oxford, Ohio. No. 66 was told by D. K. WILGUS in Bowling Green, Kentucky, where he teaches English at Western Kentucky State College. He heard the story while attending Ohio State University. No. 67 was told by GEORGE GLUSKI, my brother-in-law, in Detroit. Nos. 68–69 were told by GLEN WARREN, my sister-in-law's husband, in Royal Oak, Michigan. No. 70 was told by JULIAN LEE RAYFORD, the writer and artist, in Mobile, Alabama. Nos. 71–72 were told by ULICK LEONHARDT, who was born in England and lived in Germany before coming to the United States. She teaches German at Michigan State University. No. 73 was told by NANCY GIBBONS, from South Bend, Indiana, a former classmate of my wife at Michigan State University, now in the WAVES. No. 74 was told by STUART GALLACHER, born in Salt Lake City, Utah, now a professor of German at Michigan State University. He heard the story while working at Lake Tahoe, California, in the summer of 1921 or 1922. Nos. 75A and 76 were told by my former colleague in the History Department at Michigan State University, JOHN A. GARRATY, who was born in Brooklyn and attended Brooklyn College and Columbia University. No. 75B was told by JOHN W. ASHTON, Dean of the Graduate School of Indiana University.

The following bibliography lists sources that are referred to in abbreviated form in the headnotes of the stories or that are cited in the notes at the end of this paper: Nathan Ausubel, *A Treasury of Jewish Folklore* (New York, 1948); Nathan Ausubel, *A Treasury of Jewish Humor* (New York, 1953), chiefly literary; Richard M. Dorson, "Dialect Stories of the Upper Peninsula: A New Form of American Folklore," *Journal of American Folklore*, LXI (1948), 113–50; Mark Feder, *It's a Living, a Personalized Collection of Jewish Humor* (New York, 1948); Sam Levenson, *Meet the Folks, a Session of American-Jewish Humor* (New York, 1954); S. Felix Mendelsohn, *The Jew Laughs* (Chicago, 1935); S. Felix Mendelsohn, *Here's a Good One* (New York, 1947); S. Felix Mendelsohn, *Let Laughter Ring* (Philadelphia, 1941, 1952); S. Felix Mendelsohn, *The Merry Heart* (New York, 1951); Jacob Richman, *Laughs from Jewish Lore* (New York and London, 1926, 1939); Jacob Richman, *Jewish Wit and Wisdom* (New York, 1952); Bernard Rosenberg and Gilbert Shapiro, "Marginality and Jewish Humor," *Midstream*, IV (Spring, 1958), 70-80; Paul Steiner, *Israel Laughs* (New York, 1950); Elsa Teitelbaum, *An Anthology of Jewish Humor and Maxims*, Abraham Burnstein, ed. (New York, 1945).

THE STORIES

1. Ikie and the Carriage (Barry Spacks)

Well, Father came home one day and said he was going to buy a carriage. Everybody got all excited about that, and Father started to dream about how it would be.

"I'm going to be up in the front riding the hosses, with the reins in my hand; Mama's by my side; in the back is Ikie; kloppity-clop along. Oi, it's going to be nice."

Ikie said [*very high*], "No Papa, you got a little bit wrong; in front is me, playing wit de hosses, you sitting by my side; in the back is Mama."

Papa says [*very deep*], "Ikie, vere you getting dese tings? In de back is you; I'm driving de hosses; Mama is sitting in de front."

Ikie said, "Noh, noh [*shrill*]. All right, I won't drive de hosses; I'm sit next to you, but in de front I'm sitting; in the back put Mama. And you sitting in the front wit me."

Papa said, "No, Ikie, you're in the back."

"I want to be in the front."

"I want you to be in the back, Ikie."

"I want to be in the front" [*screaming*].

"Ikie, get out of that carriage" [*slow, stern*].

2. The Pogrom (Barry Spacks)

A floating tale attached to World War II, the Civil War, and doubtless other wars has a coy old spinster tripping up to the sentry of the occupying army, tapping him on the shoulder, and asking, "Pray, sir, when does the ravishing begin?" In a version associated with Jesse James, as reported by Homer Croy in Jesse James Was My Neighbor *(New York, 1949), p. 166, an old maid sits placidly in a train car the James band is holding up. A preacher sitting beside her whispers that Jesse will seize and rape her. "Run as fast as you can into the weeds and hide."*

*"Stop," says the old maid sternly. "Jesse James is the one who's running things here."**

There was a pogrom in a little town in Russia. The soldiers were running around, pillaging, breaking in doors, raping and killing people. Finally they came to this little cottage right on the edge of the mere, where lived an old babbila and her very beautiful granddaughter. As the soldiers broke through, the beautiful granddaughter threw herself in front of her old grandmother and said, "Take me, rape me, do anything you want to with me, but please, spare my old grandmother" [*fervently*].

And the old grandmother reached up and tapped on her granddaughter's shoulder and said, "Chilt, a pogrom is a pogrom" [*deliberately, with a shrug*].

3. Going to Minsk (Barry Spacks)

Other versions in the Archives (Graham P. Miles, East Lansing, from Hank Sirlin), and Ausubel, "The Strategists," A Treasury of Jewish Folklore, p. 374.

Well, these two businessmen met in a Warsaw railroad station. They were business competitors. One walked up to the other and said, "Lou [*rising inflection*], where are you goink?"

The first one said, "Goink to Minsk."

"So you're goink to Minsk [*suspiciously*]. You tell me you're goink to *Minsk* because you want me to think you're goink to *Pinsk*. But I happen to know that you really are goink to Minsk. So why do you lie?"

---

* [Here, as elsewhere in this paper, the headnotes have been supplied by the author.—The Editors.]

4A. Joe College (Barry Spacks)

This young fellow was brought up from the very start to be a rabbi. At a very young age he was sent to study with the *shammes* of the shul and learn the law and the Talmud. And he always wanted to be a rabbi. At the proper time he was sent off to *yeshiva* college. Well, he got there, he got the proper fitting skull cap, and he got himself a suit of black clothing, and he started growing the proper type of beard. And he hadn't been home for a while, and finally he came home for Passover vacation. And he walked up to the door carrying his little suitcases, his skullcap on his head and his little beard on his chin, his black suit on, with a quiet, studious demeanor. His father came to the door, threw it wide open, and said,

"So look who's *here*—Joe Collitch!"

4B. Joe College (Maurice A. Crane)

This boy went to divinity school, rabbinical school in New York, and he comes home and he's got this scraggly little beard that the kids wear in orthodox seminaries, and his long sideburns allow his hair to curl and he's got a black suit on and black shoes, long overcoat, and he is also wearing a black hat. He's got a prayer shawl around him, and he's already beginning to bend over, and he's carrying a great, huge book of the Commentaries underneath his arm. He arrives at his family's home for the first time on vacation and knocks at the door. His mother opens the door and looks at him and says,

"Hey Sam, come here, look at Joe College!" [*accented*].

5A. Anti-Semitism: in the Washroom (Barry Spacks)

None of the collections listed in the bibliography of this paper (p. 119) contains variants of the anti-Semite cycle. A French paral-

lel to the present text appears, curiously enough, in André Gide,
Ainsi Soit-il ou Les Jeux Sont Faits *(Paris, 1952), pp. 71–73. See
also Rosenberg and Shapiro, "Marginality and Jewish Humor,"*
Midstream, *IV, 76.*

Oh, this fellow was traveling in a Pullman car, and he walks
into the lavatory in the morning, and another fellow's in there
making his toilet, and the Jewish man walks up to him and says
[*very apologetically*], "Is all right I, I, I use a bissle your soap,
just a little soap?"

The fellow says, "Sure, go ahead, g'head, use the soap."

When he's finished using the soap, he says, "Is, is okay I take
your razor for a minute? I don't have nothing wit me, and I'd
like to shave wit your razor."

"Yeah, you can use it, g'head."

Well, after he's finished shaving, he says, "Can I use just a
little talcum powder, just, just some talcum powder?"

"Sure, g'head, help yourself; use the talcum powder."

When he finishes with this, he says, "Maybe just for a minute
I can use your tootbrush a little?"

The other guy turns around, "Well, I don't mind your using
my soap, my razor, and my talcum powder, but I must, I must
draw the line at the toothbrush" [*mildly indignant*].

"Aha [*triumphantly*], anti-Semitism" [*drawn out, rhyth-
mic*].

5B. Anti-Semitism: in the Washroom (Herschel Stroyman)

Well, the story is told about the salesman who spent the night
in the Pullman car in the course of a journey and came into the
washroom the next morning without any of his toilet kit, without any preparation for shaving, and so on. And he walked up
to the washbasin, and he tapped the man on the shoulder who
was using the basin next to the one he stood before, and said,
"Excuse me, meestuh, meestuh, yoohoo, you minding please
I'm using just a little bit your soap?"

The man looked at him, shrugged, "Of course not, here," and gave him his soap. The little salesman washed and then returned the soap to the other man's washbasin.

"Oh tenk you very much, very kind of you, I'm sure. Maybe also you're not minding I'm borrowing your towel?"

"No, no, certainly not. Here" [*courteously*]. He handed him a towel from off the rack.

The little chap used it, threw the towel into the waste receptacle, and said, "Oh yes, one more ting, maybe I could borrow your comb and combing my hair, please, wid it?"

"No, no, I guess not—oh well, here."

He gave him the comb, the little man combed his hair, handed back the comb, and said, "Tenk you very much. Oh, I forgot, I didn't shave, maybe I could borrow also your razor, your, your shaving brush and soap?"

"Oh now look, this is—all right, all right, here, take the damn thing. I'm in a hurry though. I get off at the next station." He looked at his watch and sat down to wait.

Well, the little fellow shaved, washed again, gave him back his tools, and said, "Oh, dat's very, very nice of you, I'm sure. Such a kind man, you're so generous, sir. Maybe you mind I'm borrowing your toothbrush, I'm slick up my tootsies a little?"

At this, the man got up, put out the cigar he had just lighted, grabbed back his things, put them into his toilet kit and said, "No, by God, I'm going to draw the line some place," and walked out.

The little man raised his finger and pointed at the departing back of the man from the next basin and, with a quavering voice, screamed,

"Enti-Semite" [*very loud*].

6. Anti-Semitism: in the Station (Barry Spacks)

Other versions in the Archives (Martha Bernstein, New York) and Mendelsohn, "A Useless Attempt," Let Laughter Ring, p. 124. Variants of this form were also told by non-Jews. Bruce Buckley

has the pest repeatedly ask a stranger waiting for a bus what time it is; Norman Johnson has him elbow his way up to the front of the ticket window and try to beat down the price of the ticket.

This fellow was worried about when the train leaves for Cincinnati. He was in the Louisville train station, and he walks up to the man behind the window and he says, "Puddon me, but could you tell me when is the next train to Cincinnati?" [*apologetically*].

"Seven-fifteen."

"Oh, thenk you very much indeed, thenk you, thenk you, thenk you."

"You're welcome."

Ten minutes later he walks up again and says, "I'm sorry, I forgot, you already told me, but ven's this train for Cincinnati, ven it's leaving?"

"Seven-fifteen" [*trace of impatience*].

"Ah, thenk you, thenk you, thenk you."

Well, he sat down again, and again he forgot and came up to the window and says, "Vould you please tell me, dis train for Cincinnati, dis, dis train, vat time does dis train leave?"

The fellow says, "Seven-fifteen" [*loud, angry*].

The next time he comes up and he says, "Please, I forgot what you told me last time [*soft, hurried*], ven is the train leaving for Cincinnati?"

The fellow says, "For Christ sakes, I told you six times, the train leaves at seven-fifteen."

And the Jewish man says, "Anti-Semite" [*low, clenched*].

7. The Absent-Minded Rabbi (Barry Spacks)

Another version in Richman, "Providence Was Against Him," Laughs From Jewish Lore, *pp. 27–28.*

This absent-minded rabbi was a very poor fellow. He always had his shirt washed and laundered for him by his wife in time for the Friday evening services. But he always forgot to turn it right side out again after his wife had finished with it. She reminded him of this all the time because, when he returned from services, she was terribly embarrassed to see the shirt on the wrong side.

One day she decided, well, she'll turn the shirt inside out—the right side out. When he returned from services that evening it was still on the wrong way. "Jake," she said, "how come I turn the shirt this time and still you come back and it's on backwards?"

And he said, "You turned the shirt the right side out. And I turned the shirt the right side out. And still it's on the wrong side out!" [*incredulous*].

8A. The Yankee (Herschel Stroyman)

It is only appropriate that Harry Golden, the Jewish refugee from New York who edits The Carolina Israelite *in North Carolina, should include this story—"You Never Saw a Yenkee?"—in* Only in America *(Cleveland and New York, 1958), pp. 117–18. See also Rosenberg and Shapiro, "Marginality and Jewish Humor," Midstream, IV, 76; Richman, Jewish Wit and Wisdom, p. 89 (Yemenite Jew on furlough asks, "Haven't you ever seen a British soldier?"); Mendelsohn, "Environment Will Tell," Here's a Good One, pp. 115–16 (successful Jew in England says "vunce a yankee, alvez a yankee"). Charles Hirschfield, born in Brooklyn, told me a variant of the latter form. Still another version is in the Archives (Naomi E. Linden, Detroit, from Julius Miller, East Lansing).*

A member of a Hasidic shul in New York City had occasion to travel to Texas to solicit funds from several small communities there for an addition which was planned for the shul. And he got off in this small Texas town, and he started to walk from the station. All the youngsters, the little Indian children, and the little boys playing around the station started following him and looking at what seemed to them his outlandish garb. The man was dressed in the typical Hasidic fashion, with long earlocks, a beard, black suit, a black, broadbrimmed, sort of squashed top hat, white socks, and black shoes. They followed him from the station, hooting and calling at him, and making all sorts of noises calculated to disturb him. The man finally turned around, put down his suitcases and his bookcases, looked at them, and said,

"Hey, vat's de matter wit you, you little monsters, hain't you never seen a Yenkee before!" [*very fast, excited*].

8B. The Jew in Mississippi (Maurice A. Crane)

This farmer would eat only the food killed according to Jewish ritual, and of course he couldn't get it down in his little community in Mississippi, so he sent for a *shohet*, a ritual butcher, to come down from New York. The butcher took a train down as far as Mobile, and then he took a bus down as far as New Orleans, and then a cab out a certain distance. Then the road ended, and he had to walk out to the man's farmhouse. He was wearing a skullcap, prayer shawl, black, old-country clothing, long beard. He was a bent-over man, a typical caricature of a European rabbi. As he walked along, the children started to gather behind him, and Negroes came out from the cotton fields, and the loafers and the people from the town started following along, until there was a pretty great big huge crowd following behind him.

Well, he gets exasperated, turns around and says, "What's de matter, you've never seen a Yenkee?" [*rising inflection*].

9. Directions (Leo Lapidus)

A French-Canadian dialect story also involving complicated directions is in my "Dialect Stories of the Upper Peninsula," JAF, LXI (1948), 129.

Well, this is a story that is rather well known, I think, about a man that stops another man on the street, and he says, "Do you speak Yiddish?"

The other man says, "Yes, I do."

"Vell," he says, "I vant to go to Blossom Street. How do you go?"

"Vell," he says [*eager to help*], "go hupstairs, take the helevator, end go on de helevator and get off at Vashington Street, end take a transfer, go downstairs, take a streetcar, end you go as far as Lincoln Evenue. Get off at Lincoln Evenue, on de corner, end go across de tracks end go down de subvay, end take a subvay train end go along the subvay train until you come to de next station, end dot's it."

10. Do You Speak Yiddish? (Leo Lapidus)

Teitelbaum, "Pantomine," Anthology, p. 289, gives this a reverse twist.

Well, there's another one that illustrates the same principle, about the man in the theater that taps a fellow on the shoulder and says, "Do you speak Yiddish?" [*rising inflection*].

"No."

Taps another fellow on the shoulder, says, "Do you speak Yiddish?"

"No."

He taps a third fellow on the shoulder, says, "Do you speak Yiddish?"

"Yeah."

"Please, vat time is it?"

11. Macy's (Leo Lapidus)

Other versions in the Archives (Joseph Rose, Detroit), and Richman, Jewish Wit and Wisdom, p. 373 (told on Gimbel's).

It's told about this old Jewish couple that had come over from Europe and lived about twenty years on the East Side, had a little grocery store, and had never left that place to see any other part of the city. They lived in back in a small room, and one day after about twenty years the old man decided to get out and see the town, and he landed up in Macy's. Well, of course, the man was quite amazed at this whole spectacle, and finally he walked up to one of the floorwalkers, and he said, "I vould like to see Mr. Macy, could you tell me vere he is?" [*high-pitched*].

Well, the floorwalker was a little bit surprised but he said, "Why yes, I'll take you up there."

So he took him up to Mr. Macy's office, and they went inside, and Mr. Macy said, "Yes, what can I do for you?"

And he said, "Vell, Mr. Macy, I vould like to buy your store."

Mr. Macy was, of course, amused, but he thought he would play along with the guy and he said, "Yes, I'm not really intending to sell it, but I might."

"Vell, how much do you vant for the store?"

"Well," he said, "well-a, I would have to sell it for about twenty million dollars."

"Pahdon me, Mr. Macy, could I use your telephone?"

"Why," Mr. Macy said, "yes, of course, go ahead."

So this little fellow goes to the telephone and calls up his wife. "Hullo, Becky."

"Yeah."

"Becky, you listen very careful, I'll tell you what you should do. You go to the back of the kitchen to the closet, up on the fourth shelf on the left-hand side you'll find a shoe box. In the shoe box you'll bring me the peckage right away to Macy's store. Right away."

Well, in a few minutes his daughter arrived with the package, and he opened the package and started taking out these wads of bills and began counting out the money. A hundred, a thousand, five thousand, ten thousand, and he got up to about fifteen million, sixteen million, seventeen million, and that's all he had. He was amazed, thunderstruck. So he said, "Just a minute, Mr. Macy, can I use your telephone again?"

"Certainly."

He calls back on the telephone, he says, "Becky. Vere did you find that shoe box?"

So she told him, "I found it back on the third shelf."

He says, "I told you it was the fourth shelf shoe box, not the third shelf."

[That has another ending, doesn't it, Leo?]

Yes, that does have another ending. The other ending consists in this, that the fellow was very anxious to buy the store, and he left his wife to look around while he went up to Mr. Macy's office. And when Mr. Macy told him it was twenty million dollars, he was right ready with the cash in his pocket. But as he was counting it out, his wife suddenly broke into the office and said, "Jake, wait a minute Jake, don't buy the store" [*loudly*].

"Why," he says, "what's the matter, Becky, it's a beautiful store, wonderful."

"Jake, but it doesn't have three rooms in the back."

[Leo, you were telling us that sometimes you add another little bit to that, when he sees the escalator.]

Oh yes, well it's rather hard to describe that in English, because actually originally it's told in Yiddish, but the essence of it is that he sees these people riding up on the escalator, he's quite amazed that they are moving and at the same time standing, and he relates this little expression that says, "Aah, clever America, people stand and move." The Yiddish is "America goniff, me steht me geht."

12. The Two Shuls (Leo Lapidus)

Another version in Mendelsohn, "More Truth Than Poetry," Let Laughter Ring, *p. 69 (two Jews on a desert island organize three congregations).*

Well, this is about a Jew who left New York City and went away because he wanted to get away from it all. He went away to an island, and he was the only Jew on this island. And he established himself there, and one day a friend of his came to visit. He took him around and showed him the island, showed him the various things on it. And he showed him this building and that building, and finally he said, "This is the shul that I go to."

"Well, it's a fine shul."

They were walking along, and they came to another building, and his friend said, "What's this building?"

He said, "Well, that's another shul."

"You mean to say that you're the only Jew on the island and there are two shuls?"

"Oh yes, this is the shul that I *don't* go to."

13. Cencer Schmencer (Leo Lapidus)

Another version in the Archives (Martha Bernstein, New York, who also gives analogues turning on "Oedipus schmoedipus" and "nifter schmifter").

This is a typical story. It's about these two friends that meet, and they're conversing one with another.

"Say, have you seen Moe Goldberg lately?"

"Ye–es, I've seen him, he's pretty good, but I don't know, something seems to be the trouble, he isn't quite right."

"Vell, what seems to be the trouble?"

"Vell," he says, "I don't know. He said he vent to see a doctor; the doctor says he's got cencer."

"Vell, cencer schmencer, as long as he's healthy."

(They tell that in Yiddish. The Yiddish would be, "Cencer schmencer, a be gesund.")

14. A Problem (Leo Lapidus)

Cf., on the gesture, Richman, Laughs from Jewish Lore, p. 259: ". . . argued the casuistic theologian, in the Talmudic sing-song, drawing with his thumb a semicircle in the air. . . ."

Well, if we were going to put this into a modern setting, we might say the *yeshiva-bochers* were whooping it up one Saturday night after the Bialystok *yeshiva* had played the Vilna boys, but, of course, they didn't have any football in those days. But anyway, it seems that these fellows got together, and one of them got drunk, and as a prank they brought him out and left him in the cemetery. And, of course, after a while he came to, and he looked around, and, in the typical fashion of a Talmudic scholar, he said, "If I'm alive, what am I doing in the cemetery? And on the other hand, if I'm dead, tell me, why do I have to go to the bathroom?"

[You were telling us, Leo, that when that story was told, the Talmudic scholar makes a certain gesture with his thumb.]

Yes, he usually takes his hand and holds his thumb up, and then as he argues, he dips his thumb down pointing to the ground, and then up again, and then down and up again. This is sort of the general gesture that goes with this tipulistic argumentation that's so commonly known in Talmudic circles.

15. Anti-Semite (Leo Lapidus)

Another version in Ausubel, "God's Impatience," A Treasury of Jewish Humor, p. 167, which lacks the "anti-semite" ending below, concluding with the incident of the falling branch.

Well, there are several stories, as you know, that illustrate the feeling Jews have about anti-Semitism. The one that I know that's rather funny, I think, is about the Jew who is walking along a lonely road on a very dark night, and it's raining and storming, and suddenly this tremendous crash of lightning comes down upon him and strikes a tree, and the tree breaks off and lands right in his path, just practically missing him. And, of course, he looks up, and he shakes his hand up at heaven, and he says, "Anti-Semite."

16. Traveling (Leo Lapidus)

Well, then there's one told about three ladies who were conversing. Again this was originally in Yiddish, but in English translation I think it's still pretty good.

One of them says, "How's your son making out?"

"Vell, my son is doink fine, he's trevelink."

"Vere is he trevelink?"

"He's trevelink in de Vest."

"Ooh."

And then they say to the second lady, 'And how's your son makink out?"

"Oh, fine."

"Vat is he do?"

"He trevels."

"Vere is he trevelink?"

"Also in de Vest."

Then they turn to the third lady. "And vat does your son do?"

"He trevels."

"Vere does he trevel?"

"Uh, he trevels in de South."

They all look at one another. "The South? Vere is de South?"

The first lady says, "I don't know. I suppose it's also in de Vest."

17. The Only Flaw (Leo Lapidus)

Well, this one here is about a marriage broker. The marriage broker is a character that figures in Jewish life. The name given to him is *shadchan* in the original Yiddish.

It seems that this *shadchan* had a match for a man, and he was telling him about the girl. He says, "Oh," he says, "I've got a wonderful girl for you."

"Yes, tell me something about her."

"She's a very beautiful girl. Marvelous."

And the fellow, the other fellow, says to the *shadchan*, "Tell me, vat's de matter wit de girl?" [*knowingly*].

"Nottink's de matter, she's very beautiful, very attrective. Well educated."

"Ye-es, but vat's de matter wit de girl?"

"Nothink at all. I tell you she's beautiful, attrective, well educated, well brought up. In fect, her father has lots and lots of money" [*persuasive, excited*].

"Is that so?"

"Yes."

"But vat's de matter wit de girl?"

"I tell you, nottink at all, she's wonderful, she comes from a fine family."

"Listen, tell me, vat's de matter wit de girl?"

"Well, nottink. She's just a little bit, but only a little bit, pregnant."

18. Not Interested (Leo Lapidus)

This girl Becky got into trouble and went to see her family doctor about it. The family doctor said, "Well, Becky, I'll tell you. I brought you into the world, and all your brothers and sisters, and I wouldn't want to see any harm come to you. I'll take care of you but it's a risky business. Just see that it doesn't happen again" [*paternally*].

Three or four weeks later Becky is back with the same complaint. She's in trouble. The doctor says, "Now, Becky, I told you, this is a dangerous thing. Now if I'm found out in this business I could lose my license, ruin my reputation."

"Vell, doctor, you know how it is, I, I . . ." Well, anyway he took care of her.

Well, after this happened several times, finally he says "Becky," he says, "this is the last time I'm going to do anything for you. But tell me, every time this happens, is it with a different man or the same man?"

"Ahh now, it's the same fellow all the time."

"Well, Becky, now why don't you marry the guy?"

"H'I dun't know—he doesn't happeal to me" [*squeaky*].

19. Catch Question (Leo Lapidus)

"Can you give me a drink that begins with *H*?"
"You caught me off guard there, Leo. No, I can't tell you a drink that begins with *H*."
"Ha malted."

20. The Value of Woman (Leo Lapidus)

This next story that comes to mind is about a lecture that's being given on the value of woman. And the lecturer is saying that, well, after all, woman is a great asset to the world, and her value is immeasurable, and he points to one little fellow in the audience, and he says, "Now you, what is your wife worth to you?" [*loud, forceful*].
The fellow says, "Hm, make me han offer."

21. In the Sahara (Leo Lapidus)

A friend of mine, George Campbell, from Lansing, Michigan, who has told me many urban anecdotes, ran this joke in the Capitol Guide, *a monthly bulletin for out-of-towners which he edited for a while.*

This story illustrates a well-known trait. This Jew had made a lot of money, and he had vowed that if he did make a lot of money some day, he was going to take a trip around the world. So this came to pass actually, and he found himself in the Sahara Desert. So he's walking along in the Sahara Desert with his bathing suit on, y'know, and he meets up with someone.
The fellow says to him, "Say," he says, "what are you doing walking along here with a bathing suit? Why, there's no water along here for miles and miles around!"
"Yeah, but you got to admit it's a beautiful beach."

22. The Baby (Leo Lapidus)

A similar story exemplifying a similar characteristic, I think, is the story that's told about a lady that is standing with a baby carriage, and someone comes up and looks at the baby and says, "You have a very beautiful baby there, madam."

She says, "Yes-s, but you should see the baby's picture" [*inflected*].

23. The Mohel's Window (Leo Lapidus)

This next story exemplifies I think a certain trait in the clever Jew. It seems that these two Jews wanted to find a *mohel*. A *mohel* is a man who does ritual circumcisions. And so one of them knew where a certain *mohel* was to be found, so they went there, and they found that the location was in a store in which there were three balls hanging outside, and, in the window, watches all over the place. So they come inside, and-a, "How do you do. I understand that you are a *mohel*."

"Yes, sure."

"What's the idea of all the watches in the window?"

"Vat do you expect me to put in the window?" [*sly, cunning*].

24. Fire, Fire! (Leo Lapidus)

Well, it's about a fire apparently. A call had gone out in the country, and the firemen answered the call, and looking around they heard someone shouting, "Fire, fire!" but they didn't see any flames. And they tried to trace the source of the fire—the source of the sound I should say—and finally traced it to the outhouse. They go in there, look around, they don't see anyone but they still hear someone shouting, "Fire, fire!"

And one of the firemen looked down and saw a man down

there up to his neck. And the fireman yelled down and said, "What are you yelling fire, fire, for, I don't see any fire around here?"

The fellow calls back, "Vat do you expect me to yell?"

25. Train for Utica (Leo Lapidus)

Well, this next one has no connection with any of the preceding and probably won't have any with the following. But it seems that this lady came up to ask the trainman a question at the train station. The trainman happened to be a Jewish person, and he is calling out "Trains for Syracuse, Schenectady, Buffalo" [*accented*].

And the lady comes up, and she says, "Pahdon me, when does the last train leave for Utica?"

He says, "Lady, ven the last train leaves for Utica, you should live so long" [*slyly*].

26. Name-Changing: Abraham to Allen (Leo Lapidus)

Another version in Mendelsohn, "Mistaken Identity," Let Laughter Ring, pp. 126–27 (Adolf Cohen wants to change the Adolf).

There are several stories told about name-changing. This story is told about this man who comes into court and wants to have his name changed. And the judge says, "Well, what is your name?"

"Vell, my name iss Abraham Stinker."

"Abraham Stinker! Well, I certainly can't blame you for wanting your name changed. What would you like to have it changed to?"

"Allen Stinker."

27A. Name-Changing: Cabot to Saltonstall (Leo Lapidus)

Other versions in the Archives (Martha Bernstein, New York, from Bernard Rauch, Cambridge—Kelly to Reilly); Mendelsohn, "Im-

proving on Ancestry," The Jew Laughs, *p. 206 (David Cohen to Donald Crane to Dudley Kingsbury); Teitelbaum, "A Binominal Theorem,* Anthology, *pp. 273–74 (Izzie Rabinovitch to Patrick Gilligan to Donald O'Brien).*

There is another one. It's about this man that comes in, and he wants to have his name changed. And the judge says, "What is your name now?"

"My name iss Meester Cabutt."

"Your name is Cabot. What do you want to have it changed to?"

"I vant to have my name changed to Saltonstall."

"You want your name changed from Cabot to Saltonstall!" he says. "I don't understand it; you've got to give me a reason."

"Vell," he says, "everytime I go in any place and say, 'My name is Cabot,' they always ask me, 'Vat vass it before you changed it?' And I don't vant to have to say it vas Korbitski. So next time if they ask me vat vass your name before you had it changed, I'll say, before it vass Saltonstall it vass Cabot" [*high, mincing*].

27B. Name-Changing: O'Hara to McGonigle
(Maurice A. Crane)

There's another one about name-changing. Mr. O'Hara comes in to change his name and he says, "Ach, you're de man vat changes de names?"

"Yes."

"So look, my name is O'Hara. End, end I'd like to change it to McGonigle, McGonigle."

"Well, certainly, Mr. O'Hara, but well, how come, why do you want to change your name? O'Hara is a perfectly lovely Gaelic name."

"Well, I'll tell ya, I talk to somebody and he asks me what my name is and I tell him, and he says, 'Yeah, but what was it *before* it was O'Hara?'"

28. Name-Changing: Jack Waters (Leo Lapidus)

This is about two men who meet on a train and find out that they're both Jews.

One of them says to the other, "What is your name?"

"My name is Jack Waters."

"Jack Waters! How does it happen that a Jew should have the name Jack Waters? Are you an American Jew?"

"Well, no," he says. "As a matter of fact, before I came to this country, I lived in England, and in England," he says, "my name was Fountain."

"Oh," he says. "You're an English Jew."

"Well, no," he says. "Actually, before I lived in England, I lived in France, and in France my name was Mr. LaFontaine. I came to England, so from LaFontaine it became Fountain. When I came to the United States, from Fountain, Jack Waters."

"Oh," he says. "I see that you're a French Jew."

"Well, not exactly. Before I lived in France, I lived in Chermany. And there," he says, "my name was Spritzwasser."

"Ohh, I see, Spritzwasser."

"Yes, and when I went to France, from Spritzwasser it became LaFontaine, from LaFontaine, Fountain, and from Fountain, Jack Waters."

"Oh, then you're a German Jew?"

"Well," he says. "Actually, I was born in Kovno *gubernja*, and there they used to call me Bevelterpisser."

29: Have a Sandwich (Leo Lapidus)

Other versions in Ausubel, "Who Counts?" A Treasury of Jewish Folklore, *p. 378; Mendelsohn, "Here's Your Hat—What's the Hurry?" Let Laughter Ring, p. 190.*

This is somewhat typical of a certain type of person, not necessarily Jewish, but this happened to be a Jewish person who was walking around among her guests, carrying a tray of sandwiches. She stopped and offered the tray to a lady guest, "Have a sandwich."

"Thenk you, I've already had two."

"Huhuh, you've had six, but who's counting?"

30: Potato *Latkes* (Leo Lapidus)

Richman, Jewish Wit and Wisdom, *pp. 392–93, gives two maniac joke-tales.*

It appears that an inmate of a certain institution was talking to some visitor who had come to visit a friend, and the visitor asked, "You sound like a rather intelligent person, how does it happen that you've been committed to this institution?"

"Well, I don't really know, but the strange thing is they put me here because I happen to like potato *latkes*." (Now you know *latkes* is simply the word for pancakes. These are very well known; in fact, they're made frequently at various occasions throughout the Jewish holiday year.)

"It's rather strange that they should put you in here just because you like potato *latkes*. I like potato *latkes*, too."

"You *do*. Well, when I get out, you'll have to come to my house and come to my attic. I have *trunks* full and *trunks* full of potato *latkes*."

31. A Question (Leo Lapidus)

Other versions in Ausubel, "Why Not?" A Treasury of Jewish Folklore, p. 437; Mendelsohn, "The Eternal Question," The Jew Laughs, p. 88; Teitelbaum, "Erotematic," Anthology, p. 333; Rosenberg and Shapiro, "Marginality and Jewish Humor," Midstream, IV, 79.

Well, a well-known question that's asked is this. Put it this way. Someone asks a Jew this question, "Why is it that when-

ever you ask a Jew a question, he always answers you with another question?"

And the answer that he gives is, "Vy not?" [*sly*].

32. Sholom (Leo Lapidus)

There's a story that I heard recently—this is a rather recent
one—from a man who came from Israel. He was telling this to
a Jewish audience, so ostensibly the end is only supposed to be
something known to Jews, but I don't think that anything is
really disclosed here of a nature that will, shall we say, violate
the security of either Israel or the United States.

It seems that someone asked an Israeli, "Why is it that all of
the different European nations have a separate word for hello
and goodbye? For example, in English, you meet a person and
say, 'Hello,' when you leave you say 'Goodbye.' In France it's
'Bonjour,' 'Au Revoir.' In Germany you say 'Guten Tag' and
'Auf wiedersehn,' and so forth. But here in Israel when you
meet a person and say hello, it's 'Sholom,' which means 'peace
unto you,' and when you leave him and say goodbye, it's
'Sholom.' "

"In Israel right now we don't know whether we're coming
or going" [*accented*].

33. Families (Leo Lapidus)

This one is about two old women friends who meet in the
United States after about twenty years, not having seen each
other since they were in Europe.

"Oh, hello Becky, how are you?"

"I'm fine. It's so good to see you after all these years. How
are you, Molly?"

"Fine. And how's your family? I suppose you hev a family?"

"Yah."

"How many children do you hev?"

"I hev six. How many do you hev?"
"I hev two."
"Huh—Yenkee."

34. At the Theater (Leo Lapidus)

This one is also, I think, typical of a certain type of Jewish woman. This person was in a theater watching a play—sitting up on the second balcony pretty close to the top where the technicians throw the spotlight on the stage. As she watched the play, she was sitting behind a woman in front of her whom she happened to know, and every once in a while this woman would say, "Hooh, hah. Hooh, hah." Just like this, you know.

Well, after the show, as they were walking out, the person tapped the woman on the shoulder and said, "I see you enjoyed the show very much. Every once in a while you kept exclaiming 'Hooh hah.'"

"Oh," she said, "no, it wasn't the show, but you know those spotlights. I got such a good bake on my shoulders."

[Leo describes Jewish women in bathing slapping their shoulders and going "Hooh hah."]

35. Braddd! (Leo Lapidus)

Another version in Richman, Jewish Wit and Wisdom, *pp. 317–18.*

Finally this last one that I have is about a man who used to patronize a certain restaurant. The first time that he went into the restaurant, the proprietor, as was his custom, came over to the man after he had finished his meal, and said, "Well, how did you enjoy your meal? Was everything all right?"

"Oih yes, everything wass fine, but you don't serve enough *braddd*."

Well, next time the man came in, the proprietor saw him coming, and he said to the waiter, "Put a little extra bread on his plate."

And so after the meal was over the proprietor again came over to the man; he says, "Well, how was everything today?"

"Oih, fine, everything iss very good, but whatsa matter, you don't serve enough *braddd.*"

Well, next time the man came in, he again told the waiter, "Give him six or eight slices." And again the same story.

"Everything fine, yeah, wonderful meal, but for heaven's sakes, why are you so stingy with *braddd?*"

So the next time this man came in, the proprietor said to the waiter, "Take the whole loaf of bread and slice it right down the middle and put the two halves on the plate."

And so this time the proprietor asked the man as he left, "Well, how did you find everything today?"

"Vell," he says, "I see you're back to two slices."

36. Thoroughly American (Alfred L. Friedman)

Well, this is a true incident which occurred in connection with my wife. When I was in Benton Harbor and St. Joe, Michigan, we had many visitors, especially from the Chicago area, who came up to vacation—it is a resort area. Well, one Friday evening a number of these people were at our services in Benton Harbor, and following the service we had a social hour during which time people met and conversed. My wife had occasion to speak to a particular lady who was well dressed, perhaps expensively so, and she was boasting to my wife, somewhat like this:

"Y'know, I belong to a reformed congregation in Chicago, and y'know vot, ve don't have services on Friday night. No sir, ve have services on Sunday morning!"

37. Santa Claus (Maurice A. Crane)

Other versions in Richman, Jewish Wit and Wisdom, *p. 374, and Rosenberg and Shapiro, "Marginality and Jewish Humor," Midstream, IV, 77–78 ("A leben an dein kepple," says Santa Claus).*

Santa Claus was sitting in this department store in a metropolitan area, and these kids start coming up to him. The first kid comes up, and Santa Claus says, "Ho, ho, ho, ho, little girl, who are you?" [*very deep*].

"I'm Sally Jones."

"Ho ho, ho, and what would you like for Christmas?"

"Well, I'd like to have a sled and a couple of dolls and a doll-house."

"Ho, ho, ho, ho. Well Sally, we'll certainly get that for you, and who is this?"

"My name is Jimmy Johnson, and I'd like a bicycle and some skates."

"Oh ho, ho, ho, haw, Jimmy, I certainly will come over and get you a bicycle and some skates. Oh, ho, ho, ho. And who are you little boy?"

"Well Santa, my name is Sammy Cohen, and I, I just came to be with the other kids. You see, I don't, I don't really believe in Christmas. I'm Jewish."

"Oh ho, ho, ho, Shmuel, a gezinta an dein kepple." [Translation: "Ha, ha, Sammy, God bless your little head," or "Good health to your little head."]

38. The Radio Announcer (Maurice A. Crane)

Similar texts in the Archives (Martha Bernstein, New York), and Mendelsohn, "Trouble, Trouble, Everywhere," The Merry Heart, p. 197.

A whole genre of Jewish jokes are the anti-Semitism jokes—the false anti-Semitism jokes.

The man meets a friend on the street and says, "I-I-I-I-I jus', I jus'—I whooo—I-I-I-I was—I was down at—I was down at—I whoo—hooh ah—I was down at the radio sta—I who—I wanted to get a job at the radio station."

"Well, Jake, what did you want to do?"

"Well, well, I-I-ooh-I wanted—I wanted to be a radio, a radio announcer—a spi-spa-spi-spo-sportscaster."

"Well, did you get the job?"

He says, "No-no-no-no-nah-no. They hate Jews."

39. The Priest and the Rabbi (Maurice A. Crane)

There are seven variants in the Archives, two of which are close to the present text in having the priest and rabbi meet on a train (Herbert F. Dykema, Jr., Grand Rapids, from C. B. Simkins; and Marguerite Emmerling, Detroit, from Dave Siegel). Often this story is told in the form of a snappy comeback; see Mendelsohn, "Theology and Logic," Let Laughter Ring, p. 37, and Teitelbaum, "Mendelsohn's Answer," Anthology, p. 356.

This is the one in the service where they're coming back on the train. They're several of them—I don't know why it is they always pick on priests. But it always seems to be a priest and a rabbi arguing. This time the men are coming back from overseas. They both live in New York, and they're coming in from the Pacific, and they get on the train the first day, and the meals on a troop train are pretty much the same. For breakfast it's bacon and eggs, and for lunch it's pork chops or pork sausages, for supper it's ham. The first day, of course, the rabbi doesn't eat anything at all. The priest asks him what's the matter. He says, "I can't eat this because it's against my religion, I'm not allowed to eat swine's flesh."

And the second day, of course, he gets quite hungry, and it's an extremely hot day. This troop train is rather typical, moving along at about twelve miles an hour—and the rabbi's getting hungry, but he holds out. The third day, however, they're getting along in the Colorado mountains, and he's very famished.

And the priest says, "Come on, have some of my ham." And sure enough he does, and boy, he likes it, and he eats it up. And he goes around to all the soldiers there, and anybody's got leftover ham; and he eats, and he eats, and he eats.

"Boy is this good, boy oh boy is this good!"

Finally they get to New York, they get to the station, and the rabbi rushes out, and this beautiful, gorgeous woman comes up to him, hugs him, kisses him, throws her arms around him. "Jake, it's wonderful to have you home. Let's go home immediately."

He says, "Wait a second, Sarah, I want you to meet my good friend, Father O'Reilly. Come on over here, Pat."

Pat comes over, and he [the rabbi] says, "Father O'Reilly, I want you to meet my wife Sarah."

"How do you do, Father."

"Say, Father, where's your wife?" he says.

"Oh, no, no, I'm, I'm, I'm not allowed to have a wife. You see it's, it's against my religion" [softly].

"Oh," says the rabbi, "You ought to try it, it's better than ham!" [enthusiastically].

40. Salmon (Maurice A. Crane)

The lady goes into the delicatessen. She goes in, and she says to the man behind the counter, "Listen, Mr. Rapalport." She points—she says, "Could I have some of that selmon."

"Selmon, that's not selmon, that's hem!"

"So who asked ya?"

41. Name-Changing: John Kelly (Maurice A. Crane)

Another version in Mendelsohn, "True to his Heritage," Let Laughter Ring, p. 207 (Yankele becomes John Kelly).

There are a number of name-changing jokes. There is one about the typically Jewish man in New York whose name is John Kelly. He had gone to Ellis Island, they asked him his name, and he said, "Yankele," which is the affectionate diminutive for Jacob.

42. Name-Changing: Cohen or Levy? (Maurice A. Crane)

Other versions in the Archives (Martha Bernstein, New York, from Bernard Rauch, Cambridge—which O'Reilly: Birnbaum, Schwartz, or Cohen); Mendelsohn, "Be Specific, Please," Let Laughter Ring, p. 159 (which O'Connor: Friedman or Solomon); Richman, Jewish Wit and Wisdom, p. 394 (which Ryan: Rabinowitz or Levy); Teitelbaum, "Nominal Change," Anthology, p. 284 (which O'Reilly: Steinberg or Goldberg).

A very famous story is about Cohen and Levy, who have a pretty flourishing business, but they think it could do even better if they would change their names. So Cohen decides he's going to change his name, and he goes down and has it officially changed to Vanderbilt. And the firm of Vanderbilt and Levy prospers, does very well indeed, until Levy says, "You know, you know, Sam, I think we could do even better if I were to change my name, too."

So he goes down to the office and pays them the two bucks, and sure enough he changes his name to Vanderbilt, too. And the firm is now called Vanderbilt and Vanderbilt, Incorporated.

So now, the girl in the office—the girl at the switchboard—answers the phone, and someone asks to speak to Mr. Vanderbilt. She says, "Sure, which Vanderbilt do you want, Cohen or Levy?"

43. The Lobster (Maurice A. Crane)

I'm not sure this is a typically Jewish joke, but it works well with an accent.

A man goes into Hackney's Restaurant and orders a lobster. He sits back to eat it, and this lobster is brought before him and he looks at it, and these sad lobster eyes look at him. And this compassion fills his heart, and he looks at this pitiful winsome face of the lobster, and he says, "Take it away, please." And he walks out, and he doesn't eat at all.

The next day he goes back to Hackney's, he's just dying for lobster. He sits down, and the exact same thing happens. This sad-faced lobster comes out and looks at him and tears come to his eyes. He says, "Please, take it away, please."

And the third day the same thing happens. He's going to Hackney's, and again the same sad-faced lobster. He decides, no more of this, I'm not going to eat here any more.

The fourth day he goes into Kornblau's. He sits down at Kornblau's—these are in Atlantic City, and it's quite a ways from Hackney's—and he sits back ready to eat. A lobster is brought before him, and he looks down at the lobster, and the lobster looks up at him.

"Hey, Jake, how come you're not eating at Hackney's any more?"

44. The Water Cure (Maurice A. Crane)

I heard this from Jack Baker, who was a master of ceremonies of mine, at the Erin Isle Café in Atlantic City. And he could tell a fine Irish joke. This was an Irish nightclub, and he told mostly Irish jokes. But the truth of the matter is, he was less of a Gael than a Gaelitsiano. At the end of the summer I discovered that he had a wonderful store of Jewish jokes. One of them was this.

A man comes down to Atlantic City to cure his arthritis. He's got to go bathing in salt water. The water is cold, and he can't go in the water, so he decides to go and buy a couple of tin buckets, get water, and take the buckets up to the hotel room and rub the water on his legs.

He goes down early in the morning, and the lifeguard says, "This man is a fool. I'll see if I can't make some money from him."

So the man's taking his two buckets of water up. "Wait,"

says the lifeguard, "just a minute. What do you think you're doing?"

"Hm, I'm taking water up to my room, I should put it on my legs so I'll cure my arthritis."

"Well that's all very good but um, what do you think I'm here for? I'm guarding this water. If you want to take a bucketful of water I'll have to charge you twenty-five cents a bucket."

"Well, it's hokay." He goes into the pocket of his bathing suit, he gets out fifty cents and gives it to the lifeguard.

He comes back late in the afternoon. He needs some more water, but now the tide's gone out. Before it was high tide, now it's low tide. Before he goes in to get his water at all he goes up to the lifeguard, taps him on the shoulder, and says, "Boyy, are you making money!" [*loud, admiring*].

45. The Convert (Maurice A. Crane)

Another version in Richman, Jewish Wit and Wisdom, *pp. 350–51.*

This is a long, long, long story, and it's a moral story. A lady wants to get into a hotel, and she's a very, very typically Jewish-looking woman, and this is up in Saratoga in an exclusive hotel, and they would like to keep her out if they could. They try a number of ruses, but it comes out that she needs a room very much for the night, and they say finally, "Well, we can't allow you because it's our policy not to admit Jews in this part of town."

"Wat, is that the honly trouble? [*high scream*]. Listen," she says, "I don't know where you got the idea, but the truth of the matter is, I'm not a Jewish lady. The truth of the matter is, I'm a convertible."

"A what?"

"A convertible. I used to watch this Fulton Schine on the radio. He made me into a Cadillac."

He says, "You're a Cadillac convertible!"

"Yeah, yeah" [*high scream*].

He says, "Wait, I'll ask you. It just so happens that I'm a product of a parochial school, and I'm going to ask you the catechism. How was Jesus born?"

"Of course, he wass born by himmaculate concepsion. And his fadder wass Josiph, and his mudder wass Mary."

"Yes, but where was Jesus born?"

"Oih, he wass born in a man–ger."

"That's right. Now why was he born in a manger?"

"Because *some dirty dog* like you wouldn't geeve a Jewish lady a room for the night!"

46. Groucho Marx (Maurice A. Crane)

A similar version in Mendelsohn, "Half a Loaf Will Do." The Merry Heart, p. 183.

Well, I don't know whether this was actual or not. I read it in Leonard Lyons' column a long, long time ago.

Groucho Marx stopped at a hotel, and he was admitted as a celebrity, but somebody—one of the people connected with the administration of the hotel—told him that they'd just as soon not have him in the pool. This was the barrier they put up; they didn't want Jews in the swimming pool.

"Well," Groucho said, "that's all right. I certainly admit that I'm Jewish. I'm not much of a swimmer, anyway. But the truth of the matter is, my wife's an Episcopalian, and my children are, of course, therefore half Jewish and half Episcopalian. I wonder if you would let them go into the pool up to their knees?"

47. The Mohel's Sign (Maurice A. Crane)

Louis C. Jones of Cooperstown, New York, has related the same story. Mendelsohn, "Nothing But the Best," Here's A Good One, p. 134, tells of a registered nurse who put up the sign, "Diplomatic Midwife."

This *mohel* moved to Scarsdale, and, of course, he put up a big neon sign: Moshe the Mohel—the circumciser. The people from the Chamber of Commerce said, "We're very glad to have you in our community, Mr. Moshe, but this sign is not in good taste" [*courteous but pointed*].

" 'Sokay." He takes down the sign.

The next day there's a new sign up: Maurice, the Yankee clipper.

48. The Mohel Goes Fishing (Maurice A. Crane)

This is the oldest of the *mohel* jokes. There's a man sitting trying to catch some fish, and he sees people go by with big loads, so he decides he's going to stop them. There's a man carrying a great big load of fish.

"Well, what are you using for bait?"

"Well, I'm a physician. I take out appendixes, and I operated this morning. I cut out an appendix, and gee, muskies just love it."

The next man comes along, "What do you use for bait?"

And he's got this huge load larger than the first one, and he says, "Well, I'm a doctor, and I just took out somebody's tonsils last week, and I preserved them in formaldehyde, cut 'em up this week. Boy, those bass, they just love 'em. They just love tonsils."

The third man's got the biggest load of all. And again the questioner asks him, "What do you use for bait?"

He says, "Well, you see, I'm a *mohel*."

49. No Cheating (Maurice A. Crane)

Other versions in Ausubel, "No Admittance," A Treasury of Jewish Folklore, p. 434; Mendelsohn, "Stop Thief!" The Jew Laughs, pp. 180–81. Cf. also Arthur Koestler, The Age of Longing (New York, 1953), pp. 55–56.

It's part of Hebrew law that nobody works on a prayer day. And so it was instituted the tradition that nobody carries money, and it's still practiced. People do not carry money or do any business on a holy day. Therefore, passing the collection plate as is familiar to everybody, it just doesn't take place in Jewish tradition. Instead they sell tickets for going on high holy days, and this is the source of revenue.

One high holy day things got very very crowded, and a man comes rushing up to the usher and says, "I gotta get in, I gotta get in, I'm in a hurry, I gotta get in" [*excited*].

"So where's your ticket?" [*dryly*].

"I don't have a ticket, but listen! I'm from Gold-Goldberg-Goldfarb and Cohen, and I'm, I'm Cohen, and Goldfarb's in there, and the warehouse is burning down, and I gotta talk to Goldfarb, I gotta talk, I'm in a hurry, I gotta go in and see him" [*breathless*].

"Well, I guess it's an emergency, I'll let you in. *But if I ketch you praying!*"

50. Eggtwist (Maurice A. Crane)

Barry Spacks also told this story. For a joke about chaleh, *see Ausubel, "Price is No Object," A* Treasury of Jewish Folklore, *p. 282.*

I don't know how the darn thing goes. You want to find somebody who talks Jewish.

It's a very, very big loaf of bread. You've probably seen it in Boston—C-H-A-L-E-H—they call it "Shale" in Boston. They sell it everywhere in Cambridge.

Anyway, this man's got his arm out, holding the loaf of bread, and somebody steals it. And standing there he looks like a homosexual. The punch line is, "Ooie, who stole my *chaleh?*"

51. Last Words (Maurice A. Crane)

Bruce Buckley related a close variant at Bloomington, Indiana, as did Rabbi Friedman in Lansing, Michigan. See Mendelsohn, "Busi-

ness Before Pleasure," Let Laughter Ring, *p. 165; Teitelbaum,* "*Business to the End*," Anthology, *p. 318.*

Jake's dying and he's in his last death throes, about to shuffle off the mortal coil, and, in some pain, he says, "Sam, are you here?" He can't even look around.
"Yeah, I'm here, father."
"And Becky, are you here?"
"Yeah, Pop, I'm here."
"Rose, Rose here?" [*louder*]
"Yes, Jake, I'm here" [*softly*].
"What about Uncle Yitzok, you here?"
"Yes, Jake, I'm here, I'm here" [*very soft*].
"And, and Jake, you here?"
"Yeah, yeah, yeah, I'm here."
"Benny?"
"Yeah, yeah, I'm here."
"So who's watching the store?" [*rising inflection*].

52. Relativity (Maurice A. Crane)

Other versions in Ausubel, "From What Einstein Makes a Living," A Treasury of Jewish Folklore, pp. 357–58; Richman, Jewish Wit and Wisdom, p. 20. A remoter variant is in Mendelsohn, "What an Awful Business," Here's a Good One, p. 202.

"Look, you're such a smart man, Jake, explain to me, what is this, what is this Einstein's relativity?"
"It's simple, look. You sit on a hot stove for one minute, it seems like two hours. But you're wit' your girl friend, and you're huggin', and you're kissin', and you're settin' on the couch in the dark for two hours, it seems like a minute."
"So tell me, Jake, from this Einstein makes a living?"

53. Sizing Them Up (Maurice A. Crane)

It's a story of the war. A man is purchasing some undergarments as a surprise to his wife, and he's extremely embarrassed.

He's an elderly man, and he's going through the negligees and finally he's trying to buy his wife a brassiere and he can't talk sizes, he's so embarrassed.

"Well," the girl says, "just give me this—are they big, or are they small?"

"Hooh, hooh, hoooh, are they big! [*rising inflection*]. Hitler should have 'em for tonsils."

54. Surprise (Maurice A. Crane)

Someone calls on the phone and says, "Hello. Is this the Levy house?" [*heavy accent*].

"Yeh, yeh, yeh, this is the Levy house. Yeh, yeh, yeh, that's it, that's it" [*high, shrill*].

"So who's this? Is this Mrs. Levy?"

"Nah Mrs. Levy."

"Well, you mean Sadie?"

"Nah. Mrs. Levy is downtown, she's shopping for somethin'."

"So who's this? This is Mr. Levy?"

"Nah Mr. Levy. Mr. Levy is in de store, he's got beezness today, it's a workday, he's got beezness."

"So this is maybe—Becky?"

"Ooy, Becky is in school. She goes to school, she's learning to be a stenographer."

"So this is—this is little Abe?"

"Ooy, little Abe is out playing baseball wit' de American Legion. They play baseball—bat, bat wit' de baseball."

"So tell me, who's dis?"

"Dis is Magnolia de Schweitzer."

(Schweitzer is a common term; it's the German word, the Jewish word for black, the black one.)

55. A Friend in Need (Maurice A. Crane)

This story is so well-known in some circles that simply the punch line is mentioned in conversation.

This man's buying a house on a land contract, and if he doesn't pay the hundred dollars for the month, the house will be taken away, and he happens to be very very much saddled with debts and insurance and so forth, this time of the year. And he goes up to his good friend Sam, says, "Sam, would you lend me a hundred bucks or they'll take my house away, and they'll kick me out in the street."

Sam says, "Noh!" [*high, emphatic*].

"What you mean, No. Sam listen, you remember in 1926, when you wanted to start into beezness, you came to me, you asked for ten thousand dollas; fifteen thousand I give you. I *gave* ya fifteen thousand. Later, your first boy was born, I gave ya five thousand dollas. In 1929 comes the depression you're wiped out, fifty thousand dollas I give ya, I set you up in beezness again. And when your daughter Rosie gets married in 1933, I give ya twenty-one thousand dollas you should have a nice wedding."

"Yeah, dat's true, dat's all true [*musing*], I admit. But what have you done for me recently?"

56. A Toast (Maurice A. Crane)

I always knew this as an Irish joke, but you can certainly tell it in Jewish.

Two men are arguing. They've been enemies for a long time, and they finally get together, and they're sitting over their cups, and they decide to make up, so they pour a little Mannishevitz in each glass.

Jake says, "Sam, let's make up. Here's a toast. Here's wishing you everything that you're wishing me."

"Haw, haw, starting in again!"

57. Rabbi Shulz (Maurice A. Crane)

This takes place in New Guinea during the war, in one of these jerry-built prefabs. And a GI urinal is just a wall with a drainboard. And these men are performing matutinal ablutions.

One says to the other, "Hey [*rising inflection*], you're from Philadelphia?"

"Yeeeh, yeh, yeh, yeh. South Philadelphia."

"Broad Street perhaps?"

"Broad Street exactly—exactly Broad Street."

"Uh, uh, five hundred block?"

"As a matter of fact, 612, 612 South Broad."

"You go to shul by Rabbi Shulz?"

"Yeeh, yeh—oh, he's been our rabbi all my life, he's been our rabbi. How d'ye know?"

"Well, he always circumcises on the bias, and you're p——— all over my leg."

58. At the Football Game (Maurice A. Crane)

Other versions in Ausubel, "Babe Ruth and the Jewish Question," A Treasury of Jewish Folklore, p. 426; Mendelsohn, "Hebraic Egocentricism," Here's a Good One, p. 12 (Is the antelope's escape good or bad for the Jews?); and Richman, Jewish Wit and Wisdom, p. 358 (Is the Giants' victory good or bad for the Jews?).

A man sends his son to the University of Pennsylvania in the heyday of Ray Dooney and Skippy Manisi and their great backfield. And as it so happens, they were at the ball game a short time, and Manisi breaks away and runs ninety-four yards for a touchdown. Everyone jumps up. "Hurray, yay, yay."

They're all cheering, and the son gets up, and, of course, he's cheering, and the father says, "So nu, what happened?"

"Well, papa, Skippy Manisi got the ball, and he ran ninety-four yards for a touchdown."

"Hooh hah, is it good for the Jews?"

59. The Poor Rothschilds (Maurice A. Crane)

Other versions in Ausubel, "Rothschild's Poverty," A Treasury of Jewish Folklore, p. 396; Mendelsohn, "The Acme of Niggardli-

ness" (told on the rich Brodsky), Here's A Good One, *pp. 195–96; Richman, "Who Said Brodsky was Rich?"* Laughs From Jewish Lore, *p. 120–21.*

There's a cycle about Baron Rothschild, as there are, I guess, in all folklores about the wealthy man in the community. The one I remember is about the man who says, "Ooy, I'm really worried for the Rothschilds, I think they're getting poor. I was in their house the other day in the living room, and *two* of his daughters were playing on *one* piano!"

60. Thirsty (Maurice A. Crane)

Another version in Ausubel, "It's Terrible," A Treasury of Jewish Folklore, p. 325. Bernard Stroyman gives this a slightly different twist; a man on the sleeping car groans in great distress, and asks a fellow to get him some water. He does so and then asks what was the matter. "Oy, was I thirsty!"

I wish I knew my geography a little better. This man is going from one point to another in Texas, and these points are about four hundred miles apart, and in the middle there's just this one stop at a two hundred mile point and no stops anywhere in between. The train's very crowded, it's an extremely hot day in Texas, and as fate would have it, the water cooler is on the blink. There is no water. All the passengers are uncomfortable but they are trying to make the best of the situation, except this one elderly Jewish man who says, "Ooy, am I thirsty! Ooyaya-yayay, am I thirsty. Ooy am I thirsty!" And on and on until lips become parched, and throats begin to choke up, and people are sympathetic with him, but he's making them thirsty, too. And he continues, "Ooy, ooy, ooy, ooyee. Am I thoistee, I'm thoistee, thoistee, am I thoistee, ooy" [*series of groans and cries*].

This goes on for two hundred miles farther. The people can't stand it. And they come to the stop. There's only a five-minute stop but they all rush out and get buckets full of water and hoses full of water, and they get glasses and cups and bottles, and everybody brings some water, and he drinks and drinks and drinks till he drinks all the water there is. And the people unload the last bucket, and the train starts out again. The people themselves haven't had anything to drink, they've been too busy bringing him water. But at least they feel he's not going to be tortured, and he's not going to torture them.

Well the train pulls out of the station, and it's gone five minutes on the last two hundred miles of the journey when he starts in, "Ooy, was I thirsty, ooyee, was I thirsty!"

61. On the Subway (Maurice A. Crane)

In a related type, a British soldier captures nine German Jews by asking for a minyan: *Ausubel, "Secret Strategy,"* A Treasury of Jewish Folklore, *p. 424; Mendelsohn, "The Power of Judaism,"* The Jew Laughs, *p. 34; Richman, "Playing on the Enemy's Sentiments,"* Laughs From Jewish Lore, *pp. 207–8. In the American setting, the tenth man is sought in a train, and a prize-fighter prepares to deal with the seeming anti-Semite: Ausubel, "Only a Civil Question" (told on Benny Leonard),* A Treasury of Jewish Humor, *p. 640; Mendelsohn, "Jewish Sensitiveness,"* The Jew Laughs, *p. 216. Richman's text, "Goliath of the Bronx,"* Laughs from Jewish Lore, *pp. 203–5, is closest to the present one.*

This happens on a subway train in New York City, and this particular car, as frequently happens, is filled with many Jews. A very, very big, tough-looking bruiser comes into the car and says, "Hey [*deep, gruff*], are there any Jews in this car?"

Well, they're all afraid, but this one fellow's unfortunately on a date with his best girl, and he's got to show up, and he says, "Yeah, yeah, mister, I'm Jewish" [*meekly*].

The big bruiser says "Hey, would ya come into the next car, we need a tenth man for the *minyan*, we're *davening Kaddish* for my own *Seder*."

62. Misunderstanding (Maurice A. Crane)

Two little boys are coming home from Hebrew school, and a matron comes up. One of the boys, who happens to be schooled in politeness, offers her a seat, and she says, "Much obliged." The boy immediately sits down again.

Sammy says to him, "What's the matter, Ben, how come you sat down?"

"Well, I wanted to offer her my seat, but when I got up to give it to her, she said, 'Moishe, bleib'."

63. Understanding (Maurice A. Crane)

Another version in the Archives (Ray Must, Detroit). Barry Spacks has also told the story.

A very distinguished looking man sits down next to a rather distinguished looking lady. He's obviously a rabbi, a man of learning. He sits in the train, and the conductor comes by to pick up the tickets, and he's sleeping. The conductor figured there's no sense bothering this man, that he'd get him next time. He comes by the second time and the man is deeply engrossed in reading what appears to be a religious text. So the conductor says, "Could I have your ticket?"

The man says, "Annh."

"Can I have your ticket?"

"Annnh" [*higher*].

"Let me have your ticket."

"Wha–a–a–t?"

Well, the conductor figures the man's deaf and goes away. The lady next to the rabbi says, "What's the matter, why didn't you give the conductor your ticket when he came?"

The rabbi turns to her and says, "F—— him" [*shrill*].

64. Sam Feinman (Maurice A. Crane)

A close parallel, without the Jewish aspect, is in Ken Murray's Giant Joke Book (New York, Ace Books, 1954), pp. 116–18, where the astonished man on the scales at LaGuardia Airport misses his plane; he is pictured on p. 117. Richman, "It Was No Machine, but an Anti-Semite," Laughs from Jewish Lore, pp. 85–87, has a candy machine baffling a Jew.

Sam Feinman comes in a railroad station. He's got to make the 10:20 train. It's 9:15. He's got to while away the time, and wandering around looking for something to do in a rather barren station he sees a scale which says, "Your weight and your fortune, one cent."

"Hooh hah. What ken I lose?" says Feinman. "I'll try it."

He takes out a penny. He throws caution to the winds, puts it into the scale. So he's on the scale, comes out a little card saying, "Your name is Sam Feinman, you're a Jew, you weigh 135 pounds."

"Smart aleck, it's a smart aleck. I'll fool it."

He walks around the corner, comes back in, puts in another penny, steps on it, comes out a card says, "Your name is Sam Feinman, you're a Jew, you weigh 135 pounds."

He sees a porter walking by, says, "Hey, boy, come over here will you, come over here." He says, "A smart aleck machine I got here. Step on this, will you please."

So he puts in a penny in the machine, comes out a card, says, "Your name is George Botkins, you're a Negro, you weigh 185 pounds."

"Mh, umh, such a machine. Thank you very much. I'll see how it gets dis way," he says, "I'll find somebody." Comes by a man. He says, "Would you step on this machine, please?"

"Sure."

He puts in a penny in the machine; comes out a card, "Your name is Thomas J. O'Hoolihan, you're an Irishman, you weigh 160 pounds."

He says, "Tenk you. I'm gonna get dese guys now. I'm gonna get 'em" [*rising inflection*].

He goes across the street, he gets an Archie Mandrake out of the Armenian church next door. He says, "Hey Archie, come on, would you stand on this?"

"Surrre" [*high*].

He stands on it. Comes out a card says, "Your name is Stanislaus K. Impopulous, you weigh 194 pounds, and you're an Archie Mandrake in the Armenian Church."

Well, Sam Feinman happens to know someone he thinks can really fool them. On the other end of town there's a girl he knows who's half Hawaiian, half Moslem. He goes takes a taxi, gets her, and he says, "Listen Leilani, I want you to do me a favor" [*confidentially*].

"Sure."

She comes down, she gets on the scale, he puts in a penny. The scale says, "Your name is Leilani Poppananadalou, you're half Hawaiian, half Moslem, and you weigh 112 pounds."

He says, "Thanks very much," gives her carfare home. He's gonna try one last time. He goes into the shoeshine parlor, gets some black shoe polish, smears it over his face, gets a piece of rope, puts it on like a mustache, goes over to the counter and buys himself some sunglasses, puts them on, pulls his hat down over his head, wears his scarf up high, puts up his collar, puts some weights into his overcoat, gets on the scales, and puts in a penny. The scale says, "Your name is Sam Feinman, you're a Jew, you weigh 135 pounds, endt you chust missed your train!"

65. Moving Day (Bruce Buckley)

Papila is down at the store and tells Rosila to go home and tell mama to get packed and get ready to move, for he has just bought a house for the family.

Rosila runs home very excited and runs in the door and yells, "Mamila, mamila, tear down the wallpaper and pull out the nails, we're moving" [*sing-song*].

66. An Insight (D. K. Wilgus)

A longish Negro version, "John and the Twelve Jews," was re-
corded at Pine Bluff, Arkansas, in July, 1953 (R. M. Dorson, Negro
Tales from Pine Bluff, Arkansas, and Calvin, Michigan *[Blooming-*
ton, Indiana, 1958], pp. 125–26).

Two Jewish businessmen were traveling from the coast to
Chicago, and they were making the porter run all over the train
for them, getting them glasses, shining their shoes, taking orders
for this and that. When they got to Chicago, they got off the
train without tipping him and started to walk off.

One said to the other, "Did you give George a tip?"

"No, I thought you did."

So he goes back to the porter and says, "Here's twenty-five
dollars."

The porter says, "Now I know that you Jews didn't crucify
Christ, you just scared him to death."

67. Clouds (George Gluski)

Fuller texts in the Archives (Richard Berglund, Minneapolis, from
Robert Killackey, Grand Rapids; and Norette Droste, Detroit,
from Helmann Brenner, Detroit).

In heaven the Catholic was complaining, "I've just got a plain
cloud and an ordinary halo, but the Jew has got that fancy
cloud, with white side-walls and TV antenna."

"Ssh, he's one of the boss's relatives."

68. So Soon (Glen Warren)

Another variant in the Archives (Henry H. Katz, Detroit, from
Joe Rose, Detroit.)

A Jew was swimming at the beach and got caught in the
undertow. He yelled for help, and a man swam out and pulled

him out. When the Jew came to on the beach, a crowd was standing around.

"Who saved me?"

A man there said, "I did."

"I'll do anything you want, or give you anything you'd like."

"Well, I'm a priest, and I'd like very much to convert you."

"All right." So the priest got some water and baptized him.

The Jew went home and called his wife. "Sarah, I've got something to tell you."

"Not now, I'm in a big hurry, I've got to go to town and play bridge with the girls. Give me $500."

So he gave her the $500, and called his daughter. "Becky, I must tell you what happened."

"Not now, Papa, I've got to go downtown and do some shopping. Give me $150."

So he gave her the $150 and said, "Well, I'll tell Sammy. Sammy, come here, I want to tell you what happened to me."

"I can't stop now, I've got to go to the Boy Scout's meeting. I'm four weeks behind in my dues, and I need $5."

He gives him the $5 and says, "I've been a Christian only an hour, and already these Jews are bleeding me white."

69. In the Convent (Glen Warren)

There are two variants in the Archives (Fred J. Baumgartner, Milwaukee, from J. Thomas Pearlman, Battle Creek; Frances M. Davey, Milford, Mich., from Dr. M. B. Sheffer), and another, a nicely accented version, was told by Kenneth Goldstein of Hicksville, N. Y., in July, 1958. Cf. Mendelsohn, Let Laughter Ring, *p. 14.*

Little Sammy went to work at a convent, to make some pocket money. One day the Mother Superior called him aside and said, "Sammy, you're doing all right, but there's three things I want to tell you about. First, don't wash your hands in

the holy water. Second, don't hang your coat on the crucifix.
And third, don't call me Mother Shapiro."

70. The Way It's Done (Julian L. Rayford)

*For a comparable joke in Italian dialect, see "Dialect Stories of the
Upper Peninsula," JAF, LXI (1948), p. 146, "Dominick in Church."*

Two Jewish boys ran a pawn shop. And one morning Abie
says to Ikie, "Ikie, business ain't so good. But the Catholic
church across the strit is doing good business, always lots of
pipple there. I want you should go and see how they get so
much trade."

So Ikie went. And on Monday morning he came into the
shop. Abie asked him, "Did you find out?"

"Yes."

"What happened?"

"I went into the synagogue, and the rebbi came out, and he
got up into the pulpit. He took off one hat and put on anudder
hat. And he faces the congregation. And he sings out:

" 'Can anybody here play dominoes?' And nobody answers.
And he sings again, 'Can anybody here play dominoes?' And
with that, away in the back of the synagogue, somebody in the
barbershop quartet says, 'Yes, we can play dominoes' [*dominoes is chanted throughout*].

"So the rebbi says, 'I challenge you to a game of dominoes, of
dominoes.'

"So they say, 'We take up the challenge, we play you a
World Series game of dominoes.'

"So the rebbi says, 'All right, we play dominoes.'

" 'Dominoes.'

" 'Dominoes.'

" 'Dominoes.'

"And after that they pass the hat and everybody in the synagogue lays a bet."

71. The Marriage Broker (Ulick Leonhardt)

A man goes to a marriage agent, and she trots out pictures of all the prospects. The good-looking ones had no money, so finally the agent pulls out a picture of this boss-eyed witch who had a lot of money, but had gone through several major operations, had no hair, no teeth, and a wooden leg.

When the man complained, the agent said, 'Well, if you marry a nice bright young thing, she gets sick, and her hair falls out, and you have to buy a wig, and her teeth fall out, and new teeth cost money, and she gets in a car accident, and loses her leg, and you have to pay all the hospital bills. So here you have a ready-made job."

(I heard this in German Yiddish. It could have been in Königsberg.)

72. The Same Old Story (Ulick Leonhardt)

These emigrants go to the Supermarket in Florida in search of oranges, and the salesperson there says, "Juice?"

The little Jew nods his head, "Yeah." So the storekeeper wraps up the little juice oranges for him.

When he goes home to his wife, he says, "It's just the same discrimination as it was in Germany. The first thing he asks, are we Jews. Then he gives me the smallest oranges."

73. Embarrassing (Nancy Gibbons)

It seems that one day Abie came home from work, and he got his paper and slippers from Rosa, and he sat down to read the paper, and all the time he was reading, Rosa sat in the chair sighing, very, very deep sighs.

Finally he said, "Rosa, vat's de matter? You had bridge club today. Vat's wrong, you lose some money maybe?"

She said, "Oh Abie, it was terrible. I vas so embarrassed. Yah, I vent to bridge club, and Mrs. Brown vas dere. And vat you tink she vas vearing—emerald rings on her fingers, emerald bracelets, emerald earrings—just dreeping mit emeralds. And Mrs. Cohen vas vearing a mink hat, mink stole, mink earrings—just dreeping mit minks. And de rabbi's vife, here she sits—not only does she have diamond earrings, diamond rings on her fingers, diamond lavaliere, diamond bracelets, just dreeping mit diamonds. Oh, the shame of it all. Such embarrassment. Dere I sat in my old blue suit just like a damn Gentile."

74. Abie and Ike (Stuart Gallacher)

Cf. Mendelsohn, "Where a Weakness Is an Asset," Let Laughter Ring, p. 209. A related tale involves the Jew who cannot talk over the telephone if he has to hold both hands on the instrument. See Mendelsohn, "An Impossible Task," The Jew Laughs, pp. 34–35; Teitelbaum, "Unhandy," Anthology, p. 305.

These two fellows, Abie and Ike, were going to take this excursion boat. And so their friend said, "I vouldn't take de boat if I vas you, zince you don't know how to swim."

So Abie says, "Ve vant de trip, ve vant de trip, so ve take de boat."

The boat rams another boat and sinks. The friend is worried about Abie and Ike, since the casualty list was almost a total affair. Several days elapse, and the friend sees Abie and Ike again talking to one another, and asks with great surprise, "Zince you couldn't svim, how come you two got saved?"

Then Abie says, "Vell, it vas yust like zis. Ve yust started to talk to one another, and ze fust zink you know, ve came right to shore."

75A. The King's English (John A. Garraty)

Cf. Mendelsohn, "Environment is Contagious," The Jew Laughs, pp. 203–4, where the story is told on a Yale professor.

It seems there was this Jewish businessman who made a big fortune, and he was trying to get somewhere socially. And naturally one of the things he wanted to do was get his son accepted in polite society. But the trouble was that, like him, his son had a very thick Jewish accent. So he decided that the best thing to do would be to send his son to a good boarding school, where he could associate only with people who spoke in the most cultured accents. So he asked around and found out about a little school in New England which was very highly recommended. He made an appointment with the headmaster and took his son to see him, explaining the problem.

"Vell, Mr. Headmaster," says the businessman, "I'm wanting you should make my son speak with poifect English. Could you do it?"

"My good man," replied the headmaster, "there's nothing to it really. After all, a year's association with our boys, with our highly trained teachers, will make your young Jacob a master of the English language. Of that I am certain. You have my guarantee."

So he leaves his son at the school and goes away. But at the end of the year when he goes back to get him, Jake is speaking just the way he always has. And when his father complains to the headmaster, the headmaster admits defeat. "Vell," says the businessman, "vat should I do now? I want mine Jakela should speak English. Is dere notting to be done?" The headmaster leans back in his chair, thinks for a minute or two, and then suggests as a last resort, that he send the boy to Eton.

Well, this is a very difficult problem. After all, even English boys have to be entered at birth at Eton, so the businessman had an awful time getting Jake admitted on short notice. But he pulled a lot of strings, called up some of his business associates abroad, and finally got Jake accepted. He was determined that his son would learn to speak English properly at all costs. They took the boat to England and went to Eton. He explained the problem in detail to the headmaster and asked him if he could solve his problem. "Well, my good man," said the headmaster, "it may be that your American schools have not been able to teach your son to speak properly, but here in addition to the most modern technical methods we have the tradition of centuries to reinforce our pedagogical techniques. Fear not. When you return at the end of the semester, you will not be able to distinguish your son's pronunciation from my own."

So the businessman went back to America and worked hard for another year making money to pay for his son's tuition. And at the end of the school year he rushed back to England to see the results. When he arrived at Eton, he hurried to the boy's dormitory but discovered that all the students were away attending a cricket match at Harrow. While waiting for him to get back, he walked over to the headmaster's office to see how things had gone. The headmaster's secretary admitted him to the office, and the headmaster rose to greet him. "Vell, Mr. Headmaster, how ju make out? Mine Jake he's speaking de King's English, nu?"

"Netchally," replied the headmaster, "vat else?"

75B. Doing Fine (John W. Ashton)

A Jewish family sent their son to a fashionable boarding school to learn good English.

"Please, you being sure titch him right," the father told the headmaster.

"You need not have the slightest concern whatsoever," replied the headmaster.

At the end of the school year the father called on the headmaster. "Und how is my boy doink?"

"Dun't esk!" said the headmaster.

76. Weinstein, Feinstein, and Katz (Jack Garraty)

This is an unreported classic of modern American storylore, for which I suggest the general title, "The Man Who Knew Every-

body." Shortly after hearing Jack Garraty tell this story, I heard a second version from another close friend, Norman Johnson, then national sales-promotion manager for Chevrolet, in Detroit, who possessed a fund of stories that he delivered at sales conventions. His text possesses no Jewish elements.[8] Subsequently I heard many variations. An American serviceman from California, Hank Mangeti, regaled a party in Tokyo, in April, 1957, with a number of stories, and told this one on Harry Garrett, of Kokomo, Indiana, who "knew" Eisenhower, Churchill, and the Pope. Leo Lapidus recalled it with a Yiddish ending: "Wer ist der Goy dortin mit ihm?" ("Who is the Gentile with him?"). William H. Jansen, professor at the University of Kentucky, told me in June, 1958, an Irish version, with a reverse twist, which he had known for at least twenty years. In this version, which was told on Oliver St. John Gogarty, Gogarty is successively instructed to call on his priest in Dublin, the bishop in Belfast, and the pope in Rome. Each time he apologizes for the intrusion, saying, "But I am only a poor simple farmer." Finally he stands on the balcony with the Pope overlooking the crowd, and a man below says, "Who is that little fellow with Gogarty?" This is similar to the text printed in Eric Partridge, The 'Shaggy Dog' Story (London, 1953), pp. 95–98, "Paddy's Visit to Rome"; the Soviet envoy asks his assistant, "Tell me, Ivan, who is that, standing there with Paddy?" Two of my graduate students in folklore at Indiana University know variants. Guthrie Meade, from Kentucky, heard it told on "Old Bill Jones." Ester Gayo, from the Philippines, heard it from a college student at Silliman University in 1957, and her friend heard it from a tuba-gatherer. Juan, the braggart culture hero of the Tagalog-speaking Filipinos, is the man who knows everybody.

There are five variants in the Archives. One follows the story printed here in presenting three Jewish boasters, Goldstein, Abie, and Izzie (collected by Sharon M. Johnson from Jim Mortinsen, 1954). The punch line has one man saying to another, "Who's that sitting in the garden with Izzy?" A long text is told on Sam, who knows Bobby Jones, Ike, and the Pope (Sharon M. Johnson from Harold Johnson, 1954). A brief text about Sam Jones ends with a tramp saying to Sam's friend, "Can't tell who the fellow with the beret is, but the other guy is Sam Jones" (John Toucany, 1955).

The same tag occurs in a fourth example, where the American friend asks the Italian who the elderly man with the skull cap is (Nan Olin from Jim Ware, 1955). Or the Pope may be identified as a man dressed all in white (Isamay Addis, 1952).

The appeal of this tale reflects the ethics of modern American business society, with its premium on "contacts" and "knowing the right people" as the means of "getting ahead."

Once there were three Jewish businessmen who were named Weinstein, Feinstein, and Katz, who were attending a clothing convention in New York, and got into a friendly argument as to which of them was the most important. For a while the argument got no place. One of them pointed out how much income tax he paid, another talked about his contributions to charity, the third quoted statistics on the volume of his business. But no one convinced the others as to his superiority. Finally Weinstein said, "Chentlemen, all dese figures mean notting. Let me tell you a little story about something dot happened to me in Vashington just a few months ago. Vun day I'm walking down Pennsylvania Avenue ven zuddenly up next to me comes a great big Cadillac. Who's in it? President Roosevelt.

" 'Why, Weinstein,' said the President, 'what are you doing here in Washington?'

" 'O, nutting, your excellency, I'm just down here on business.'

" 'Well, where are you staying?' says Roosevelt.

" 'Oh, I'm staying in a small hotel the other side of town.'

" 'Nonsense,' says the President. 'Weinstein, when you're in Washington, you stay in the White House with me. Get in the car.' "

Then he says, "Dot's how important I am."

The other two listen politely and shrug. They're not impressed. "Dot's notting," says Feinstein. "But it reminds me of a story, that shows how important I am. Copple years ago I'm in London on a business trip. Von day I'm valking through Hyde

Park. Suddenly a silver coach wit twelve vite hosses pulls up next to me. Who's in it but King George.

" 'Why Feinstein, what are you doing here in London?'

" 'Vy nothing, your Highness, I'm just here on business.'

" 'Well, where are you staying?' says the King.

" 'Oh I'm staying in a small hotel the other side of town.'

" 'Nonsense,' says the King. 'Feinstein, when you're in London you stay in Buckingham Palace with me. Get in the coach.' "

Then he says, "Dot's how important I am."

Well, Weinstein is kind of impressed with this story. After all, Roosevelt is more powerful than the King, but there is a certain social prestige associated with royalty which the democratic presidency does not have. But Katz merely smiles smugly. "Dot reminds me," he said, "of something dot happened to me a few years ago ven I vas in Rome on business. Von day I'm walking down de street minding my own business and suddenly up next to me comes a solid gold chariot, pulled by twenty-four vite horses. Who's in it but the Pope. 'Why Katz, what are you doing here in Rome?'

" 'Vy notting, your Holiness, I'm just down here on business.'

" 'Well, where are you staying?' says the Pope.

" 'Oh, I'm staying in a small hotel the other side of town.'

" 'Nonsense,' says the Pope. 'Katz, when you're in Rome, you stay in the Vatican with me. Get in the chariot.'

"So I'm getting in the chariot and we're driving through Rome on our vay to the Vatican. But on the vay we have to stop for a traffic light. And vile ve're vaiting for the light to change, up next to us comes a great big chromium-plated limousine. Who's in it but Mussolini and King Victor Immanuel. Mussolini looks across the chariot and sees me and the Pope stending there talking. Mussolini frowns and nudges Victor Immanuel. 'Hey Vic,' he says, 'who's de skinny ginny stending dere in de chariot talking to Katz?'

"Dot's how important I am."

Notes

1. P. 265. He further quotes Freud that "The Jewish jokes made up by non-Jews are nearly all brutal buffooneries in which the wit is spoiled by the fact that the Jew appears as a comic figure to a stranger." Actually, as this collection will show, non-Jews get many Hebraic jokes from Jews.

2. In "Dialect Stories of the Upper Peninsula: A New Form of American Folklore," *Journal of American Folklore*, LXI (1948), 113–50. Folklorist friends have described to me the same story-making process among Mexican-Spanish communities in the Southwest and in a Danish community in Utah.

3. Texts are given in Mendelsohn, "An Animated Conversation," *The Jew Laughs*, p. 21; Ausubel, "Conversation Piece," *A Treasury of Jewish Folklore*, p. 431.

4. Cf. my text in "Maine Master-Narrator," *Southern Folklore Quarterly*, VIII (1944), 282, with variants in Ausubel, "Miracles and Wonders," *A Treasury of Jewish Folklore*, pp. 376–77; Mendelsohn, "A Compromise," *The Jew Laughs*, p. 79.

5. Cf. No. 68 in my "Dialect Stories of the Upper Peninsula," p. 147, with Mendelsohn, "Misery Loves Company," *Here's A Good One*, p. 65.

6. Richman, *Jewish Wit and Wisdom*, p. 347.

7. Richman, *Jewish Wit and Wisdom*, pp. 269, 288. I have a text of "The Priest's Guest and the Eaten Chickens" (Type 1741). Cf. "Negro Tales," in *Western Folklore*, XIII (1954), 162–63.

8. (The following story, told me by Norman Johnson, is given in full as an interesting parallel to "Weinstein, Feinstein, and Katz"— No. 76.)

I heard it first from Julius Lyell, our sales promotion manager in New Orleans. He had been using this story as part of his training program with retail salesmen, and the story illustrates a very important principle of salesmanship, and that is that the retail salesman should know the greatest possible number of people.

The story as it is told has to do with one Malcolm Campbell, a retail salesman who was very well known in his community. And a very close friend of his became quite impressed with the number of people that he seemed to know. And talking to Malcolm Campbell one day, the friend remarked that he seemed to know a great many people, and Malcolm Campbell replied, "Well, you know, a good salesman has to know everyone."

Whereupon his friend said, "Oh, you're exaggerating, surely you don't mean everyone."

"Well, I certainly do," said Malcolm Campbell.

Whereupon the friend proceeded to challenge him, "Well, I'm sure you don't know Eisenhower."

"Why," he said, "I certainly do know Eisenhower. I know him very well."

"Well," his friend said, "you will have an opportunity to prove this statement, because Eisenhower is coming to town next week, and you and I will station ourselves along the route of the parade, and as he comes by, we'll see if Eisenhower knows you."

So on the day of the parade Eisenhower came by, seated on the top of this open car. And as he approached and came abreast of the friend who was accompanied by Malcolm Campbell, he stopped the car and jumped out, rushed through the crowd, and shook Malcolm Cambell's hand heartily, and said, "Malcolm, I am certainly glad to see you again." And they exchanged several reminiscences of the past, and Eisenhower got in his car and went on his way.

Well the friend was naturally impressed, but he thought he could pursue this a little farther because he still didn't believe the statement. So he said, "Well you may know Eisenhower but you certainly don't know Winston Churchill."

"Well, I certainly do," said Malcolm Campbell. "Winston Churchill and I are old friends, too."

So nothing would do but the friend charter a plane, fly across the Atlantic, and appear at Number Ten Downing Street. So Winston Churchill was then prime minister. They knocked on the door, and when the man came, they said they would like to see Mr. Churchill. The man said, "Under no circumstances, Mr. Churchill is occupied with great affairs of state, and it just wouldn't be possible for anyone to see him today." So Malcolm Campbell said, "If you don't mind, would you just send word in to him that Mr. Campbell from the United States is here to see him."

So rather dubiously the man went back inside, and in a few minutes he reappeared and said, "Mr. Churchill will be very, very happy to see you. Come on in." So Mr. Campbell disappeared and was closeted with Mr. Churchill for about thirty minutes, after which he came out and found his friend overcome with amazement.

So the friend was still not sure that Malcolm Campbell knew every-one, so he said, "I'm sure that there's one person that you don't know and that's the Pope at Rome."

"Well it just so happens," said Malcolm Campbell, "that the Pope and I are very well known to each other and that we are good friends."

So again the friend chartered the plane and they flew off to Rome. And they arrived at Rome when they were having quite a public reception in the Square, in front of the Vatican. And in the crush of the tremendous population that had turned out to hear the Pope, why the friend became separated from Malcolm Campbell. So he was pushing around through the crowd. And the harder he pushed, the harder it became to get anywhere near the balcony where the Pope was to appear.

So after about an hour's waiting and still not able to get very close, the time came for the public gathering when the Pope was going to speak to the people. And Campbell's friend looked over toward the balcony, and although he was about half a mile away, he could dimly see what he thought was a couple of figures who appeared on the balcony. So he was looking and looking, trying to see who was on the balcony, and he finally turned to an Italian who was standing near by, and he said, "Is that the Pope who is out on the balcony now?"

And the Italian looked very carefully, and he says, "I'm not sure it's the Pope," he says, "but the fellow standing next to him is Malcolm Campbell."

A Spaniolic-Jewish
Version of "Frau
Holle"

WARREN E. ROBERTS Indiana University

by *Warren E. Roberts*

AARNE-THOMPSON Type 480, often called "Frau Holle" from
the name borne by the Grimm brothers' version, is one of the
world's widely known folktales. The story is a relatively simple
Märchen which deals with a mistreated stepdaughter who sets
out on a trip for one of a variety of reasons. After some adven-
tures on the way, she encounters one or more old women,
witches, fairies, or the like. The girl is kind to the being whom
she encounters and follows the instructions she is given. In return for her kindness, the girl is rewarded with a box of gold,
or great beauty, or with some other desirable gift. The spiteful,
jealous stepsister tries to emulate the heroine, but the stepsister
is disrespectful and unkind to the being whom she encounters
and is punished in some way: She is given snakes or toads in a
box, or she is made ugly, or she is given some other undesirable
gift. Despite the apparent simplicity of this story, it has had an
amazing vitality in tradition, for it is found in nearly all parts of
the world.[1] The tale is widely known in eastern Europe from
Spain to Finland, in all Slavic countries, in southern Europe,
and in the Balkans and Greece. In India, southern Asia, and
Japan the story seems common. Collectors in Africa have recorded over forty versions of the story, and it has been brought
to the New World, both North and South America, in many
different forms and by many different peoples.

When we turn to the Near East, we find that the story is likewise well known in many parts of this area, which is of great
importance for folktale study. Over thirty versions of the story
have been recorded in Turkey[2] and at least a few versions are

included in the meager collections published from Iraq and Persia. It is therefore surprising that only one version of this widely spread tale has ever been recorded in print from Jewish storytellers.

The one version that I speak of was collected from Spaniolic Jews by M. Grunwald and published in 1947 in the second volume of *Edoth*, pages 226–27. It is not made clear whether the story was recorded in the Balkans or in Palestine. In this version a young girl lives happily with her father and mother, but a widow who lives nearby falls in love with the girl's father. The widow works upon the girl and finally convinces her that she should kill her mother by dropping the lid of a chest upon her mother's neck when she looks into the chest. The girl's father subsequently marries the widow, who also has a daughter. Instead of the good treatment that she had been promised, the girl receives only mistreatment at the hands of her stepmother. The girl is helped by a cow in the many tasks that she is assigned, and the stepmother tells the girl that she must kill the cow and wash its intestines in a river. (Although it is not explicitly stated in this version, in other forms of the story the helpful animal which is slain is often the girl's mother in a transformed shape.) As she is washing the intestines, the river carries them off. The girl runs along the river bank searching for them and comes to the castle of three fairies. They promise her marvelous gifts: pearls will drop from her mouth when she opens it, and her feet will leave golden tracks. The stepmother sends her own daughter to the fairies, but they are disgusted with her and curse her so that spittle falls from her mouth and mud is left behind in her footprints.

This Spaniolic version is of great importance for a study of the origin and whole development of Type 480, for it shows obvious connections with the forms of the tale known in two widely separated areas. First of all, the introduction in which the girl kills her mother by dropping the lid of a chest upon her is similar to one commonly found in Persia. In several Persian variants of the tale the widow tells the girl to ask her mother for oil from a huge jar and to push her mother into the jar so that she will drown.[3] In many Spanish and Spanish-American versions the heroine sets out in pursuit of animal intestines which are carried off by a river, just as she does in the Spaniolic version.[4] Accordingly, one motif in the Spaniolic form of Type 480 closely resembles the Persian variants, while another motif resembles Spanish versions. At first sight, one might assume that these similarities arise because the Spaniolic version has retained a motif from Spain, but has also been influenced in the Balkans by Near Eastern, possibly Turkish, versions of the tale. There is, however, a Majorcan version of Type 480 (the closest analogue to the Spaniolic version in question) which throws a great deal of light upon the problem of determining the provenance of the Spaniolic version. Outlines of the two versions in parallel columns will make clear the close similarities which exist between them.

Spaniolic Jewish	*Majorcan*[5]
1. A widow with a daughter tells the heroine to drop the lid of a chest on her mother's neck when her mother looks into the chest.	1. The same.
2. The heroine's father marries the widow, and the heroine is mistreated.	2. The same.
3. A cow which helps the heroine is killed, and the girl is sent to wash its intestines in a river. The river carries off the intestines, and the girl runs after them.	3. The same, except that it is a sheep which helps the heroine.
4. She comes to the castle of three fairies.	4. She meets four old women.
5. Rewards: pearls fall from the heroine's mouth, and her feet leave golden tracks.	5. Rewards: diamonds and pearls fall from her hair, and a gold star appears on her forehead.

6. The evil stepmother's own daughter, who tries to imitate the heroine, is punished: spittle falls from her mouth, and her feet leave behind mud.

6. The evil stepmother's own daughter, who tries to imitate the heroine, is punished: lice and nits fall from her hair, and an ass's tail appears on her forehead.

The relationship between the Spaniolic and the Majorcan versions is obviously very close. It would therefore seem logical to assume that the Spaniolic Jews who were driven from Spain in 1492 carried with them the Spanish form of Type 480 which was current at that period and that they have retained this form with relatively little change for a period of over four hundred years. During this period, however, most of the Spanish versions of the tale have undergone change, so that the introduction (the heroine killing her mother by dropping the lid of a chest upon her neck) has almost disappeared. Only on the periphery of the area, namely, in Majorca, and in an isolated group, the Spaniolic Jews, has the older form been retained. It is of some interest to note that none of the Spanish-American versions of Type 480 contains the introduction specified above, which leads one to the conclusion that by the time the Spanish colonists came to the New World with versions of the story, the story had already lost the introduction in most parts of Spain. The Spaniolic Jewish version, therefore, represents an early Spanish form of the tale while the Spanish-American versions seem to represent a somewhat later form. The form of Type 480 known in Spain around the year 1500 must have been essentially like the form represented by the modern Spaniolic Jewish and Majorcan versions. These two versions coincide so closely that no other conclusion seems possible. It would be too great a coincidence to expect that the older Spanish form was something different, but that the Spaniolic and Majorcan versions have independently developed in almost exactly the same way.

The Spanish ballad scholar, R. Menéndez Pidal, has found that the Spaniolic Jews have retained in substantially the original form ballads which have disappeared or which have been greatly altered in Spain itself.[6] The evidence afforded by Type 480 gives further proof of the great conservatism of this group.

With the aid of the Spaniolic Jewish version, therefore, it is possible to establish the fact that Type 480 existed in Spain prior to the year 1500. But the Spaniolic Jewish and the Majorcan versions, when considered together, do even more: they tell us what the early Spanish form of the story was like. Once we have this earlier Spanish form, we are able at once to see the close tie that exists between the Spanish and the Near Eastern forms of the tale. Most of the present-day Spanish versions of Type 480 do not, at first glance, resemble the Near Eastern versions very closely; but when we know that the earlier Spanish form of the story contains the motif of the girl who kills her mother by dropping a chest lid upon her, we can see the similarity to the Persian variants in which a girl kills her mother by pushing her into a huge oil jar. The Spaniolic Jewish version of Type 480, therefore, affords important information that helps us in reconstructing the history of the origin and dissemination of the entire tale.

We have seen that the only Jewish version of Type 480 that has ever been recorded and published is undoubtedly of Spanish origin. We have also seen how popular Type 480 is in most parts of the Near East, but we must remember that it is seldom safe to speculate upon the basis of negative evidence in folktale studies. Because a tale has not been collected in a given country or from a given people does not necessarily mean that the story does not exist there; it may mean only that collectors have never searched for that kind of material in that country or among those people. When one of the most eminent of American ballad scholars, George Lyman Kittredge, stated in 1904 that "Ballad-making . . . is a lost art; and the same may be said of ballad-singing,"[7] he was generalizing upon the basis of negative evidence, for practically no ballads had been collected in America at that time. Little did Kittredge know how false later collecting would prove his statement to be. It is to be hoped that there will be extensive future folktale collecting in Israel, for it is obvious from the foregoing remarks that if more Jewish versions of international folktales can be found, they will be of great assistance to students of comparative folklore.

Notes

1. General comments concerning the distribution of Type 480 are based upon the author's study, *The Tale of the Kind and the Unkind Girls* (Berlin, 1958).

2. W. Eberhard and P. N. Boratav, *Typen Türkischer Volksmärchen* (Wiesbaden, 1953), Type 59, pp. 65 ff.

3. D. L. R. and E. O. Lorimer, *Persian Tales* (London, 1919), pp. 79–88; A. Christensen, *Märchen aus Iran* (Jena, 1939), pp. 90–96; W. Ivanow, "Persian as Spoken in Birjand," *Journal and Proceedings of the Asiatic Society of Bengal*, N. S., XXIV (1928), 258–61.

4. See, for examples, A. de Llano Roza de Ampudia, *Cuentos Asturianos* (Madrid, 1925), pp. 95–97; J. B. Rael, "Cuentos Españoles de Colorado y de Nuevo Mejico," *Journal of American Folklore*, LV (1942), 76–84 (three versions).

5. "El Romancero judío-español" in *El Romancero* (Madrid, 1927). See also W. J. Entwistle, *European Balladry* (Oxford, 1939), p. 188.

6. H. C. Sargent and G. L. Kittredge, eds., *English and Scottish Popular Ballads* (Cambridge Students Edition, 1904), p. xiii.

4 | Jewish Folksong

The Musical
Vocabulary of
Ashkenazic
Hazanim

H A N O C H   A V E N A R Y   Tel Aviv, Israel

by Hanoch Avenary

UP TO THE middle of the 19th century, the *hazanim* in Eastern and Central Europe formed a secluded social class of their own. They remained "wandering minstrels" during their lifetime. Occasionally they settled in one of the communities on their way; but even then they took care to reserve the right of "roaming through the country" periodically (*iber di m'dine geyn*). A successful *hazan* was highly appreciated and won the deep affection of the people. Nevertheless, he had to fight continually for his personal and professional status and to defend the freedom of his art against the restrictive tendencies of certain rabbis.

The pressure on his civil and professional life from the outside was counterbalanced by the strong intrinsic cohesion within the class of the "sweet singers of Israel." As a rule, a *hazan* was the descendant of a *hazan*, was raised and educated by a *hazan*, and married a *hazan's* daughter. The apprentices of *hazanuth* came from the ranks of the young choristers (*M'shor'-rim*) who often shared the roving life. They obtained their instruction and training by listening to other *hazanim* and performing in accordance with the oral tradition of the profession.

It is usual and natural for a specialized trade, executed by a secluded guild, to develop an idiom of its own. Its vocabulary may be restricted merely to technical terms, but at times it extends to other spheres of life and forms a secret language not understood by outsiders. The latter was the case with the popular musicians (*klezmerim*) of Eastern Europe. Their particular slang has been introduced into literature by Sholom Aleichem[1] and has also attracted the attention of folklorists and linguists.[2]

As compared with the popular musician, the *hazan* represented a higher social level; he belonged to the *kley kodesh* of the synagogue. He developed a professional language, not a slang, but a vocabulary of idiomatic musical terms. In the present study an attempt (the first to our knowledge) will be made to collect these musical terms and to assemble and verify current explanations of them.

The terminology of the *hazinim* may be divided into two main categories, which may also be differentiated by the use or non-use of purely Hebrew words:

(1) Terms taken over from European music, sometimes with a rather archaic meaning, or with a change of sense. Examples: *bass, pastuchel, trop, redel, zuhalten* (see below). There are no Hebrew words in this category.

(2) Terms referring to particular features of Jewish music which are expressed either by foreign words that have to be understood in a special, narrow sense or by genuine Hebrew words. Examples: *misinay nigunim, meìnyano nigunim, m'shoyrer, nusah, n'ginoth, sagen, leynen, gust* (see below).

As we can assume that most of the terms in (2) represent an idea peculiar to the art of *hazanuth* or to Jewish music in general, the musicologist may find valuable hints in the mere existence of a term. From linguistic findings the folklorist may draw conclusions about cross-cultural communication and trends.

The present collection has been drawn mainly from literary sources and hence does not exhaust the available material. Further research in this vanishing field of Ashkenazic *hazanuth* remains an urgent task.

Musical Terms of the *Hazanim*

ADOJSHEM MOLOCH-SHTEYGER. A *shteyger* (q.v.) or "synagogal mode" with a scale which, among other peculiarities, contains a diminished seventh. It is named after the beginning of Psalm 92, which was sung in this "synagogal mode" on *Shabath* eve.

AHAVOH RABOH-SHTEYGER. Synagogal mode so-called after the section *Ahavah rabah* in the morning prayer. Its very characteristic scale includes a superfluous second and a semitone descending to the final note. The *hazanim* in Hungary and Austria used to call it also *Yishthabah-Shteyger*.

AV HORAHAMIM-SHTEYGER. Synagogal mode often referred to as a *shteyger* "which always sweeps." Its scale contains two superfluous seconds which stress its mournful, lamenting character. The name of this mode was taken from the elegy *Av harahamin*. Sometimes it is called *Mi Sheberach-Shteyger*, after the beginning of a prayer which precedes the elegy.

BASS. The bass part was sung by a *m'shoyrer* (q.v.), a chorister who accompanied the singing of the *hazan*. Hence the word *bass* was often added to the name of the *m'shoyrer* and subsequently became a surname. A well-known example is Shabthay Bass (1641–1718), who was a *m'shoyrer* at Prague and who, having become a printer and bibliographer, put musical notes on the title pages of his books as a printers' mark.[3] The unknown author of *Tokhehah laHazanim*, a pamphlet dating from the beginning of the 18th century, characterizes the *bass* with this rancorous remark: "And the second [*m'shoyrer*] is standing on his [the *hazan's*] right side . . . he is the man accepted by him as a *bass* who bawls like the treaders of grapes, and his voice is low and rough."[4]

CHOR SHUL. A modern ("reformed") synagogue where a mixed choir of male and female voices is heard (as in Paris since 1822, in Vienna since 1826, in Munich since 1832, in London since 1841). ". . . In opposition to the Slavonic and other orthodox Jews who detest the *chor shul* with all their hearts."[5]

CONTRABASS. A second bass part performed by a *m'shoyrer*, using a special voice technique in order to imitate an instrument, such as the bassoon or some other instrument like it. ". . . a Soprano and a Bass, joined by a so-called Contrabasso, . . . a voice formed by a violent pressure in the throat; the timbre of the voice, in spite of its strong force, remained very unpleasant. This part was intended to imitate the Serpent"[6] (a coarse-sounding Contrabass-Cornetto).

DIBUR. Recitative style of chant, as contrasted with the singing of true periodic "melodies" in the European sense. Performing the *dibur* was designated by the term *sogen* (q.v.). "That which the former *hazanim* plainly called *dibur* in contrast with *kol*, i.e., the skill of creating an effect by means of a melodic *parlando*. . . ."[7]

DRONG. "An expression peculiar to the *hazanim*, meaning literally a log of wood; having an unmusical, wooden voice."[8]

DVEJKELE. *Dvekuth* is a term of Jewish mysticism, meaning the close attachment of the soul to God. Hence *Dvejkele* is "a religious melody which inspires a pious mood."[9]

FAGOT-BASS. A *m'shoyrer* having the ability, hence the duty, to imitate the sound of a bassoon. "This last imitated . . . . a bad bassoon —sometimes continued one note as a drone base; at other times, divided it into triplets and semiquavers iterated on the same tone."[10]

FISTEL-SINGER. A *m'shoyrer* of the high-voice class (*singer*, q.v.) having the particular task of imitating the sound of a flute or a violin in high falsetto or *fistel shtim* (from the Latin *fistula*, "flute"). "One of these voices was a falset, more like the upper part of a bad *vox humana* stop in an organ than a natural voice. . . . He had a facility for running divisions, and now and then mixed them with passages of taste which were far superior to the rest."[11] A. H. Heymann provides the following description: "The singer whose name was Teberich was what is called a *Fistelsinger*, which means that he generally sang solo. Mr. Lion [the *hazan*] suddenly paused, and Mr. Teberich screamed and shrieked for some minutes, and this he supposed to be tirades."[12]

FLEYT-SINGER, FLETEL-SINGER. A *m'shoyrer* of the class of *singers* having the ability to imitate the sound of a flute or clarinet and also to perform the characteristic flourishes of those instruments. The grandfather of the composer Michael Gnessin was called Y'shayah (Sheyke) Fleyt-singer and was well-known as a *badhan* and popular singer in Vilna.

GUST. A term once used by the *hazanim* in Russia, having the same meaning as *shteyger* (q.v.) in Western Ashkenazic communities. It is equivalent to the Hebrew word *taàm*. "The word *gust* comes from the Latin *gustus* and means taste."[13]

KLAVANER. Name of a secondary *shteyger*, also called *Oz b'kol* or *K'vakoras-Shteyger*, according to the relevant prayers of the Penitential Feasts. The origin of this name is not known, but it seems to come from the Austro-Hungarian dialect. The *klavaner* is said to be of a "gipsy-like, droll character."[14]

KOL. Singing in which the melody is even and regularly built, as contrasted with plain recitative. Cf. *dibur*.

K'VAKORAS-SHTEYGER. A secondary synagogal mode named after a part of the *Un'thaneh thokef* prayer. It is identical with the so-called *Oz b'kol-Shteyger* or *Klavaner* (q.v.).

LEYNEN, LEYENEN. To read, and in particular to recite from, the Bible with the melody indicated by the Masoretic accents. ". . . . A term, familiar to every *hazan*, for the cantillation of the *sidrah*, *haftarah*, *m'gilah*, and *Eykhah*."[15] Cf. also *Trop*, *N'ginojs*.

MEINYONO NIGUNIM. "*Meinyono* melodies—i.e., traditional melodies which were destined for a certain feast and lent a special feature to it."[16] Such melodies are transmitted, e.g., for the *Shalosh r'galim*, and also serve as musical hints in the *Yor Kadish* (q.v.). The term itself was adopted from the Talmud,[17] where it designates one of the modes of interpretation of the Law. Accordingly, its musical meaning may be explained as a melody which is related to the concerns or features of the feast.

MI SHEBERAKH-SHTEYGER, MI SHEBERAKH-GUST. Term used by the *hazanim* in Russia for the synagogal mode which is called *Av Horahamim-Shteyger* (q.v.) in Central Europe.

MISINAY NIGUNIM, NIGUNIM MISINAY. Certain traditional melodies which the *hazan* was not allowed to change, as *Aleynu l'shabeah*, the *kadish* of *musaf*, and *n'ilah*, *bar'chu* of the *Yamin noraim*, etc. The term parallels the Talmudic expression *Halakhah l'Mosheh miSinay*, and hence its meaning is an old, time-honored tradition which is generally accepted, though it cannot be traced to the Pentateuch. In its musical meaning, this term appears in the *Sefer hasidim* as early as the 12th or 13th century.[18] See also *Skarbowe Nigunim*.

MOGEN OVOYS-SHTEYGER. Synagogal mode named after a prayer of *Shabath* Eve. Its scale is "natural minor."[19]

M'SHOYRER. Chorister standing near the *hazan* and accompanying his singing. Commonly, there are two *m'shor'rim*, the *singer* (soprano) and the *bass;* sometimes there were additional choristers, among them those who imitated the sounds of certain instruments with their voices. "The *hazan* was given two, three, or more assistants (*m'shor'rim*) who either had to accompany his tunes with hummed harmonies or who intermingled their voices with the melody itself and executed a kind of concertant antiphony similar to the symphonic play of instruments. The performers went so far, in their simple-minded copying, as to imitate the characteristic passages of certain instruments. There was not only an assistant with a high voice (the *singer*) and one with a low range (the *bass*) but also a *Fletel-singer* or *Fistel-singer*, who endeavored to perform the runs of the flute or clarinet by falsetto, a *fagott-bass*, who copied the rough staccati of this instrument, a *sayt-bass, etc.*"[20]

N'GINOYS. The Masoretic accents in the text of the Bible, and their melody. Cf. *Trop.*

NUSAH. (1) In a general sense, the manner in which the *hazan* performed the traditional melodies. "This *hazan* has a good *nusah*" means that he executed the traditional tunes correctly and in a pure style. (2) In a narrower sense, the particular tune of certain prominent chapters of the Pentateuch, such as *B'reshith*, *Shirath hayam*, *Assereth Hadivroth.*

OZ B'KOL-SHTEYGER. A secondary synagogal mode, identical with the *K'vakoras-Shteyger* and the so-called *Klavaner* (q.v.).

PASTUCHEL. A tune composed in the style of a *pastorale*, perhaps from French *pastourelle*. The *hazanim* would sing a *pastuchel* when it was required by the text, e.g. in *K'vakorath roeh edro* and others.

PHRYGISH. In musicology this term designates an ecclesiastical mode with a diatonic scale based on *mi;* accordingly, the Phrygian mode has a semitone just above its final note. The *hazan* Hirsh Weintraub (1811–81) adopted this term for any synagogal mode closing with a semitone above the tonic, disregarding inner construction of Jewish modes.[21] Several *hazanim* and writers on music followed this use in a rather indiscriminate manner, and sometimes they called any tune of another character than plain major or minor *Phrygish* or *Yiddish-Phrygish*.

POLNISH SINGEN. "To sing in the *Polnish* manner" meant to the Western *hazanim* in the first half of the 19th century a Slavonic *capriccioso* style. It is called *Bolacko* in the manuscript of Josef Goldstein Bass, written c. 1791–99;[22] *Polnisch* in the manuscript of Leb Wolf, written c. 1809–10;[23] *Air polonais* by Israel Lovy.[24] Later on, *Polnish singen* was associated with the old style of Eastern Ashkenazic *hazanuth*, as contrasted with the reform-style of Solomon Sulzer and his followers.[25]

REDEL. The word means "wheel" in Yiddish. This expression (Latin *rota* and derivatives) has had several different meanings in musical history, but here it should be understood in a very specific sense, as a Hasidic tune without words changing from a slow tempo and a sad mood to a quick and gay rhythm, with tempo and mood change and return—like the parts of a revolving wheel. "A *redel* as it is sung: slower—it sweeps, then quicker—it is prepared to dance. . . . The first time one should sing it slowly; the second time more quickly and more gaily."[26]

SARKA. One of the Masoretic accents governing the recitation of the Bible. It is the first in the table of accents as taught in school. Accordingly the whole table of accents is called the *sarka*.[27]

SAYT-BASS. *M'shoyrer* with a deep voice, a *bass* (q.v.), who had to imitate the sound of the deep-toned stringed instruments.

SETZEN. To adapt a foreign tune to the words of a Hebrew prayer or hymn. Adaptations of vernacular melodies were common practice also in the church, where they are called *contrafactus*. "We had a unique *hazan*, indeed! . . . This man used to sing arias of the opera, too. And how well it went together! as if the tune were composed for it. . . . It formed a part of it [the art of a *hazan*] to know *setzen* well, that is, to adapt the melody to the text."[28]

SHTEL. A tune built in even periods like most of the European melodies. "The recitation is the free melodic effusion of the soul . . . in opposition to the *gestellten* pieces (as it is generally expressed by the *hazanim*) or, more accurately expressed, 'in contrast to the composed piece.' "[29] Bernstein notes that ". . . . in the old times, the *hazanim* also used to sing melodies without text—commonly called a *shtel*—which served to introduce the prayers."[30]

SHTEYGER, STEIGER. The term *shteyger* designates the joint me-. lodic character of a group of tunes with regard to their scale, their motives, and their most important notes. It is sometimes erroneously associated with the German word *steigen* (i.e., "to ascend") and is accordingly explained as being equivalent to "scale." In Yiddish, however, the word means "manner, mode" (e.g., *lebens-shteyger*, "mode of life"). The musical meaning of the term comprises the melodic features of a group of synagogal tunes and parallels the medieval concept of *modus* and that of the Arabic *maqām*. "The peculiarity of the melodies of Jewish liturgical song is known under the term *Steiger*, which performs the same function as the ecclesiastical modes, so that we are correct in replacing the designation *Steiger* with 'synagogal modes.' "[31]

SHTUBEN-TROP. The tune of the students of the *Mishnah* and *Gemara* in the *shtub* (room) of the *Beyt haMidrash*. A simple kind of recitative differing from that accorded the Bible in the synagogue. The term is mentioned by Yaaqov Moelln (about 1355–1427): "The Maharil used to sing the recitation of the Bible in the morning and afternoon prayers [of the Day of Atonement] in the manner of the youngsters, which is called *shtuben trop.*"[32] See also *Trop*.

SHUL-TROP. The melodic recitation of the Bible as performed in the synagogue, as contrasted with the simple humming melody of the students in the *Beyt haMidrash.*[33] See also *Trop, Shtuben-Trop*.

SINGER, SINGERL. One of the *m'shor'rim* who accompany the singing *hazan*. In general, the *singer* was a boy soprano, but men also performed this task, using the falsetto range. The *singer* often served as a soloist and inserted runs and coloraturas into the song. The title *singer*, like that of *bass*, has frequently become a family name, as with Shlomoh Singer, a well-known popular poet and minstrel at Prague (about 1650). "His [the young Lewandowski's] soprano voice was as clear as a bell and full of deep feeling, and helped him to be accepted as a *singerl* with the former *hazan* Asher Lion."[34]

SKARBOWE NIGUNIM. Official melodies of the Ashkenazic synagogue which should not be altered. The term is equivalent to *misinay nigunim* (q.v.). It has erroneously been connected with the Latin *sacra*, "holy."[35] In fact, this term is derived from the Polish *skarb,* "treasure," and *skarbowe* (according to the information supplied by A. Yaari, Jerusalem) means "from the treasure, official."

SOGEN, SAGEN. To chant a prayer in the recitative style, and not as in a European periodic melody. Steinthal writes, "His *sagen* was unique, deeply stirring, and it would not have been so if every sound were not pronounced clearly. I should like to abandon any other musical education in favor of this *hittuch hadibur* [pronunciation].[36] Singer, referring to the art of the former *hazanim,* says, "Exclusively he was held in great respect as one who knew how *woyl zu sagen,* that is, to recite in an artistic manner."[37]

TROP. Recitative performed with the reading of the Bible in the synagogue, and regulated by the Masoretic accents. In medieval Latin writings on music, melismatic phrases are often called *Tropi,* and in particular such melismata as served for instructional purposes. This term appears to have been adopted by the Jews in early medieval times for the melodic phrases of their Bible chants, for it is quoted by as early a commentator as Rashi.[38] ". . . . quae a Judaeis graece Tropi, hebraice *Neginoth,* hoc est soni, appellantur." See also *Shtuben-Trop, Shul-Trop.*

UNTERHALTER. Designation of the *m'shoyrer,* a variant of the term *zuhalten* (q.v.). It possibly refers to the voice of the *bass,* which was below (*unter*) the voice of the *hazan.*

WOYL SINGEN. To sing in accordance with the style and the special features of traditional *hazanuth* as well as with the *nusah* (q.v.). "This *woyl singen* culminates in the scrupulous endeavor to use exclusively intervals proper to the occasional *shteyger,* and it was considered sacrilegious to disgrace the style with intervals which are strange to it."[39]

WULACH, WOLOCH'L. A tune expressing an elegiac mood, in the manner of Wallachian folk music. The *hazanim* used to sing a *Wulach,* for example, for the verse *Ana haShem* in the *Halel* prayer, in contrast to the gay melodies that preceded.

YISHTHABAH-SHTEYGER, YISHTHABAH-GUST. A synagogal mode named after a prayer in the morning service. Its melodic character varies in Eastern and Western Ashkenaz: (1) In (former) Russia and Poland, the second note of its scale was a tone when ascending and a semitone when descending; as there was a major third, a superfluous second was formed in descending. (2) In

Hungary and Austria, it was almost identical with the *Ahavoh Raboh-Shteyger* (q.v.).

Y'KUM PURKON-SHTEYGER, Y'KUM PURKON-GUST. A *shteyger* which was popular with the *hazanim* in Russia and which was distinguished by a major third in an ascending tune and a minor third when descending.

YOR-KADISH, YAHRES-KADISH. A *kadish-shalem* sung in a tune composed of the most characteristic melodies of all the feast tunes of the year, and hence its name, "*Kadish* of the Year." Hanoch ben Avraham ben Y'hiel reports in his *Reshith Bikurim* (written about 1650, printed in 1708) that the *hazan* used to sing the "*Kadish* of the Year" after *Hazkarath N'shamoth* in order to lead the mood of the congregation back to the joy of the feast. Today, it is a musical topic of the feast of the Rejoicing of the Law.

ZUHALTEN. To perform ". . . an harmonious accompaniment which had to be invented by the choristers from their own inspiration."[40] According to Friedmann," . . . to sing, or (as was the technical term of the *hazanim* at that time) to perform the *zuhalten*, with one's father. . . ."[41] This function of performing an extempore accompaniment was usual also with the *klezmerim*: ". . . and the members of the orchestra performed the *zuhalten* with all their instruments."[42]

Notes

1. Sholom Aleichem, *Shtempenyu*, chap. iii.

2. S. Weissenberg, "Die Klesmersprache," *Anthropologische Gesellschaft in Wien, Mitteilungen*, XLIII (1913), 127–42; A. Landau, "Zur russisch-jüdischen Klesmer-Sprache," *ibid.*, 143–49; N. Prilutzki, "L'shon haKlezmerim b'Polaniah," *R'shumoth*, I (1918), 271–347; J. Trivaks, "Di yidishe jargonen, II: Klezmer-Loshen," *Bey uns Yiden* (Warsaw, 1923), pp. 167–71.

3. Cf. A. Yaari, *Kiryath Sefer* (Jerusalem, 1943), XIX, 264.

4. Cf. A. Freimann, ed., *Hebräische Bibliographie* (Frankfurt a.M., 1911), XV, no. 5.

5. I. Schwarz, "Ueber Chasonus und Steiger," reprinted in A. Friedmann, ed., *Dem Andenken Eduard Birnbaums* (Berlin, 1922), p. 205.

6. Samuel Naumbourg *Z'miroth Yissraél* (Chants liturgiques des *Grandes Fêtes* [Paris, 1847]), Introduction, p. iii.

7. B. Jacobsohn, "Die Konservierung der juedischen Melodien," *Allgemeine Zeitung des Judenthums* (1896); reprinted in *Dem Andenken E. Birnbaums*, p. 171.

8. A. Z. Idelsohn, "Song and Singers of the Synagogue," *Hebrew Union College Jubilee Annual* (Cincinnati, 1925).

9. A. M. Bernstein, *Musikalischer Pinkas* (Vilna, 1927), p. 84.

10. Charles Burney, *The Present State of Music* (London, 1775), II, 299.

11. *Ibid.*

12. A. H. Heymann, "Lebenserinnerungen," reprinted in H. Bach, *Juedische Memoiren* (Berlin, 1936), p. 116.

13. P. Minkowski, "Hazanuth," *Otzar Yisrael* (1907–13), IV, 262b.

14. I. Schwarz, *op. cit.*, p. 202. Cf. also J. Singer, *Die Tonarten des traditionellen Synagogengesanges* (abridged reprint in *Dem Andenken E. Birnbaums*, p. 98).

15. J. Singer, "Das Leienen mit dem Trop," *Dem Andenken E. Birnbaums*, p. 49.

16. A. Friedmann, *Der synagogale Gesang* (Berlin, 1908), p. 70.

17. Sanhedrin, 86a.

18. J. Freimann, ed., *Sefer hasidim* (Frankfurt a.M., 1924), p. 207; cf. A. Z. Idelsohn, "Der Missinai-Gesang der deutschen Synagoge," *Zeitschrift fuer Musikwissenschaft*, VIII (1925), 449–72.

19. Cf. A. Z. Idelsohn, "The Mogen-Ovos-Mode: A Study in Folklore," *Hebrew Union College Annual*, XIV (1939), 559–74.

20. A. Marksohn and W. Wolf, *Auswahl alter hebräischer Synagogal-Melodien* (Leipzig, 1875), Introduction; reprinted in *Dem Andenken E. Birnbaums*, pp. 183–84.

21. Hirsh Weintraub, *Shirey Beyth Adonay* (Koenigsberg, 1859).

22. Cf. Idelsohn, *Thesaurus*, VI, No. 19; 23.

23. *Ibid.*, No. 39, pp. 40a, 40b.

24. Israel Lovy, *Chants réligieux* (Paris, 1862).

25. E.g.: L. A. Frankl, *Nach Jerusalem* (Leipzig, 1858), I, 351; II, 103; J. Singer, "Polnisch-Singen in der modernen Synagogue," *Dem Andenken E. Birnbaums*, pp. 191–97; I. Lachmann, "Unsere synagogale Nationalmusik," *Der Juedische Cantor* (Bromberg, 1880), quoted in A. Friedmann, *op. cit.*, pp. 57–58.

26. Z. Kiselgof, *Lider-zamelbuch* (Berlin, 1911), p. 79.

27. D. E. Jablonski, *Biblia Hebraica* (Berlin, 1699), Introduction, section 29: "Habent enim. . . . tabulam quandam, universos accentus complexam, atque ab initiali voce *Sarka* apellatam. . . . In qua tabula pueri a magistro viva voce edocti canere discunt."

28. H. Steinthal, "Ueber Juden und Judentum," reprinted in Hans Bach, *Juedische Memoiren* (Berlin, 1936), p. 142.

29. A. Nadel, "Gebet und Musik," *Der Orden Bne Briss* (1935), Nos. 9–10, p. 94.

30. A. M. Bernstein, *op. cit.*, p. xv.

31. J. Singer, *Die Tonarten des traditionellen Synagogengesanges, op. cit.*, p. 93.

32. *Sefer Maharil, ed. Lemberg* (1860), fol. 66b. Cf. A. Friedmann, *op. cit.*, p. 13, for several theories regarding this term.

33. Cf. J. Singer, "Das Leienen," *op. cit.*, p. 52.

34. A. Friedmann, *op. cit.*, p. 137.

35. P. Minkowski, "Nigun," *Otzar Yisrael*, III (1907–13); A. Z. Idelsohn, "Missinai-Gesang," *op. cit.*

36. H. Steinthal, *op. cit.*, p. 143.

37. J. Singer, "Polnisch-Singen," *op. cit.*, p. 196.

38. Talmud, *Commentary to Kidushin*, fol. 71a. Cf. also Johannes Reuchlin, *De accentibus et orthographia linguae Hebraicae* (Hagenoae, Germany, 1518), Liber III; Shlomoh Lifshitz, *Th'udath Shlomoh* (Offenbach, Germany, 1718); B. Heller, "Von tropos und troparion zum Trop," *MGWJ* (1936) pp. 125–27.

39. J. Singer, "Duerfen alte Synagogenmelodien modern harmonisiert werden?" *Die Wahrheit* (1911); reprinted in *Dem Andenken E. Birnbaums*, p. 104.

40. *Ibid.*, p. 108, n. 1.

41. A. Friedmann, *op. cit.*, p. 137.

42. Sholom Aleichem, *Shtempenyu*, chap. iv.

Social Background of
East European Yiddish
Folk Love-Songs

YEHOASH DWORKIN   Columbia University

by Yehoash Dworkin

THE PURPOSE of this study is to show how the cultural pattern of courtship and marriage in the Eastern European Jewish community, from the mid-eighteenth century to the latter part of the nineteenth, produced a distinctive type of folk love-song. In order, however, to understand the influence of the Jewish community on the folk love-song, we must first examine the general cultural framework within which the activities described in the songs occurred.

The Jew in the Eastern European countries lived behind a wall of laws and prohibitions imposed on him by the various Slavic nations, and within a *self*-imposed spiritual ghetto. He adjusted to the outside or majority culture only when such adjustment did not interfere with his Jewish identification or disturb his adherence to traditional mores. The community functioned according to a rather strict and dogmatic code of behavior which regulated the life of each individual. Disputes were settled in conformity with the traditional precedents of the Talmud, based on Biblical law rather than on the jurisprudence of the particular nation. By the mid-nineteenth century the Jewish community had acquired an officially sanctioned semi-autonomous status, at least in regard to religious and fiscal matters. In Russia, in 1804, under a series of *ukazay* (decrees) popularly known as the "Jewish Constitution," the Rabbinate was given permission "to look after all the ceremonies of the Jewish faith and decide all disputes bearing on religion,"[1] while the community was ordered "to see to the regular payment of the State taxes."[2]

Parental control and not free choice was favored in respect to courtship and marriage. "Falling in love without benefit of parents or marriage-brokers was frowned upon."[3]

Primarily, the choice of a "proper match" was based on social position and a desire for security. Position was measured according to a dual standard: (1) scholarship and (2) economic status. As for scholarship, a man was judged by his proficiency in the intricacies of the Bible and Talmud, by his acquaintance with traditional Jewish studies, by his absorption in scholarly activities, and by the extent to which he abided by the moral precepts of the Torah. The ideal Jewish *male* was pious, compassionate, and scholarly.

The economic stratification consisted of three conventional classes—upper, middle, and lower—but the evaluation of each of them always took into account the almost intangible elements of piety and learning. The wealthiest man, were he a boor or a dullard, could never achieve maximum recognition, while the lowliest drudge, possessed of a facile and scholarly mind, could rise above his material environment, in the esteem of his neighbors. The upper and middle classes differed essentially on the basis of income, although both were expected to employ their resources for the good of the community. The man who was not himself a scholar could gain a measure of acceptance by supporting the indigent student. Each member of the community was expected to feel an intimate relationship with the charitable and social institutions which served almost all of his social and religious needs. In short, it was not the accumulation of money but the use to which it was put that elevated a man in the eyes of his neighbors.

The poorest class was composed of manual laborers and artisans. They were held in the lowest esteem, and even the highly skilled craftsman occupied a minor, status-defined position (undoubtedly because he was obliged to live frugally and was prevented by lack of time and money from having an opportunity to pursue learning).

It thus becomes clear that the Jewish community was involved in the question of "status" in almost every aspect of its existence. Despite the great distance between the classes, however, it must be realized that close ties, both personal and social, existed within the community. "The poor and ignorant look to the wealthy and learned for assistance; the latter in turn depend upon their dependents for earthly and heavenly rewards."[4]

A proper match could be considered one between two members of the same social class, or one in which a young student was matched to a wealthy girl. It was not uncommon for a father-in-law, in the latter case, to support the young couple for as long as was necessary or possible so that the young man could continue with his studies. In many instances, if the wife did not have a substantial dowry, she would assume the family's economic burden. Hence, one of the primary considerations in marriage was the problem of enabling the husband to continue with his studies.

Since the young person desired to choose his own mate, a marked conflict arose from the differences between the ideal of free choice and the parental and community concept of controlled and arranged marriage. The community ties and affiliations were so strong, however, that open revolt rarely occurred, except under conditions of complete disaffiliation. Therefore, most folk love-songs deal with secret and fleeting affairs rather than with open meetings, since both lovers were aware of the temporary nature of their relationship and knew that to transform longing into reality was either impossible or could be achieved only at a prohibitive cost.

YIDDISH

Oy, helf mir, gotenyu, oy, got in himl,
Helf mir, gotenyu, s'iz mir nit git.
Shoyn tsayt dray yorelach, vi mir shpiln a libe,
Un oys-shpiln di libe konen mir nit. . . .[5]

TRANSLATION

Help me God, God in heaven,
God help me, I'm so unhappy.
We have loved each other for three years,
And we cannot resolve our love.

The folk love-song served as an expression of the spiritual
unrest and frustration of the younger generation, and not as a
call to revolt against an established order of affairs. It was not
so much that young people rejected the importance of parental
consent in marriage as that they desired the right to choose their
own mates. As a matter of fact, the choice was usually in keeping with the community's and parent's concept of a proper
match. In one song a girl, when asked whom she would like as a
husband, rejects the tailor, the shoemaker, and the doctor because she is not the daughter of a tailor, shoemaker, or doctor
and is herself unfamiliar with these occupations. When a scholar
(a rabbi) is suggested, however, her reaction is quite different.
Not only is she the daughter of a scholar, but she is also well-
versed in the traditional studies; a scholar is just the type of
husband she desires.

YIDDISH

Vos-zhe vilstu, vos-zhe vilstu?
A shnayder far a man?
A shnayder far a man vil ich nit.
A shnayder's a tochter bin ich nit.
Kleydlech neyen ken ich nit.
Zits ich oyf a shteyn
Shtilerheyt un veyn.
Ale meydelech hobn chasene
Nor ich blayb aleyn.

Vos-zhe vilstu, vos-zhe vilstu?
A shuster far a man?

A shuster far a man vil ich nit.
A shuster's a tochter bin ich nit.
Shich laten ken ich nit.
Zits ich oyf a shteyn. . . .

Vos-zhe vilstu, vos-zhe vilstu?
A doktor far a man?
A doktor far a man vil ich nit.
A doktor's a tochter bin ich nit.
Rfues shraybn ken ich nit.
Zits ich oyf a shteyn. . . .

Vos-zhe vilstu, vos-zhe vilstu?
A rebn far a man?
A rebn far a man vil ich doch.
A rebn's a tochter bin ich doch.
Toyre lernen ken ich doch.
Zits ich oyfn dach
Un kuk arop un lach.
Ale meydelech hobn chasene
Ich mit zey baglaych.[6]

TRANSLATION

Do you want a tailor?
As a husband?
I do not want a tailor for a husband.
I am not a tailor's daughter.
I cannot sew dresses.
So I sit on a stone
And cry to myself.
All my friends are getting married,
But not I.

Do you want a shoemaker
As a husband?
I do not want a shoemaker for a husband.
I am not a shoemaker's daughter.
I cannot patch shoes.
So I sit on a stone. . . .

Do you want a doctor as a husband?
I do not want a doctor for a husband.
I am not a doctor's daughter.
I cannot prescribe cures.
So I sit on a stone. . . .

Do you want a Rabbi as a husband?
Yes, I want a Rabbi for a husband.
I am a Rabbi's daughter.
I study the Torah (Bible).
I sit upon the roof,
And laugh to myself.
All my friends are getting married,
And so am I.

Even those institutions established for the purpose of keeping control over the young people in the hands of the family or community were not despised by these same young people. This was a logical consequence of their integration into the institutionalized life of the community from the very first moment of birth. The reliance placed upon these institutions is exemplified in the song "Yome, Yome, shpil mir a lidele,"[7] wherein a young girl's worries are dispelled by her parents' promise that the matchmaker will find her a proper husband:

YIDDISH

Yome, Yome shpil mir a lidele
Vos dos meydele vil.
    Dos meydele vil a chosn'dl hobn
    Muz men geyn dem shadchn zogn,
Yo mameshi, yo
Du konst mich shoyn farshteyn
Du veyst shoyn vos ich meyn.[8]

TRANSLATION

Yome, Yome, play a song for me,
And tell me what the maiden wants.

> The maiden wants a bridegroom
> So we must go and tell the marriage-broker.
> Yes, mother, yes
> Now you understand me,
> Now you know what I mean.

In those few cases of open rebellion against authority, the rebellion was only of a temporary nature and was followed by a return to the family—which, symbolically, indicated a return to, and acceptance of, the precepts of the family.

YIDDISH

> Oy, ch'ob geton aza zach,
> Ch'ob gornit batracht;
> Ch'ob gemeynt az s'iz tog—
> Tsum sof iz gor nacht!
> Oy, mame, mame,
> Du binst doch gerecht:
> Az men folgt nit kayn eltern,
> Kumt aroys shlecht![9]

TRANSLATION

> Oh, I did such a [terrible] thing,
> I thought it was day,
> And in the end it was night!
> Oh, mother, mother,
> You are right:
> If one disobeys one's parents,
> The outcome is unfortunate.

So far our emphasis has been placed on those component elements of the community which influence the folk love-song. For the purpose of further developing our theme and in order to accentuate the individual moments in the cycle of courtship and marriage, we shall make a preliminary attempt to classify these songs. To be sure, this rough categorizing takes into account only the more salient aspects of an individual item, without any thorough analysis of each facet of the song.

It should be noted that the term "folk love-song" is used throughout to include only those songs which deal with the conditions surrounding courtship and marriage, or with actual love affairs. Wedding and family songs are not included in this definition. Perhaps the term "courting songs" would be more applicable, but only if we understand that the courtship described in these songs is a secret, and not an open, relationship.

The songs fall into five general categories: riddle songs, songs of desertion, songs of separated lovers and clandestine love, and songs expressing a desire for marriage.

Of the five categories, only the riddle songs include subjects other than love; actually "riddle song" is a generic term for a type of song which, unlike the other four categories, is differentiated by its structure rather than its content. The form used is a conversation between two parties, one questioning and the other replying. In some cases the conversation is only implied, with the singer both posing the question and furnishing the answer.

YIDDISH

Du meydele du sheyns, du meydele du fayns,
Ch'vel dir epes fregn a retenish a fayns.
Vos iz hecher far a hoyz,
Un vos iz flinker far a moyz?

Du narisher bocher, du narisher trop,
Du host nit kayn seychl in dayn kop.
Der roych iz hecher far a hoyz,
A kats iz flinker far a moyz.[10]

TRANSLATION

Pretty maiden, fine maiden,
I will ask you a fine riddle.

What is higher than a house,
And what is quicker than a mouse?

You silly boy, you foolish boy,
You haven't a brain in your head.
Smoke is higher than a house,
A cat is quicker than a mouse.

The love motif is not always strongly expressed in these riddle songs, but there is a noticeable element of heartbreak and longing in the last two lines of the following example:

YIDDISH

Shteyt a bocher un er tracht,
Tracht un tracht a gantse nacht,
Zol er zi nemen um nit farshemen? (2)
    Tumbala, tumbala, tumbalalayka (2)
    Tumbalalayka, shpil balalayka,
    Tumbalalayka, freylach zol zayn.

Meydl, meydl, ch'vel bay dir fregn,
Vos kon vaksn, vaksn on regn,
Vos kon veynen, veynen on trern,
Vos kon brenen un nit fartsern?
    Tumbala, etc. . . .

Narisher bocher, vos darfstu fregn,
A shteyn kon vaksn, vaksn on regn,
A harts kon veynen, veynen on trern,
Un libe kon brenen un nit fartsern.
    Tumbala, etc. . . .[11]

TRANSLATION

A young man stands and thinks,
Thinks the whole night through,
Should he take her and not put her to shame?
    Tumbala, etc.

Maiden, maiden, I will ask you,
What can grow without rain,
What can cry without tears,
What can burn without consuming?
    Tumbala, etc. . . .

Silly boy, why need you ask,
A stone can grow without rain,
A heart can cry without tears,
Love can burn without consuming.
    Tumbala, etc. . . .

As has been previously mentioned, attachments formed during clandestine love affairs were very unlikely to lead to marriage. Consequently, the lovers appreciated, and were affected by, the fleeting quality of their relationship. Such a situation was not conducive to constancy, and fickleness is an ever recurring theme.

YIDDISH

Oyfn barg shteyt a taybele,
Un tut zich troyerik brumen;
Ch'ob amol gehat a gutn fraynt,
Ch'kon shoyn tsu im mer nit kumen.

Oy mome, mome, shtay oyf fun keyver,
Un helf mir oys in mayne neytn!
Fun der libe gey ich arumet,
Vi an aristant in keytn.

Oy shvach bin ich, oy shlaf bin ich,
Af mayne fis kon ich nit shteyn;
Oy di tsores vos ich layd zich onet,
Leygn mich shoin in dr'erd arayn![12]

TRANSLATION

A dove stands on the mountain,
And coos in sorrow;

I once had a good friend,
But I can no longer find him.

Oh mother, mother, arise from the grave,
And help me in my sorrow!
Love has shackled me
Like a prisoner in chains.

I am weak and weary
And can no longer stand.
The sorrows that I suffer
Drive me to the grave.

Many a poor maiden, sure of her conquest, found herself deserted when a greater charmer beckoned:

YIDDISH

Oy, vos ch'ob gevolt, hob ich oysgefirt,
Zol ich azoy lebn!
Ch'ob gevolt a sheyn yingele,
Hot mir got gegebn.

Ch'ob gemeynt az er iz shoyn mayn,
Ch'ob im shoyn bakumen;
Iz gekumen a shener meydele
Un hot im tsugenumen.[13]

TRANSLATION

All my life, as I lived,
I had what I wanted,
I wanted a handsome lad
And God gave him to me.

I thought that he was already mine,
That I had already gotten him,
But along came a prettier maiden
And took him away from me.

The deserted girl is left to mourn, realizing that men are fickle and unworthy:

YIDDISH

In droysn iz a regn,
Ale shteyner zaynen nas;
Itztike bocherim iz tsu gloybn
Vi di hint afn gas.[14]

TRANSLATION

The rain wets the cobble stones
And the street is wet.
A young man is not to be trusted—
Like a dog in the street.

Finally, she warns others to avoid the same mistakes:

YIDDISH

Hert nor oys, ale meydelach!
Kayn libe iz nit gut tsu kenen;
M'zol tsuzamennemen ale falshe yingelach
Un oyf'n fayer zey farbrenen.

Oyf'n fayer zol me' zey farbrenen
Biz oyf drobne koyln.
Finf yor tsu firn a libe,
Un nisht tsu kenen poyln![15]

TRANSLATION

Oh, listen all ye maidens,
It hurts to know of love.
All false young men should be gathered together
And burned.

They should all be burned,
'Till nothing but embers remain.
Five years have I loved—
And all in vain.

Actually, the songs of separation might also be included with the songs of desertion since the frustration resulting from unrequited love often culminated in separation. Here, however, we are dealing only with those songs of separation in which the separation is due to external pressures. Whereas the songs of desertion reflect the conflict between youthful desires and the traditions of the family and the community (i.e., internal conflict), the songs of separation are an outgrowth of escapism, fear of conscription, desire for economic security—all involving conditions beyond the control of the family or the community. In the songs of desertion the woman is the central figure, but in the songs of separation we find that the man plays the dominant role. Even when the singer is a woman, it is the absent lover who figures most prominently:

YIDDISH

Her nor, du sheyn meydele,
Her nor, du fayn meydele,
Vos vestu tun in aza vaytn veg?
    Ich vel geyn in ale gasn
    Un vel shrayen "Vesh tsum vashn!"
    Abi mit dir tsuzamen zayn!

Her nor, du sheyn meydele,
Her nor, du fayn meydele,
Oyf vos vestu shlofn in aza vaytn veg?
    Ich bin noch a yunge froy
    Ich ken shlofn oyf a bintl shtroy,
    Abi mit dir tsuzamen zayn.[16]

TRANSLATION

Tell me, pretty maiden,
Tell me, lovely one,
What will you do in such a far-off land?
    I will go up and down the streets
    And become a washerwoman.
    If only I can be with you.

Tell me, pretty maiden,
Tell me, lovely one,
Where will you sleep in such a far-off land?
I am still a young woman
And can sleep on a bundle of straw.
If only I can be with you.

It is interesting to note that many of the songs in this group contain an element of constancy rarely found in the other four categories:

YIDDISH

Lomir beyde a libe firn,
Lomir beyde zayn fun got a por;
Shvern shver ich dir bay got un bay mentshn,
Az vartn vel ich oyf dir tsvey-dray yor.

Tsvey-dray yor vel ich oyf dir vartn,
Afile finf yor iz mir oychet k'day;
Gelt in polk arayn vel ich dir shikn
Un ich vel mich mutshn bay der shnayderay.[17]

TRANSLATION

Let's fall in love,
We will be a pair created by God;
I will swear to you before God and man
That I will wait two-three years for you.

I will wait two-three years for you,
And even five years;
I will send money to you in the army
While I suffer at the tailor's trade.

At this point it should be quite clear that the theme of thwarted lovers pervades the Yiddish folk love-song. In the case of the man his frustration (at least on the level of folk expression) leads to a concrete course of action. Because the commu-

nity frowns upon courtship without an intermediary, his wooing must be done circumspectly; he is forced to arrange clandestine trysts with his beloved. Although secret meetings are mentioned in a large percentage of the songs falling into the other
categories, they are usually sub-themes within a more dominat-
ing framework. Thus, only those songs dealing exclusively with
clandestine meetings, or with the mechanics involved in these
meetings, are included in the category of clandestine songs.

As is to be expected of an environment in which parental
and community control were so strong, clandestine wooing
could never progress naturally:

YIDDISH

Fun vanen nemt zich a libe?
Fun zitsn un fun reydn un fun lachn;
Unzer libe hot zich bashlosn
Fun eyns biz tsvey in der nacht.

B'shas unzer libe hot zich bashlosn,
Hot doch keyner nit gevust;
Un haynt klingt doch in ale gasn,
Az unzer libe iz shoyn oys!

Genug shoyn dir tsu reydn un tsu shmuesn,
Fir shoyn mich op aheym!
Vos far a terets vel ich zogn
Bay mayn mamen in der heym?

Genug dir shoyn tsu redn un tsu shmuesn,
Fir shoyn mich op aheym!
Der zeyger hot shoyn tsvelf opgeshlogn,
Di tir iz farshpart in der heym![18]

TRANSLATION

How does love begin?
From sitting, talking, and laughing;

Our love was sealed
Between the hours of one and two [at night]

When our love was sealed,
No one knew of it;
But today it is known in all the streets,
That our love is at an end!

Enough conversation and talk,
Take me home!
What sort of an excuse will I give
In my mother's home?

Enough of your talk,
Take me home!
The clock has struck twelve,
The door is locked at home!

A series of songs falling within the category of clandestine love is directly traceable to the Swiss "Kilt-Lied."[19] These songs follow a unique and strictly defined structural form, consisting of conversation between two lovers separated by an actual (physical) barrier:

YIDDISH

Ver klapt es azoy shpet banacht?
Yankele volyantchik?
 —Efn, efn, Brontchele,
 Ich bin dayn kochantchik!

Vi kon ich dir den efenen,
Ch'ob moyre far dem tatn.
 —Efn, efn, Brontchele,
 S'vet dir gor nisht shatn.

Vi kon ich dir den efenen,
Ch'ob moyre far mayn mumen.
 —Efn, efn, Brontchele,
 Anit vel ich mer nisht kumen.[20]

TRANSLATION

Who's knocking there so late at night?
Yankele the ruffian.
   Open the door, Brontchele,
   I've come to be your suitor.

How can I open [the door] for you?
I'm afraid of my father.
   —Open the door, Brontchele,
   It won't hurt you to.

How can I open the door for you?
I'm afraid of my aunt.
   —Open the door, Brontchele,
   Or I will never come again.

   Despite the fact that most Yiddish folk love-songs are in the minor mode, a great number of the marrying songs are humorous and, at times, even burlesque. They are usually instruments of ridicule satirizing the institution of marriage as well as many of the situations connected with courtship. The old maid becomes an object of fun, the lack of dowry is treated as a joke, and the marriage-broker is made a clown. Yet, interestingly enough, the importance of a dowry and the services of a marriage-broker are accepted, and the decisive role of parents is clearly indicated.

YIDDISH

Mameshi, mach mir chasene.
   Tochter, s'iz noch tsayt.
Mameshi, mach mir chasene,
A gelechter on a zayt.

Mameshi, mach mir chasene.
   Tochter, shvayg shoyn shtil
Mameshi, mach mir chasene,
S'iz nit kayn kindershpil.

Mameshi, mach mir chasene.
Tochter, s'iz nito kayn gelt.
Mameshi, ch'vil nit visn,
Ch'vil oych visn fun a velt.[21]

TRANSLATION

Mother, marry me off.
Daughter, you still have time.
Mother, marry me off,
This is no laughing matter.

Mother, marry me off.
Daughter, be quiet.
Mother, marry me off,
This is no child's play.

Mother, marry me off.
Daughter, there is no money.*
Mother, I don't want to hear of it,
I also wish to know of the world.

YIDDISH

Ich bin shoyn a meydl in di yorn,
Vos hostu mir dem kop fardreyt;
Ich volt shoyn lang a kale gevorn,
Un efsher take chasene gehat.

Un efsher geyt dir, ketsele, in nadn,
Di mame vet farkoyfn di shtib;
Mir veln beyde chasene hobn,
Vayl ich hob dich lib!

Un efsher vilstu visn mayn yiches,
Der zeyde iz geven a rov;
Lomir-zhe beyde chasene hobn,
Un zol shoyn nemen a sof . . .[22]

* For the dowry.

TRANSLATION

I'm already an old maid,
Why did you turn my head;
I would have been a bride long ago,
And would have been married.

Perhaps you are worried about my dowry,
Mother will sell our house;
Let us get married
For I love you so.

Perhaps you would like to know my background,
My grandfather was a Rabbi;
Let us get married
And put an end to this.

In a way, these songs, more than any others, indicate that the revolt of youth against parental control was emotional rather than stemming from any deep-rooted conviction. While ridiculing the traditional attitudes of their parents, the young people accepted the customs of their elders, and perhaps secretly even admitted the wisdom of this acceptance.

In our summary of the influence of the Eastern European Jewish community on its love-songs, there are certain facts to be especially noted. These songs describe a pattern within a pattern, the manner in which one segment of the population deals with a problem peculiar to it within the framework of the customs and traditions of the entire population. Although the actions described in the folk love-songs seem to be in direct conflict with the ideology of the community, it cannot be said that this behavior is abnormal, since the activities sung about are an integral part of the over-all life of the community. The behavior is therefore deviant only in the sense that the projected course of action differs from the established ideal.

The love-songs indicate that the emotional revolt was directed only against parental control and not against the instituions surrounding courtship and marriage or even against the preconceived image of the ideal or proper match. In a sense, the song was an escape valve for the frustrations and repressions which, had they been directed against their actual source, would have resulted in the ostracizing of the individual from the community. No song suggests that the singer is willing to relinquish identification with the Jewish community and the traditions of his Jewish heritage.

Notes

1. S. M. Dubnow, *History of the Jews in Russia and Poland* (2 vols.; Philadelphia, 1916), I, 366.

2. *Ibid.*

3. Ruth Rubin, *A Treasury of Jewish Folksongs* (New York, 1950), p. 47.

4. M. Zborowski and E. Herzog, *Life is With People* (New York, 1952), p. 420.

5. Rubin, p. 53.

6. Taken from a series of song-sheets published by the J. L. Cahan Folklore Group of the Yiddish Scientific Institute—YIVO (New York, n.d.), p. 8, song 4.

7. M. Kipnis, *One Hundred Folksongs* (Buenos Aires, 1949), pp. 45 ff. Printed in Yiddish.

8. *Ibid.*, verse 5.

9. S. M. Ginzburg and R. S. Marek, *Jewish Folksongs in Russia* (St. Petersburg, 1901), No. 196, pp. 156 ff. Printed in Yiddish.

10. *Workmen's Circle Folksong Book* (New York, n.d.), p. 24. Printed in Yiddish.

11. Sung to me by Mrs. A. Twersky, New York.

12. J. L. Cahan, "Yiddish Folksongs," *Pinkos*, I (New York, 1930), p. 28.

13. J. L. Cahan, *Yiddish Folksongs* (New York, 1912), II, p. xxxv.

14. S. M. Ginzburg and R. S. Marek, No. 141, p. 113.

15. J. L. Cahan, *Yiddish Folksongs*, pp. 230 ff.

16. S. P. Schack, *Yiddish Folksongs* (New York, 1947), pp. 32 ff.

17. Kipnis, p. 78 ff.

18. Ginzburg and Marek, No. 177, pp. 138 ff.

19. J. L. Cahan, "Yiddish Folksongs," from a footnote on p. 8: "This type of not very modest song is usually credited to a Swiss source, although the Swiss themselves try to disprove it. L. Tabler, for example, in the introduction to his *Swiss Folksongs* (1882), I, 136, shows that these 'Kilt-lieder,' which relate specifically to nocturnal visits, were an old, widespread custom, especially amongst the Celtic population in England, where it is in part practiced to this very day. . . . Although it could lead to promiscuity, it was not any worse than similar practices in the Middle Ages. Therefore, the 'Kilt-lieder' are exactly the same as the 'Tage-lieder' of the Minnesingers and troubadours."

20. Kipnis, pp. 41 ff.

21. Cahan, *Yiddish Folksongs*, II, 15.

22. Kipnis, pp. 29 ff.

Synthesis and Symbiosis
of Styles in Jewish-
Oriental Music

EDITH   GERSON - KIWI

Hebrew University, Jerusalem

by Edith Gerson-Kiwi

ALL OVER the world, the tide of time is now working against the folk arts and their stylistic purity. Whereas until recently the main subject of ethnomusicology was the authenticity of folksong as the decisive factor in the process of its description, analysis, and final definition, a new category of questions—motivated by the growing mixture of folk styles—has recently been opened. The new view is likely to reverse everything which was thought to be irrevocable. The phenomenon of "impurity" in any given folk art now seems to be as essential for its definition as its "purity," or the absence of foreign elements, used to be.

The change of approach in the study of folk music is gaining a deeper significance. In general, ethnomusicology has already undergone several phases of development. Whereas in its early days, some sixty years ago, the accent was mainly on the exhaustive collection of musical material from closed folkloristic areas—as exemplified in the Smithsonian publications on American Indian tribes, or in Hornbostel's monographs on single primitive tribes—some twenty years later the interest shifted to the investigation of possible interrelations among the peoples of the globe. By means of comparative research, and with the help of speculative musical theories laid down by the ancient civilizations of China, India, Arabia, or Greece, certain principles of world-wide validity—e.g., Hornbostel's "standard norm" of tuning and M. Schneider's "cycles" of early tonality—were established. In line with the approach suggested in Robert Lachmann's *Music of the Orient* (where the musical history of the individual Asiatic nations is continually trespassed in favor of a division based on their common musical problems), a further step was taken to deepen the "comparative" method of research concerning non-European—i.e., non-written—music by stressing every possible evidence of interdependence in musical thought, instruments, melody, intonation, or form. But the spell of this wondrous, barrier-less world of music, where cultural contacts cause a never-ending fluctuation, migration, and mutation of musical elements, lends itself to various interpretations. Are certain parallel occurrences of, say, three-tone scales, microtonality, and temperature indeed interdependent, or should we rather acknowledge that there are *independent creations of a basic thought at unconnected places?* Perhaps we have been too zealous lately in detecting numerous cultural contacts and interdependencies. Man, as the one species of *homo sapiens*, is likely to strive along similar lines and to arrive at similar conclusions—under given circumstances—without working under direct influence. How could we otherwise hope to define Scottish songs as Scottish, Negro as Negro, or Mexican as such, if their melos, with its five-tone foundation, were only a dependency of the "Chinese" scale? It seems more probable that we are here facing spontaneous formations which appear in unrelated places and civilizations and point to quite heterogeneous phases of evolution. The same may be the case with all those Asiatic, and some non-Asiatic, peoples working upon the *Maqām* system, or with the many basic cultures revealing primitive polyphony, like the South-African Negroes, the Malayans, and Polynesians, or—in the context of European folklore—with the fishermen of Genova, the Jews of Corfu, the Russian peasants, with their organum-like part-singing, or with the Dalmatians, with their howling of parallel seconds.

In this multitude of independent formations from a basic musical spur, there is, on the other hand, as little "pure" folksong as there are tones without overtones. Nearly every song on earth appears to be mixed, and its inimitable character is due precisely to its specific mixture and synthesis of styles. In particular, we can speak of synthetic folk styles if certain foreign elements have been assimilated to a creative new blend. The cardinal examples of this kind of blending are the liturgies of the early Christian churches—the Gregorian chant and the Byzantine chant—together with the Oriental sections of Armenian, Jacobite, Nestorian, or Coptic chant, which, through an amalgamation of ancient Jewish cantillations to their own folk traditions, led to the foundation of entirely new music cultures. Besides, many a secular folk tune on local ground may have been converted into chant, and it is only the sanctity of clerical tradition which makes us forget how many folk melodies have crept, and are still creeping, into official liturgy. Though all the monotheistic religions of Western Asia adopted the same principle of chanting, drawing on similar stores of basic melodies, we readily accept each new synthesis on local ground as an original creation.

Israel today is a unique phenomenon in this respect. With the return of the Jewish exiles, the nation is now sheltering a multitude of synthetic musical traditions which, in spite of their diversity, and often complete unrelatedness, point among themselves to one common source, transparent behind the many later layers and the strongest peculiarities of Diaspora formations. This common source is the Book of the Bible. Its reading, or better, its chanting, was, in the centuries of exile, the magic means of keeping the balance between the true and the adopted "ego." Adopted were the various local traditions—particularly, in Eastern countries, the Arab-Persian styles of singing—which were assimilated to the true Jewish style to the extent that entirely synthetic forms were evolved. Whether we shall ever be able to isolate the components and uncover the underlying *cantus-firmus* remains an open question. What we hear today is, so to speak, an endless row of variations on a forlorn theme, and who could ever tell the ultimate line of its original melos?

In the following example,* some "variations" of the Pentateuch cantillation (mainly from the first chapter), as recorded
from various communities, are given. They clearly reveal the
same fundamental melos, notwithstanding the divergent orna-
mentation and intonation (see Example I).

Israel today offers another interesting and curious phenomenon, the symbiosis, or nestling together, of different styles. The
same Babylonian cantor, for instance, who has chanted to you
just now some precious examples of age-old Jewish Bible reading, would be ready—as through the pushing of a magic button
—to render you a beautiful Arab-Iraqian art song, in the vernacular and with the full impact of local color. The same is true
of the Moroccan, the Yemenite, the Persian, or the Indian Jew.
Here, we are obviously confronted with the bilingual, sometimes polyglot, grounding of many Jewish folk traditions. In
this case, the dependence on the Diaspora style is easily to be
recognized. It has not reached the border of a new synthesis of
styles—quite the contrary: the Diaspora elements retain their
properties rather obstinately and nestle side by side with the in-
herited Jewish properties, in a kind of peaceful coexistence.

It seems that the dividing line between synthetic styles
(which may stand for genuine expressions of a folk tradition)
and symbiotic styles (which contain residues of an adopted,
but not integrated, host culture) runs through the liturgical and
secular forms. Thus in the Afro-Asiatic countries of the Diaspora the secular song and folk dance, or the reciting of folktales and sagas, were adopted from the respective host countries
but not assimilated to the proper "ego," as in the case of Jewish
Bible cantillation and religious poetry. In this sphere of sacred
song, resistance against wholesale adoption of foreign elements
was strongest, and still is. Even so, Jewish cantillation developed
numerous dialects, i.e., synthetic folk traditions, but the foreign

* Music examples one and two were recorded and transcribed by the author
at the Research Institute for Jewish and Oriental Music, Hebrew University,
Jerusalem.

EXAMPLE I

Comparative Pentateuch Cantillation (beginnings)

I Yemen—Hadramaut

Ex. 19:1 Ba-ho-deš haš-šě - li - si —— lǎ-ṣēt bě-nē Yis-ra-'el me-e-res Miṣ-ra-yim:

M. 1333

II India—Cochin

Gen. 1:1 Bě-re-šit ba-ra' e-lo-him et haš-ša-mayim wě-ēt ha - 'a - res:

M. 2225

III Iraq—Bagdad

Gen. 1:1 Bě-re-šit ba-ra' e-lo-him et haš-ša-ma——yim w'et ha-'a ———— res:

M. 1562

IV Kurdistan

Gen. 1:1 Bě-re-šit ba-ra' e-lo-him et haš-ša-mayim wě-ēt ha - 'a - res:

M. 1583

V Italy—Rome

Gen. 1:1 Bě-re - šit ba - ra' e-lo-him et haš-ša - ma —— yim w' et ha-'a-res:

M. 1434

VI Ashkenaz

Gen. 1:1 Bě-re - šit —— ba - ra' e - lo-him et haš-ša-ma-yim wě-et ha-'a-res:

M. 167

VII Morocco

Gen. 21:1 W'a-do-nay———— pa-qad et Sa-rah ka-'a-šer 'a - mar wa-ya-ás a-do-nay

VIII Tunis—Djerba

Gen. 1:1 B're-šit ba-ra' e - lo-him et haš-ša - ma - yim w' et [ta] ha - a-'res:

M. 2250

IX Samaritans

Gen. 1:1 Ba - rā - she - ti ba - ra e - lo - mi - te - sha-mez wit - ti —— o - rez:
(Phonetic:)

M. 1695

elements were entirely absorbed and thinly strewn out over the older strata of cantillation style. Local languages, cultural influences, and social conditions may have served as the main vehicles of this kind of synthesizing procedure.

On the other hand, symbiotic forms of singing are nearly always discernible when there is a wide divergence from the liturgical style, especially when there is a complete change-over in general expression, musical behavior, and performance—an interesting physio-psychic "moment" which cannot be rendered in written examples but must be seen and heard.

In the small country of Israel there is nowadays the unique opportunity to study simultaneously the liturgical traditions of the various Jewish communities as well as a number of non-Jewish folklore traditions from a wide circle of Mediterranean and Asiatic countries, as most of the new immigrants—our main source of research—are musically double-tongued and carry with them many of the long-hidden musical treasures of Islamic, Persian, and Indian countries.

To what extent the Jewish-liturgical and the vernacular-secular forms of singing differ within the same community, or even in the repertoire of the same person, may be approximately shown by the following two examples (one, a traditional Babylonian chanting of a verse from the Psalms, the other, an Arab dance tune), both rendered by the same singer (see Example II).

At present both musical form and folk tradition are increasingly endangered by contamination with the popular songs of urban areas. The resulting "border style"—in itself deplorable—is nevertheless a new symptom confronting musical ethnology. The picture is rather somber: ditties and "hits" are leveling the archaic strata of musical language and making short shift of valuable ethnic and local variations. Geographical inaccessibility, which, in a way, has been considered necessary for the preservation of folk traditions, is now bridged by modern means of transportation and communication. Films, television, the radio,

EXAMPLE II

(a) Psalm 113 (beginning), chanted by Y. Agassi
(b) Lebanese Hora (central part), played on the 'Ud by Y. Agassi

Dal segno al fine

and the phonograph are all helping to wipe out precious local peculiarities of style in singing and playing and will eventually cover widely divergent areas with pitiful residues of Western civilization. Easy communication, ambitious competition, and mutual imitation of songs replace the splendid immobility of time-honored tradition. As we have tried to show in the foregoing discussion, authentic folksong does not necessarily vanish in the synthesis or symbiosis of different folk styles, but in the present situation the authenticity of folksong is drastically threatened by an invading urban mentality.

Some Aspects of

Comparative Jewish

Folksong

R U T H   R U B I N   New York City

by Ruth Rubin

JEWISH LORE since the dispersion has reflected a cluster of communities in different parts of the world, spanning many centuries. Shifted historically a number of times, the lore embraces *several* cultural expressions, couched in a number of tongues.

The basic ethical and moral teachings of the Torah remained constant to all Jewish communities, but the daily religious rituals and customs differed from one Jewish community to the other. Thus, through the centuries, the lore of the Jews developed along several lines. Basically, it was related to its own Biblical and historical past and to particular mores within a specific period and environment. At the same time, it also took on some of the coloration of its surroundings. In spite of the social ostracism to which the Jews were subjected, they were strongly influenced by their Christian neighbors, simultaneously enriching the folklore of the Western peoples.

This process of cultural exchange was occurring among most European peoples during the Middle Ages. Referring to folksongs, the eminent Yiddish folklorist J. L. Cahan (1881–1937), wrote in 1910: "Already in the Middle Ages, there came about a regular exchange of folksongs, not only between such neighbor peoples as the German, Dutch and Danes; Swedes and Norwegians; Spaniards and Portuguese; Serbians and Bulgarians; Lithuanians and Latvians, but also between people of quite distant origin."[1] This process made no exception of Jewish folksong. Yet, further along in the same essay, Cahan makes this interesting statement: ". . . among the 700 Yiddish folksongs

235

which have been collected to date [1910] . . . I have, after careful searching and checking, found only a score or so which belong to parallels of other peoples. . . . Most of these trace their origin to the early Middle Ages."[2]

In this paper we shall illustrate six Jewish folksongs which have their parallels in the folksongs of other peoples and which are still current among Yiddish-speaking Americans and Canadians today. These are given along with their American (English) parallels, five of which undoubtedly came to the New World, brought by "carriers" from Europe at a time of active cultural interchange.

One of the oldest Jewish folksongs, which is chanted in Hebrew toward the end of the Passover Feast (Seder), is "Ekhod Mi Yodea" (Who Knows One?). This song uses the question-and-answer form in a pattern of numerals related to religious symbols. In an important paper entitled "Songs of the 'Twelve Numbers' and the Hebrew Chant of 'Ekhod Mi Yodea'," L. C. R. Yoffie states that "the song was well known in many sections of Europe as early as the 16th century."[3] Comparing Latin texts and French, English, and other Continental versions, Spanish songs, and American versions of the old chant, the author further states that "interest in numbers as an intellectual or spiritual interpretation of experiences is of very ancient and practically universal origin"[4] and concludes with the statement that "the Hebrew chant printed in the Haggadah is the first song of its type to set the pattern for a number-song which has spread over two continents and been transmitted through many languages and among many nations."[5] Of interest here is the observation made by I. Rabinovitch in one of his essays on Jewish music,[6] that in the Haggadahs of the Spanish, Portuguese and Yemenite Jewish communities, the "Ekhod Mi Yodea" chant is not to be found.

The thirteenth stanza of the Hebrew chant (Ekhod Mi Yodea") is given below, with an English translation. It is followed by the twelfth (concluding) stanza of an American parallel.

The Hebrew transliterated text here follows the Ashkenazic pronunciation.

HEBREW (transliterated)

Shloysho-osor mi yodea?
Shloysho-osor ani yodea.
Shloysho-osor midayo,
Shneym-osor shivtayo,
Akhad-osor kokhvayo,
Asoro dibrayo,
Tisho yarkhey leydo,
Shmoyno y'mey milo,
Shivo y'mey Shabato,
Shisho sidrey Mishno,
Khamisho khumshey Toyro,
Arba imohoys,
Shloysho ovoys,
Shney lukhoys habris,
Ekhod Eloheynu
Shebashomayim uvo-orets.[7]

TRANSLATION

Who knows thirteen?
I know thirteen.
Thirteen [are the] Attributes of God,
Twelve–Tribes of Israel,
Eleven–stars of Joseph's dream,
Ten–Commandments,
Nine–months of pregnancy,
Eight–days of circumcision,
Seven–days of the Sabbath count,
Six–orders of the Mishna,
Five–Books of the Torah,
Four–Matrons [Sarah, Rebeccah, Leah, Rachel],
Three–Patriarchs (Abraham, Isaac, Jacob),
Two–Tables of the Covenant,
One [is] our God
In the heavens and on earth.

AMERICAN

I sing of twelve oh,
Green grow the rushes, oh.
What is your twelve oh?
Twelve for the twelve Apostles,
Eleven for the eleven who went to Heaven,
Ten for the Ten Commandments,
Nine for the nine bright shiners,
    [or, Nine for the choirs of Angels]
Eight for the April rainers,
    [or, Eight for the eight bold rangers]
Seven for the seven stars in the sky,
Six for the six proud walkers,
Five for the symbols at your door,
Four for the Gospel-makers,
Three, three the rivals,
Two, two the lily-white boys
    clothed all in green-oh,
One is one and all alone
    and ever more shall be so.[8]

Secular symbols were later applied to number songs, which assumed a wide variety of forms in all languages. For example, a Yiddish children's song utilizes the number symbols as a counting-out-rhyme,[9] and "A Partridge in a Pear Tree," a well-known English Christmas carol, is popular, as we should expect, at Christmastime.

Intensive research, similar to that done on the "Ekhod Mi Yodea" chant, was also conducted on the "Khad Gadyo" (One Kid) song, which is sung in Aramaic toward the close of the Passover Feast. Like the famous number song, it is universally popular and part of the song treasure of practically every country in Europe. W. W. Newell[10] traces variations of this cumulative theme to old French secular sources of the 12th or 13th century. Several scholars who have found variants of the "Khad Gadyo" chant in Siam, Persia and India maintain that it is of ancient origin and came from the Far East. I. Rabinovitch[11] comments that, although the Spanish and Portuguese Jewish communities do not include the "Ekhod Mi Yodea" song in their Passover Haggadahs, they do have the "Khad Gadyo" song.

The tenth (last) stanza and the refrain of the "Khad Gadyo" chant are given below; the pronunciation is Ashkenazic. This is followed by the first, seventh, and eighth stanzas of an American parallel, entitled "Kid Do Go."

HEBREW (transliterated)

Ve-oso Hakodoysh Boruch Hu,
V'shokhat l'malakh hamoves,
D'shokhat L'shoykhet
D'shokhat l'soyro,
D'shoso l'mayo,
D'khovo l'nuro,
D'soraf l'khutro,
D'hiko l'kalbo,
D'noshakh l'shunro,
D'oklho l'gadyo,
 D'zaben abo bitrey zuzey,
 Khad gadyo, khad gadyo.[12]

TRANSLATION

And the Holy One, Blessed is He, came,
And killed the Angel of Death,
That slew the slaughterer,
That slaughtered the ox,
That drank the water,
That quenched the fire,
That burned the stick,
That beat the dog,
That bit the cat,
That ate the kid,
 That father bought for two zuzim,
 One kid, one kid.

AMERICAN

As I was going over London Bridge
I found a penny ha'penny, and bought me a kid.
Kid do go.
Know by the moonlight its almost midnight,
Time kid and I were home an hour and a half ago.

Went a little further, and found rope.
Rope do hang butcher,
Butcher won't kill ox,
Ox won't drink water,
Water won't quench fire,
Fire won't burn stick,
Stick won't beat kid,
Kid won't go,
Know by the moonlight, etc.

Rope began to hang butcher,
Butcher began to kill ox,
Ox began to drink water,
Water began to quench fire,
Fire began to burn stick,
Stick began to beat kid,
Kid began to go.
Know by the moonlight it's almost midnight
So kid and I got home an hour and a half ago.[13]

About the 15th century, riddles were a favorite form of balladry in Europe. As a means of testing sharp wits, however,
riddles seem to be an ancient custom which may have come
from the Orient. In folk ballads where the riddle is employed,
a series of difficult questions are posed by the young man to the
girl whom he is courting. Very often the marriage depended
upon her answers.

Some popular Yiddish riddle songs are: "Du Meydele Du
Sheyns" ("Pretty Little Maiden"), a children's song in which

the marriage theme is absent; "Nem Aroys A Ber Fun Vald" ("Lead a Bear Out of the Woods"); the cumulative "Velkhes Iz Dos Shenste Fun Der Velt?" ("What is the Loveliest in the World?"), and "Tumbalalayka," which is said to be of American vintage.[14] Several American (English) parallels to the above are: "I Gave My Love a Cherry"—riddling stanzas which, though appearing separately, are often part of "Captain Wedderburn's Courtship" (Child No. 46); "The Devil's Nine Questions," an American form of "Riddles Wisely Expounded" (Child No. 1); "Blow Ye Winds Blow" or "The Elfin Knight" (Child No. 2).

"Nem Aroys A Ber Fun Vald," transcribed from the recitation of a 67-year-old woman, born in Lithuania, is given below, together with "Blow Ye Winds Blow," or "The Elfin Knight."

YIDDISH

[She] Nem aroys a ber fun vald
Un lern im oys shraybn,
Demlt vestu, demlt vestu
Eybig mayner blaybn.

[He] Ikh vel aroysnemen a ber fun vald
Un vel im oyslernen shraybn.
Ney mir oys zibn hemder
On nodl un on zaydn.

[She] Ikh vel dir oysneyen zibn hemder
On nodl un on zaydn,
Boy mir oys a leyter hoykh
Tsum himl zol er shtaygn.

[He] Ikh vel dir oysboyen a leyter hoykh
Tsum himl vet er shtaygn,
Hobe-zhe mir zibn kinder
A meydl zolstu blaybn...

[She] Ikh vel dir hobn zibn kinder
A meydl vel ikh blaybn,
Boy mir oys zibn vign
On holts un on getsaygn—

[He] Ikh vel dir oysboyen zibn vign,
On holts un on getsaygn—
Bizt a kluge un ikh kayn nar—
To lomir beyde blaybn!

TRANSLATION

[She] Lead a bear out of the woods
And teach him how to write,
Then you may, then you shall
Forever mine remain.

[He] I will lead a bear out of the woods
And teach him how to write.
If you will sew seven shirts for me
Without needle or silk cloth.

[She] I will sew seven shirts for you
Without needle or silk cloth,
If you will build me a ladder tall
To reach into the sky.

[He] I will build you a ladder tall
To reach into the sky,
If you will bear me seven children
And virgin yet remain...

[She] I will bear you seven children
And remain a virgin,
If you will make seven cribs for me
Without wood or tools.

[He] I will make seven cribs for you,
Without wood or tools—
But you are wise and I no fool—
So let us both be married!

AMERICAN

[He] You must make me a fine Holland shirt,
Blow, blow, blow ye winds blow,
And not have in it a stitch of needle-work,
Blow, ye winds that arise, blow.

You must wash it in yonder spring, blow, etc.
Where there's never a drop of water in, blow, etc.

You must dry it on yonder thorn, blow, etc.
Where the sun never yet shone on, blow, etc.

[She] My father's got an acre of land, blow, etc.
You must dig it with a goose quill, blow, etc.

You must sow it with one seed, blow, etc.
You must reap it with your thumbnail, blow, etc.

You must thrash it on yonder sea, blow, etc.
And not get it wet or let a kernel be, blow, etc.

You must grind it on yonder hill, blow, etc.
Where there yet has ne'er stood a mill, blow, etc.

When you're done and finished your work, blow, etc.
Bring it unto me, and you shall have your shirt, blow, etc.[15]

A theme not ordinarily found in Yiddish folksong is that of the unfaithful wife, yet parallels of the old English and Scotch song "Our Goodman" (Child No. 274) are included in certain European collections of Yiddish folksongs.

This type of song was quite popular in England, Scotland, the Scandinavian lands, Hungary, Germany, France, Italy, and Russia. It is still current in certain sections of America, and several years ago two variants of the Yiddish song were recorded by the writer in New York City. Dorothy Scarborough, in a note to the Yorkshire variant, which she gives in her book *A Song Catcher in Southern Mountains*, maintains that it is "of unquestionable antiquity."[16] The Child *A* version, the earliest collected, dates from the 18th century.

One of these variants, entitled "Gey Ikh Mir Arayn Tsu Mayn Gelibter Froy" ("I Come To My Beloved Wife"), was collected from a forty-five-year-old man, born in Vilna, Lithuania. The text is given together with an American example entitled "The Sailor's Return."[17]

YIDDISH

Gey ikh mir arayn tsu mayn gelibter froy
Ze ikh mir, eyns un tsvey.
Oyfn vant hengen shverdn,
Eyns un tsvey un dray.
Tu ikh mir a freg bay mayn gelibter froy:
Vos fara shverdn dos iz?
Enfert zi mir—brokmessers,
Di mame shikt dos mir.
Oy, di brokmessers
Mit di shvartse sheydelekh,
Oy, vey, vey, in mayn harts tut mir vey,
Az ikh bin dokh dayn man,
Farvos zol zayn azoy?

Ge ikh mir arayn, etc.
Ze ikh mir, etc.
In kikh shteyen shtivl,
Eyns un tsvey un dray.
Tu ikh mir a freg, etc.
Vos fara shtivl dos iz?
Enfert zi mir—shtek-shikhelekh
Di mame shikt zey mir.
Oy, di shtek-shikhelech,
Mit di hoykhe kholevkes,
Oy, vey, vey, etc.

Gey ikh mir arayn, etc.
Ze ikh mir, etc.
In bet lign kepelekh,
Eyns un tsvey un dray.
Tu ikh mir a freg, etc.
Vos fara kepelekh zenen zey?
Enfert zi mir—kinderlekh
Di mame shikt zey mir.
Oy, di kinderlekh,
Mit di shvartse vontselekh,
Oy vey, vey, etc.

TRANSLATION

I come to my beloved wife,
And I see, one and two.
Swords hang on the wall,
One and two and three.
I ask of my beloved wife:
What kind of swords are these?
She answers, they are chopping-knives
My mother sent to me.
Oh, the chopping-knives,
In their little black sheaths,
Oh woe, woe, my heart pains me so,
For I am your own husband,
And why should this then be?

I come to my beloved wife,
And I see, etc.
Boots stand in the kitchen,
One and two and three.
I ask of my beloved wife,
What kind of boots are these?
She answers, they are slippers
My mother sent to me.
Oh, the little slippers,
With the high tops,
Oh woe, woe, etc.

I come to my beloved wife,
And I see, etc.
Heads lie in the bed,
One and two and three.
I ask, etc.
What kind of heads are these?
She answers—they are children
My mother sent to me.
Oh, the little children,
With the little black moustaches,
Oh woe, woe, etc.

AMERICAN

Home came the sailor, home from the sea,
And there in the stable a strange horse did see.
O wife, now tell me, what can this mean?
A strange brown horse where my mare should have been?
You old fool, you danged fool, you son-of-a-gun, said she:
It's nothing but a milk cow my mother sent to me.
Miles have I sailed, five thousand or more,
But a cow without an udder I never saw before.

Home came the sailor, etc.
And there in the parlor a strange coat saw he.
O wife, etc.
A coat that's not mine where my coat should have been?
You old fool, etc.
It's nothing but a blanket my mother sent to me.
Miles have I sailed, etc.
But buttons on a blanket, I never saw before.

Home came the sailor, etc.
And there in his bed a strange face did see.
O wife, etc.
Another man's head where my own should have been?
You old fool, etc.
It's nothing but a cabbage head my mother sent to me.
Miles have I sailed, etc.
But whiskers on a cabbage head I never saw before.

A theme very common to the folksongs of many peoples is the marriage theme. True to the social pattern which prevailed in many lands for generations, young folks did not select mates by themselves. This task was performed by the parents, with the aid, often, of professional matchmakers. In many songs, the problem is treated in a conversation between mother and daughter and conducted in the question-and-answer manner. The mother may ask the daughter what it is that she wishes. Given a choice of a series of things, the daughter, in the end, chooses a man. In many cases, there is an element of urgency, or pleading, on the part of the daughter. Sometimes the mother is understanding and kind. At other times, she may roundly scold "the young hussy" for being in such a hurry. In each song, there will be reflected a particular locale and the specific mores that prevail.

Below is a variant of the Yiddish "Yome, Yome, Zing Mir A Lidele" ("Yome, Yome, Sing me a Little Song"), which is very popular among Yiddish-speaking communities the world over and which this writer recently recorded from a group of first- and second-generation American-Jewish children. An American example entitled "Whistle, Daughter, Whistle,"[18] follows.

YIDDISH

Yomele, Yomele, zing mir a lidele,
Vos dos meydele vil?
Dos meydele vil a kleydele hobn,
Darf men geyn der shnayderin zogn.
Neyn, mamenyu, neyn,
Du kenst mikh nit farshteyn,
Du veyst nit vos ikh meyn.

Yomele, etc.
Vos dos, etc.
Dos meydele vil a por shikelekh hobn,

Darf men geyn dem shusterl zogn.
Neyn, etc.
Du kenst, etc.
Du veyst, etc.

Yomele, etc.
Vos dos, etc.
Dos meydele vil a khosendl hobn,
Darf men geyn dem shadkhendl zogn.
Yo, mamenyu, yo,
Du kenst mikh shoyn farshteyn,
Du veyst shoyn vos ikh meyn!

TRANSLATION

Yomele, Yomele, sing me a little song,
What does the little maid want?
The little maid wants a little dress,
We must go to the seamstress.
No, Mother, No,
You cannot understand me,
You don't know what I mean.

Yomele, etc.
What, etc.
The little maid wants a pair of shoes,
We must go to the cobbler.
No, etc.
You cannot, etc.
You don't, etc.

Yomele, etc.
What, etc.
The little maid wants a bridegroom,
We must go to the matchmaker.
Yes, Mother, yes,
You now do understand me,
You now know what I mean!

Whistle, daughter, whistle, and you shall have a cow,
I can't whistle, mother, because I don't know how.

Whistle, daughter, whistle, and you shall have a goat,
I can't whistle, mother, because it hurts my throat.

Whistle, daughter, whistle, and you shall have a pig,
I can't whistle, mother, because I am too big.

Whistle, daughter, whistle, and you shall have a man
(Daughter whistles) . . . I've just found out I can!

A nineteenth-century theme which appears both in the folksong and literature of almost all European peoples, as well as of
the United States, is the theme which contrasts rich and poor,
extols the creativeness of man and decries the powers that de-
prive him of the fruits of his labor. Rooted in the conditions
brought about by the Industrial Revolution in England, this
theme later drew sustenance from the literary trends describing the rapid industrialization of labor and turbulent historical
occurrences in England and on the Continent. It is sometimes
maintained that this theme first appeared in English literature
in a poem entitled "Song To The Men Of England," written
by Percy Bysshe Shelley in 1819, following the tragic Peterloo
massacre.

With the spread of literacy and communication, a kind of
"semi" folksong sprang up among the people. These often consisted of texts by *known* authors, set to tunes by *anonymous*
composers. Toward the end of the nineteenth century, these
increased considerably, and many a song, even with both author
and composer known, achieved the popularity of a folksong.
Such were the "sung" poems, for instance, of the three Ameri-
can-Yiddish poets Morris Winchevsky, Morris Rosenfeld,
David Edelshtat. During the eighties and nineties of the nineteenth century, a number of their poems were set to music by

anonymous composers and gained such a wide popularity that they were sung in a number of variants, *both in the United States and in Eastern Europe.* These songs deal in large part with the theme here mentioned.

The most popular song of this type here is "Un Du Akerst Un Du Zeyst" ("And You Plow And You Sow"), which is a Yiddish translation made by Dr. Chayim Zhitlowsky (1856–1946), in 1889, of a text by the German poet Georg Herwegh (1817–1875), written in 1863, which in turn seems to have been inspired by the Shelley poem mentioned above.

Below, three stanzas of a Yiddish folksong are given. This well-known lullaby, "Shlof Mayn Kind, Shlof Keseyder" ("Sleep My Child, Sleep"), deals with the theme of rich versus poor. Also included are four stanzas of an American version which reflects the sentiments of a West Virginia factory hand.

YIDDISH

Shlof mayn kind, shlof keseyder,
Zingen vel ikh dir a lid.
Az du mayn kind vest elter vern,
Vestu visn an untershid.

Az du mayn kind vest elter vern,
Vestu vern mit laytn glaykh.
Demlt vestu gevoyre vern
Vos heyst orim un vos heyst raykh.

Di tayerste palatsn, di shenste hayzer,
Dos alts makht der oriman,
Nor veystu ver es tut in zey woynen?
Gor nisht er, nor der raykher man.[19]

TRANSLATION

Sleep my child, sleep,
I will sing you a song.
When you, my child, will grow older,
You will know the difference.

When you, my child, will grow older,
You will be like all of us.
Then you will realize
What it is to be poor, and what it is to be rich.

The fanciest palaces, the finest houses,
All of these are made by the poor man;
But do you know who lives in them?
Not he at all, but the rich man.

AMERICAN

We rise up early in the morn
And work all day real hard,
To buy our little meat and bread
And sugar, tea and lard.

Our children they grow up unlearned,
No time to go to school;
Almost before they've learned to walk
They learn to spin or spool.

The folks in town who dress so fine
And spend their money free,
Will hardly look at a factory hand
Who dresses like you and me.

Well, let them wear their watches fine,
Their rings and pearly strings;
When the day of judgment comes
We'll make them shed their pretty things.[20]

We hope that in this paper we have succeeded in displaying a comparative view of several of the many vari-colored, vari-textured threads that go into the mosaic called Jewish folksong. For the student who combines an aptitude for history with a love of music and literature, there is an almost unlimited field of research in the folksong and folk literature of a single people. The comparative field, however, leads us to the world of many peoples, and to a closer understanding of the differences that separate us, as well as of the similarities that bind us.

Notes

1. *Shtudies Vegn Yidisher Folks-shafung* (New York, 1952), p. 18.
2. *Ibid.*, p. 21.
3. *JAF*, LXII (1949), 382.
4. *Ibid.*, LXII, 410.
5. *Ibid.*, LXII, 411.
6. *Muzik Bay Yidn* (Montreal, 1940), p. 154.
7. Shulsinger *Haggadah Shel Pesach*, Abraham Regelson, trans. (New York, 1951), pp. 59 ff.
8. Recorded from a 23-year-old man born in New York City.
9. Ruth Rubin, "Nineteenth Century Yiddish Folksongs of Children in Eastern Europe," *JAF*, LXV (1952), 240.
10. W. W. Newell, "The Passover Song of the Kid and an Equivalent from New England," *JAF*, XVIII (1908), 33–48.
11. *Muzik Bay Yidn*, p. 154.
12. *Haggadah Shel Pesach*, pp. 63–64.
13. W. W. Newell, *op. cit.*
14. Ruth Rubin, *A Treasury of Jewish Folksong* (New York, 1950), pp. 44, 97, 42, and 58 respectively.
15. Eloise Hubbard Linscott, *Folk Songs of Old New England* (New York, 1939), pp. 169 ff.
16. New York, 1937. "The Child *A* version of 274, the earliest collected, dates from the 18th century; the Child *B* version was translated into German by Fr. Wilhelm Meyer in 1790. It was printed as a broadside and widely sold in all parts of Europe. The Yiddish text from Lithuania is close enough to the Child *B* version to show that it *must* be derived from the Meyer broadside translation" (communication from Dr. Warren E. Roberts).
17. Frank Shay, *Pious Friends and Drunken Companions* (New York, 1923).
18. Margaret Thorne, *Songs From Story Parade* (Brooklyn, N. Y., 1945), p. 24.
19. Ruth Rubin, *op. cit.*, pp. 22 f.
20. John Greenway, *American Folk Songs of Protest* (Philadelphia, 1953), pp. 140–41.

Bridal Songs and
Ceremonies from
San'a, Yemen

JOHANNA SPECTOR New York City

by Johanna Spector

From 1951 to 1953, while working at the Hebrew University in Jerusalem, I recorded the music, the customs, and the ceremonies of Oriental Jewish communities transplanted to Israel, among them the Jewish community from San'a, capital of Yemen.

I worked primarily with new immigrants, who were not yet influenced by the new Israeli environment. Although Yemenite Jews of both sexes are reluctant to sing their songs out of context, I was permitted after much explanation and persuasion to record numerous songs.[1]

The most elaborate celebrations are those reserved for a wedding, which is the most memorable event in the life of a Yemenite Jew. Marriages are arranged by the elders of the families; women are rarely consulted. Occasionally children are betrothed at birth. More often the bride is about nine years old, and the bridegroom may be thirteen or fourteen. The feelings of the bridegroom and the bride, who may not meet until the wedding ceremony itself, are not taken into consideration. After the wedding the young couple lives with the bridegroom's family.

The wedding date is set a year in advance. In this way time is allowed for the necessary preparations, such as the storing of grain, beans, nuts, and rose water for ceremonial purposes, the making of wine and arrack,[2] the provision of elaborate wedding clothes for bridegroom and bride, and the purchase of traditionally prescribed gifts.

The wedding ceremonies themselves last two weeks. The first week is called "The Week of the Wedding," the second, "The Seven Days of Feasting." The first week is a busy one for the bride and groom, who are given special daily assignments. During the second week, which is free of special assignments and ceremonies, there are festive meals for the numerous guests, ample food (provided primarily by the guests themselves), alcoholic drinks, and entertainment furnished by professional singers and dancers.

Men and women celebrate separately, the men in the large front room (the "hall") and the women in their own quarters. Of all the women, only the bride is privileged to greet the male guests, and she only for a short time right after the wedding ceremony.

Officially, the wedding starts with the outgoing of the Sabbath, called "The Sabbath of the Beginning" (*Shabboth al-bīd*).[3] Rabbis and guests honor the bridegroom and his family with their presence. For the bridegroom, however, the wedding week starts on the preceding Thursday. He assembles his "grooms," who accompany him throughout the wedding, takes his ritual bath, has his first leisurely festive meals, visits the markets to buy narcotics and sweets, and spends an entire afternoon with his friends drinking coffee, smoking waterpipes, chewing leaves of *qat* (*Catha edulis forsk*), which produces an effect like that of opium or cola, and composing invitations to rabbis and male guests. Later on, the celebrations become religious in nature: prayers are recited, and Hebrew devotional songs are sung.

The bride's celebrations start on Sunday, after the *Shabboth al-bīd*, and are of an entirely different nature. No prayers are said, and all the songs are sung in Arabic, since the Jewish women in Yemen neither speak, read, nor write Hebrew.

The first day, Sunday (*Yōm Al-Ḥinna*), is the day when women and children assemble both in the bride's and the bridegroom's houses to be painted for the wedding. Leaves of henna

(*Lawsonia inermis*) are dried, ground, soaked in water (for the bride, in rose water), and kneaded in the presence of the bride. The resulting thick paste is then applied to hands and feet, but not beyond the wrists and ankles. The painted limbs are wrapped in cloth in order that the dresses will not be soiled After four or five hours, the bandages are removed, and the painted skin is exposed to the air. According to Rabbi Qafaḥ (see note 1), the color achieved, an orange-red, is considered "attractive to people familiar with the tradition." After a few days, the color becomes darker, and people say: "His grandmother has already arrived" (meaning "Hurry, it is getting late, the wedding is approaching!"). Weeks later the color fades, but the nails remain dark until they grow out.

While her hands and feet are bandaged, the bride sits high on a pillow, surrounded by family and friends. Next to her sits at least one married young woman (*shakma*) dressed like the bride herself. The "unclean" and "harmful" (demons) are guarded against by placing large lighted candles and vessels with burning oil in the room. In front of the bride on a low table stands a basket with eggs, flour, and durra—symbols of fertility. Rue (*Ruta graveolens*) is distributed throughout the room, and a generous bunch of this green plant is fastened to the headdress of the bride for her protection. At this time the following song is recited:

1. It Is The Hour of the Merciful
(*Recording No. 236*)

It is the hour of the Merciful,
And the devils are of no account.
The devils are in the mountains of China
And are diving into the seas.

The green rue adorns thy head, O moon,
Stretch thy hands out for adornments,
Rejoice of thy youth,

Stretch thy hand out for coloring
Since this is the custom of the girls.*

Adagio (♩=108)   Song No. 1

The adagio tempo of the song expresses dignity and awe. This sounds melancholic, as do almost all the Yemenite wedding songs, but it is difficult to say whether melancholy is intended. No dynamics, such as piano, forte, crescendo, or diminuendo, are ever used. The range of the song is a fifth. The mode sounds major to Western ears, whereas to Near Eastern people its *maqām* (oriental melodic pattern, "mode") would be *rast*. But the Yemenites do not seem to know the Arabic system of *maqāmāt* and are, of course, unfamiliar with the Western "major" and "minor" scales. Thus far it has not been possible to ascertain whether southern Arabia has a musical system of its own, or at least names for certain modes in use. The form is a three-part melody, *ABC*, in which *A* has three metrical units, *B*, two; and *C*, one. *C*, in order to fit the text, is remarkably "condensed."

The rhythm is rather simple and the meter a flexible 4/4. The instrument used for accompaniment is a *ṣaḥn*, a copper tray beaten with a metal key. The *ṣaḥn* sets the pace of the song and supplies the magical background with its sonorous bell-like sound.

---

* The texts and music appearing in this paper are from the Johanna Spector collection, Hebrew University, Jerusalem. The texts were translated from the Arabic by Johanna Spector and Rabbi Qafaḥ.

In the following music transcription and in the other transcriptions included, the first scale given is the one on which the melody is constructed.

On the second day, Monday (*Yōm Al-Tadrūfa*), the women invite singers and dancers to the bride's house, and in the afternoon the festivities start. While the bride is being dressed in her official wedding clothes (*ghalāya*,[4] *tisbūk lūlū*,[5] and other kinds of jewelry), the chief singer (*mghanniya*[6]) begins her song, accompanying herself on drums and cymbals. She starts in a slow tempo, conveying the dreamy mood of a love song, and as her song continues, sings not only of love and passion, but also of the privileges and duties of a young wife, of her joys and sorrows and marital difficulties. News of the day, recent happenings, and gossip are woven into the songs, making them a running commentary on current events, a sort of oral newspaper.[7] After the singing, professional dancers take over. They are accompanied by drums, cymbals, and wordless singing. The music is fast, stirring the dancers to swift movement. During the performance *assp* is served. This is a sweet dish consisting of raisins, dates, durra, certain kinds of roasted grain, beans, and candy. Handkerchiefs brought along by the guests serve them as dishes, since plates are unknown. Children are served twice. Singing and dancing continue until late at night while the black color, *tadrūfa*, is applied to hands and feet according to traditional patterns. The *tadrūfa* of the bride extends to the elbow, that of the other women only to the wrist.

The following song, a love song, speaks of the bridegroom's longing to see his bride and, since she is closely guarded, of the impossibility of such an undertaking.[8]

2. O Girl, O You White One
(Recording No. 232)

"O girl, O you white one,
Our[9] delight,
If you only could come to our party!"
She said: "With great pleasure,
But what about the guard?

I wish I were a wonder-bird,
I would not be ashamed
To ascend to the castle at night
And let the beloved descend before me
And the burning lamps[10] in my hands. . . ."*

Presto (♩=192)   Song No. 2

Sigha

Arabic Sigha

The tempo is presto, expressing a troubled and longing mood. The range of the melody is a seventh, A starting a fourth higher, which is not unusual in the melodic construction of

* In musical transcriptions 2, 3, 4 and 6, the symbol / appears before certain musical notes. These notes have to be performed 50 *Ellis Cents* lower than a musical note without this symbol. Such a symbol changes the intervallic structure of a musical mode. See example below:

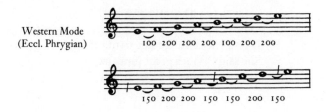

Western Mode
(Eccl. Phrygian)   100 200 200 200 100 200 200

                      150 200 200 150 150 200 150

the Near East. The mode is reminiscent of the Arabic Sigha or the Greek Dorian, only a minor third lower. The rhythm is a dance rhythm, a strict, rather regular 3/4 time, with two eighth notes and two quarter notes to a measure. The form is $A(ab)B(cd)$. The accompaniment is played again on the *ṣaḥn*, this time with bare hands on rim and center.

On the third day, Tuesday (*Al-Naqsh*), the women arrive for the noon meal and stay until late at night. Singers and dancers entertain the bride and guests while coffee is served. The bride is dressed in exquisite clothes adorned with gold and silver jewelry. Her hands and feet are painted again, now for the third time. In the painting process, called *al-naqsh*, graceful white lines and dots are applied to the face and forehead and the hands and feet.

It is an old custom that the bride should be surrounded by young women in bridal garb. The privilege of wearing wedding clothes is granted to recently married young women or to young mothers of first-born children not older than 3–4 months. These young women—sometimes as many as ten—are called *shakma*. They are dressed exactly like the bride herself so that the demons and evil spirits, who are always intent on harming the bride, will be confused. The *shakmas* provide the *assp* for the day, and the singers sing songs in honor of these special guests. After the al-naqsh ceremony, various songs are recited. Here is one for the occasion.

3. My Beloved, Do Not Come Yet
(*Recording No. 230*)

(He) "My beloved, do not come yet,
And I shall not come.[11]
But the best friendship prevails
When one meets.

Beautiful beloved, come always,
Whom do I have besides you?
Why are you worried?

I should like to be
Your umbrella against the sun
Or a cigarette[12]
To be held in your finger tips!

(She, addressing a third party)

I swear by the Lord,
Should you see the handsome one,
Tell him he should come to see us,
And we[13] will come to see him.

Rather fast (♩=132)   Song No. 3

(Prelude on ṣahn)

Sasgar

Arabic Sasgar

This is a fast, joyous love song. The range of the melody is
an octave, the first part of the melody moving from the finalis
a fifth (sixth) upward, while the second half of the melody
moves a third downward. It is also remarkable that section *A*

ends a second lower than section *B*. This always occurs in the
same manner. At the same time, the singer gradually and continually raises his pitch level, the last verse often being sung
as much as a minor third higher than the first verse. The
singer looks upon this as a performance practice, not as transposition. The mode, as put down in modern musical notation,
is reminiscent of the Greek Hypolydian or the Arabic *Sasgar*,
allowing for transposition (finalis F to finalis D).[14] In determining the mode I have omitted consideration of the passing
tone, G-natural, which is actually 50 *Ellis Cents* higher than
G-natural and 50 *Ellis Cents* lower than G-sharp. The rhythm
is a dance rhythm in 4/4 time (8/8). The form is *AABB*, and
the preceding prelude as well as the interludes before each
repetition are played on a *sahn*. The instrument is rather independent in this melody, producing complicated syncopated
rhythms and shifting accents.

The fourth day, Wednesday (*Yom Al-Ara, Yom Al
Ghalfa*[15]), has arrived. This is the most important festival day
in the home of the bride. Before sunrise, at about two o'clock in
the morning, the butcher is sent for. He brings an ox, and the
shohet (ritual slaughterer) kills the animal ritually, while the
entire household and guests look on. Final preparations are
hurriedly made, and a special messenger is sent out to invite
the guests who would not deem it polite to appear after the
first invitation, which has been sent out before the beginning
of the wedding week. This time, not only the guests of the
bride's family are expected, but the guests of the bridegroom's
family as well. On the following day all of the guests are invited to the bridegroom's house.

The noon meal of the day is called "The Meal of the Betrothal Presents." Many of the guests arrive in a formal procession, bringing the traditional gifts of bridegroom to bride.
The bearer of the gifts is an honored woman of the bridegroom's household, but never his mother.

The procession is led by a professional female singer with

drum and cymbals. Little girls and women follow in all their finery and gold and silver jewelry, carrying lighted candles in their hands. The gift bearer walks in the center of the procession surrounded by candle bearers. Into a new, colorful silk kerchief are tied the presents of the bridegroom to his bride, selected according to tradition, not individual taste. There are trousers (*kabīr*[16]) for the bride to wear on her wedding day and on special occasions thereafter, e.g., in the role of *shakma* or on Pessach night. The trousers—made of a fine woolen fabric with beautiful embroidery at the cuffs, from which they take their name—are narrow and as tight-fitting as stockings; and their price is twenty to thirty riyals (a man's wages for a month). There are also two silken kerchiefs, one for the bride, one for the mother; the black *antari* or dress (often made of velvet, embroidered with silver and gold threads, and adorned with fine jewelry worked into the dress by a silversmith); and the *qarqūsh*, a tight-fitting hood made of brocade and lined with red, green, or blue fabric. The *qarqūsh*, at this point, is still unadorned; the gold and silver coins, the silver drops, resembling a veil, for the forehead, and all the jewels which will later adorn the headgear will be given by the bride's father. This is the "dowry" of the bride, which she is permitted to take back home in case of a divorce. The bridegroom furnishes also the candles for the ceremonies, the soaps, the dyes, the rose water, and a traditional comb.

On Wednesday afternoon the bride is taken to a room on the second floor, which is called *al Hagra* (the upper story of the house overlooking the inner court.) Her hair is uncovered, combed, and arranged in the presence of the guests, and then cut over the forehead with a razor blade. From now on, no hair must escape from under the *qarqūsh*. During this ceremony no man is allowed in the vicinity of the room.

Before dark on Wednesday the bride undergoes a severe test. A piece of cotten is soaked in egg and put to the bride's cheek while a burning candle is brought close to her cheek.

If the heat of the lighted candle causes the piece of cotton to stick to her cheek, the girl is pronounced immodest and not innocent! Again singers and dancers entertain the party. The chief singer vigorously beats a drum and cymbals and creates an exciting tempo.

The following song admirably conveys the mood of the young bride, who is nervous and frightened before her official betrothal at night, and her mother's reply expresses the inevitability and beauty of the event.

4. Protect Me, O Mother

(*Recording No. 235*)

"Protect me, oh mother,
And increase your guarding!"
"One has already sufficiently guarded you,
The stars are glistening now,
Glowing candles are lit before you
In great European lanterns.
The castles of San'a are rejoicing in your honor,
And the flower-laden branches adorn the dwellings."

The transcription of this song is given on the following page. The tempo is a dragging andante, and the range of the melody is a fourth with an occasional extension to a fifth by the addition of a pitch a second below the finalis. The mode is similar to the Arabic *Bayāt* or the Greek Phrygian, only half a tone lower (C-sharp instead of D in *Bayāt*). The rhythm is a so-called "free" (flexible) rhythm, the Arabic *Tartīl*. The form is *ABA₁B₁*, with the second part of the melody embellished and shortened (*A₁B₁*). The accompaniment on the *ṣaḥn* starts with a prelude of two bars and continues throughout the song, beating a syncopated rhythm.

Wednesday night (*Lel Al-Qiddūsh*) is the night of the betrothal. Everyone has gone to the bridegroom's house, so the "hall" is deserted. The bride is led into the hall dressed in her

Andante (♩=92)   Song No. 4

precious wedding attire and wearing on her head many pounds
of gold and silver jewelry with pearls and precious stones
fashioned together with fragrant flowers into a gigantic
bridal crown. This crown, which is called a *mashbaha* and is
about a yard high, takes many hours of patience and skill to
create. While work on the crown proceeds, songs like the
following are sung.

The text of Song No. 5 is a version of No. 2, but the melody differs. The tempo is fast, the range of the melody one

5. I Wish I Were a Wonder-bird
(*Recording No. 234*)

I wish I were a wonder-bird.
I would ascend to the castle at night,
And I would bring my beloved with me
With the candles in my hands.
O girl, O white one, our delight,
If only you could be at our party!

"With great pleasure," she said,
"But who will talk to the guard?"

Presto ($\downarrow$=92)   Song No. 5

octave, and the mode similar to the European minor. The rhythm of part *B* is simple, in 3/4 time. (I could not transcribe part *A*; the pitches were very indefinite, and the singers, apparently unable to agree on them, sang two different versions.) The form consists of a four-bar question and a four-bar answer.

The bride is led by three women into a small adjoining room called *kumme* where she remains for a while. Her father locks the door from the outside and puts the key into his pocket.

As soon as the bridegroom's party arrives, the young men rush forward and post themselves at the door of the *kumme* in order to catch a glimpse of the bride at the first opportunity. This is for good luck.

Rabbis and bridegroom are seated near the door of the bridal chamber, and the hall is filled to capacity with the guests of both families. The *ketuba* (marriage contract) is ceremoniously recited by the rabbi; the coin of betrothal, which serves instead of a ring at the ceremony, is examined by three witnesses; and the marriage formula is chanted by the rabbi and repeated after him by the bridegroom word for word. During all this time the bride has remained in her chamber, which is still locked.

After the ceremony, the *kumme* is unlocked by the bride's father, and the bridegroom, accompanied by witnesses, enters the chamber and offers the bride a glass of wine. After having tasted a little, the bride returns the glass to the bridegroom. With the silver coin in his hand, he now recites the marriage formula and hands the coin and the *ketuba* to the bride. The *al-shar'a*, an expert on wedding ceremonies who dresses the bride and supervises the skin-painting, translates the Aramaic formula into Arabic for the benefit of the bride, who knows neither Hebrew nor Aramaic. She also explains to the bride the meaning of the ceremony and the marriage contract. After the bridegroom and the witnesses have left, the bride is again locked into the chamber.

The fifth day, Thursday, is the "Day of Entering." No one sleeps from Wednesday until Thursday night. A multitude of tasks (slaughtering, frying, baking, cooking, grinding, kneading, and soaking) must be finished, and neighbors and relatives are summoned to help. The noise is great; people are running in and out of house and court, calling and shouting to one another. The bridegroom is the only one who is not called upon to help, and his only concern is to find a fairly quiet spot in which to get some sleep. Meanwhile the "grooms" arrange the room assigned to the young couple by the bridegroom's parents. They bring new couches, pillows, and covers and adorn the walls with *senadar*—a gay flowery cloth— and set the low coffee table, placing it in the middle of the room. A big bowl of *assp* and a large vessel containing fried meat and two loaves of bread are placed on the table; also, the presents that the bride and bridegroom have given to each other. The bridegroom gives his bride a silver box containing twelve rings of silver filigree and two rings containing precious stones. He also gives her a small leather bag filled with perfume. The bridegroom receives in turn a fine silver narghile and a box filled with tobacco. The box is made of wood and is beautifully carved and inlaid with mother-of-pearl. The tobacco is moistened with rose water and mixed with fragrant spices. After having sprinkled the room with perfume, the "grooms" close the door tightly from the outside to preserve the pleasant fragrance for the young couple.

In the morning the bridegroom and the male guests go to the synagogue to pray, and he is given the honor of reading from the Torah scroll. The bride, meanwhile, is being dressed by the *al-shar'a* and entertained by the musicians.

The drum of the *mghanniya* announces that the bride is ready, and the bridal procession moves from the bride's to the bridegroom's house. She is accompanied by the *al-shar'a* and followed by her mother and all the women guests. Drums and cymbals are played in front of the bride, and the women voice their joyous trills. Children with lighted wax candles lead the procession. At a distance of about ten meters, the procession of the bridegroom follows. He, too, is preceded by children (but fewer in number) who are also bearing candles.

As soon as the bride arrives at the doorstep of her home-to-be, the mother of the bridegroom pours water on the threshold. She welcomes the bride affectionately, kisses her, and says: "Be it the will of the Lord that you remain my son's wife all your life." The entire group then proceeds to the big hall of the house, the music never ceasing.

While the future mother-in-law leads the young bride up the stairs into the house, women and children sing the song of the "Kadhi Flower." The kadhi flower is famous for its large, pure-white blossoms of exceptionally strong fragrance. It is used for making spices and perfume, and the Yemenites insist that the fragrance can be smelled at the distance of a two-day march! The song compares the bride to a kadhi flower.

6. The Kadhi Flower
(Recording No. 241) *

The melody is beautifully expressive. The tempo is adagio, and the range of the melody is a seventh. The mode contains two augmented seconds similar to the *Hijāz-kār*. The rhythm is free (*tartīl*); the form, *AB*.

Meanwhile, the bridegroom and the male guests have returned to the house and assembled in the "room of entering." Prayers are said, rose water is sprinkled on all the guests, wine is poured into a glass, and seven blessings are recited by the

* *Hijāz-kār* (No. 6) and *Hijāz* (No. 9), which are *maqāmāt* with augmented seconds, occur so rarely in Yemenite Jewish music that it has to be assumed that the melodies have been created under an outside influence. San'a had been under Turkish occupation as early as the 16th century, and the Turks were continually in contact with the Jews. It is not impossible, therefore, that the Jews have learned the melodic patterns, otherwise alien to their own music, from the Turks. Turkish music has both these *maqāmāt*, and they are used extensively in folk music as well as in art music. The melodies themselves (Nos. 6 and 9), however, do not seem to strike a familiar chord with Turkish musicians who have listened to them and seem to be creations of Yemen.

rabbi. Afterward, some of the consecrated wine is transferred to a small glass called the *sheva* (Hebrew, "seven," referring to the seven blessings). As soon as the guests shout "*sheva*', *sheva*'," the door to the adjoining room opens, and the bride, her face covered by a heavily embroidered scarf, appears on the doorstep, the *al-shar'a* beside her. The rabbi escorts the bridegroom to the bride, the *al-shar'a* lifts the "veil," and the bridegroom hands the *sheva* to the bride, who drinks from it. Upon the cry of *sheva*', *sheva*', all pregnant women, or women nursing children under three months of age, turn their faces to the wall for fear that they may bear their children prematurely or that their children may become feeble-minded.

After the short *sheva* ceremony, the rabbi and bridegroom return to the men, who receive them standing and singing *w'halleluya*. Prayers and blessings follow, and a small glass of wine is brought to the mother (or grandmother) of the bridegroom. Meanwhile, the women surrounding the bride eat sweets and fruit and sing various songs.

7. Who Will Tell Me?
(*Recording No. 228*)

Who will tell me
Whether I shall still have the pleasure
Of bringing good tidings to the black one?
Who will let me know
Whereto my friend has vanished,
Which way he went,
And how I can find his abode?[17]

The transcription of this song is given on the following page. The tempo is andante con moto, and the range of the melody is a sixth with an occasional extension of a lower fourth as an upbeat. The mode is in D-flat major, the melody ending on F the third. The song is almost European in character as far as

Andante con moto (♩=100)   Song No. 7

the melodic line is concerned. The form is *A* and *B*, *A* consisting of two clear cut parts, *a* and *b*, *B* somewhat condensed into a shorter phrase as originally conceived. The melismatic character of *B* suggests that originally a much longer tune was adapted to a short text. Melodically, the song is the most sophisticated of our examples. European influence can be excluded, since Yemen was always one of the so-called "forbidden countries," where strangers were not welcome and expeditions were discouraged. The rhythm of the first part is a rather steady 6/8; the second part is free. There is no instrumental accompaniment.

8. Thou Beloved of the Heart
(*Recording No. 229*)

Thou beloved of the heart
Who love passionately,[18]

Go and search for a beloved,
Whose love is as passionate as thine.
Oh, my dear one, vanished from my heart,
Whereto, my friend?

People in love should fear the Lord,
How can a beloved turn from her lover?

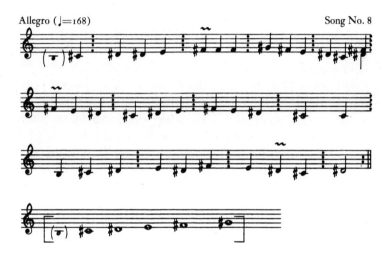

The tempo is allegro. The song is child-like in character—one which could have originated almost anywhere in the world because of its simplicity. The range is within a fifth, the mode major, beginning and ending on a third. Surprisingly, there are no changes in pitch during the repetitions. Also, the harmonic third, which is not an accidental harmonization, is repeated stubbornly each time as if intended. The song is in strict 3/4 time.

The bride is taken to the room which has been prepared for the young couple during the night and is seated on a pillow, with her husband's pillow (*farsh*) placed next to her. Since there are no chairs in Yemen, pillows or small mattresses are used for comfortable sitting.[19]

Before joining the bride, the bridegroom takes off his *Tefillin* (phylacteries), hands them to one of his grooms, and, in the company of the rabbi, enters the room of *Yiḥud* (union). Water is brought for the washing of hands; then, after removing the *Tallith* (prayer shawl) from the bridegroom, the rabbi seats him next to the bride, blesses both of them, and finally leaves the room, closing the door behind him.

For the first time the bridegroom and bride are alone. He sits uncomfortably next to the girl who is now his wife, says the blessings over the food, partakes of it, and urges the girl to do likewise. But she refuses as she has been taught, so that the young husband may not have the impression that she is greedy. He tries to make conversation, gives his wife the presents on the table before them, that is, the silver rings and the perfume; but the girl is shy and self-conscious and hardly knows what to say. "Both tremble in their entire being."[20] It is the first time that either of them has been alone with a member of the opposite sex outside the immediate family. After the bride has been offered a small glass of wine, all topics of conversation are exhausted. For one and a half hours the young couple sit cross-legged on the floor, hardly exchanging a word. Both feel relieved when the door finally opens, and the guests appear in groups to pay their respects to the young couple.

The marriage is usually not consummated because of the extreme youth of the couple and because of their fatigue after an entire week of celebration with little sleep and unusual excitement. It is reliably reported that most of these child-marriages remain unconsummated for a longer or shorter period after the wedding.[21]

The young couple receive the guests for an hour, offering everybody wine or arrack and fried fowl. The bowls of food are replenished as soon as they are empty, "until everyone is satisfied."[22] After the reception the *al-shar'a* comes for the bride's jewelry and bridal garments and leaves her in a plain dress, which she has worn underneath her magnificent bridal garments. The bride then remains at her husband's side for another half hour, afterward joining the other women, while her husband remains in "the room of entering," smoking the narghile and talking to his friends.

The *s'ūdhath miṣwō*, the most important and solemn meal of the wedding, again unites all the male guests, who first pray and then make speeches, sing, eat, and drink. The behavior during the meal is decorous, and although there is a great deal of food on the tables, the guests eat slowly and moderately. At the same time, the women celebrate in their room, singing and dancing, and eating the same dishes as the men, but not drinking alcoholic beverages. In order that the solemnity of the occasion may not be disturbed, the children are fed at home.

9. My Heart Loves Flirtation
(*Recording No. 227*)

My heart loves flirtation
And longs for delight—
Oh mother, if I only had
My musical instrument with me!

My heart loves you,
But your mother does not permit it.
I wish a snake would bite her
In the black of her eye!

The transcription of this song is given on the following page. The tempo is andante. The mode is the Arabic *Hijāz*, which never occurs in Yemenite liturgy but apparently does in folksong. The meter is a flexible 4/4, some bars being longer than others, and the melody is obviously fitted to the text. The asterisks mark the indefinite pitch of the tone, which is halfway between G and G-sharp. The chromatic ascent desired by the singers has to be indicated in modern notation by G–G-sharp. The first verse starts with B, the second verse a half tone

Andante (♩=96 increasing to 112)   1st verse   Song No.9

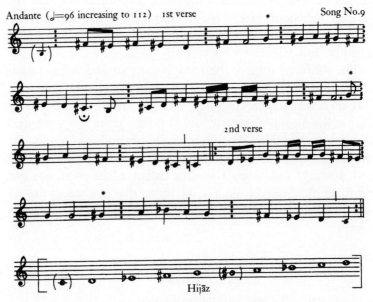

higher. The first verse is sung a half tone lower than the second verse, the singer not yet having warmed up. The form is extremely simple, consisting only of a question and an answer. This short melody, *A (ab)*, is repeated with slight variations. The song also reminds one of the Mediterranean dance songs, though European influence has to be ruled out.

10. I Would Like to Be a Bird
(Recording No. 234)

I would like to be a bird
And have wings;
I would protect my friend
From the heat of the sun.

I would like to be a bird
And have wings;
I would protect the boy
On the camel.

I would like to be a bird
And have wings wide
Like the branches of a tree;
I would protect my friend
On the horse.

Allegro (♩=138)   Song No. 10

The tempo is allegro. The mode would be pentatonic if one
disregarded the passing D-sharp. The rhythm is free, reminiscent of Arabic desert songs. The accompaniment on the *ṣaḥn*
is intricate and changing. The form is *A (abc) B (d)*.

11. The Teeth of My Friend Are Like Hail
(The melody is the same as the previous one, only slower.)

The teeth of my friend are like hail
His locks are without number.
My beloved friend has departed
And gone away burning me with fire....
Who will give me to you
And who will give you to us?[23]

12. Who Will Bring It About?
(*Recording No. 237*)

Who will bring it about
That somebody[24] shall catch you

And like one who is hunting
Put you in the crevice of a rock?

I wish I were a rue
On the top of a mountain.[25]
I would remain a bachelor
And not marry!

The text is interesting and unusual as to content. It speaks about a man who does not want to get married, who would like to be a plant with magical attributes, like the rue, that would ward off the evil spirits.

The melody is fast moving, allegro; the range is a seventh; and the mode is similar to the Arabic *Bayāt* or Greek Phrygian. The meter alternates between 3/4 and 2/4. The form is $A(aa')$, ending on the fifth, and $B(bc)$ ending on the finalis.

Friday commences the *"Seven Days of Feasting."* From this day on every guest brings his own food. Men and women continue celebrating separately, the men staying late at night, the women leaving earlier, having to care for the children at home.

On the following Thursday night (six days later) all official celebrating and feasting cease. Only the "grooms" assemble for an hour or so. The wedding is over, and on Sunday the young husband resumes his work and the normal routine of the day.

On Friday morning the young husband has breakfast in his father-in-law's house, with the male members of the family present. It is an ancient custom to invite the husband alone, the bride not being permitted to leave the house of her husband for two months.[26] If the young wife is physically mature, she will be permitted to visit her father's house once a week after a month has passed; but even these visits have to take place after dark, when "the devils are of no account" (see song No. 1).

According to the explanation given by Rabbi Yosēf Qafaḥ, brides, being very young, would refuse to return to their husbands and relatives-in-law if they were given the opportunity to visit their own families. Thus, in order that the girls may become accustomed to their new surroundings and new relatives and forget their childhood homes, they are required to remain in their new homes for at least thirty days and thirty nights.

After the official two-week celebration, the next two Sabbaths are also celebrated. On Sunday morning, after the fifth Sabbath, the doors of the house are closed to guests and are not reopened until the following year on the day of *Brith Milah* (circumcision of the first-born male child).

While tape-recording the preceding songs, I was unable to learn anything about the music from the Yemenite Jews themselves, who neither know music nor sing a melody unrelated to a text. Therefore, straight and unselective recording was required. Very often the melodies were unsure and low-pitched at the beginning, as if the singer were afraid of what he or she was doing. Many an informant asked me whether the tape-recorder would not harm him. But even the most intimidated singer became more confident after a few verses, and the melodies reflected his confidence by being on pitch. Some of the melodies were clear from the first verse on, after the singers had warmed up.

It has to be noted that in almost all cases the text is more important to the singer than the melody and that melodies are often mutilated in order to fit a shorter text. If a text line becomes longer, the melody has to be extended; if the text line becomes shorter, the melody has to be shortened as well. On the other hand, repetition of syllables and the interpolation of meaningless sounds have not been observed.

The relation of the tonality of Yemenite melodies to known Near Eastern systems has still to be investigated. In the preceding twelve songs I have tried to establish a relationship between modes used in these songs and known modes and *maqāmāt*, but I see only very loose connections from which no definite conclusions can be drawn.

Rhythms are free or metric, none as intricate as in the northern part of the Arabian Peninsula. The form of the folksongs is also simpler than in the north, and the instruments played are, as far as is known, predominantly percussion instruments—drums and cymbals. In contrast to the Uzbek Jews, the Yemenites never play solo instruments, using their instruments only for accompaniment.

The Yemenite will play anything from an empty tin can to an elaborately engraved copper tray. Occasional pipe or flute playing is also reported, but I have never had the opportunity of hearing a Yemenite Jew play a wind instrument. It is almost certain that there were no string instruments in San'a or anywhere else in Central Yemen.

These twelve wedding songs, sung by Jewish women at Jewish ceremonies, are but a fraction of the rich folk music of the Yemenite Jews. It would therefore be premature to draw conclusions as to the character and originality, modes, rhythm, or styles of Yemenite Jewish folk music. More material should be collected, transcribed, and analyzed; investigations into the non-Jewish music of southern Arabia as well as comparative studies of musical practices in neighboring countries to the east, west, and north are needed. Only after a thorough musicological study of southern Arabia and its neighbors will it be possible to get more than a fragmentary picture of Jewish folksong in that area.

MUSICAL ANALYSIS: Summary

Song No.	Modality	First Tone	Last Tone	Compass	Rhythm	Form
1	Major-like	1	3	5	4/4	*ABC*
2	Dorian (GK.) (Sigha)	4	1	7	3/4	*A(ab)B(cd)*
3	Hypolydian (GK.) (Sasgar)	1	2	8	4/4	*AABB*
4	Phrygian (Bayāt)	1	1	5	free	*ABA₁B₁*
5	Minor-like	1	3	8	3/4	*AB*
6	Hijāz-kār	1	6	7	free	*AB*
7	Major-like	1	3	7	3/4 & free	*A(ab)B*
8	Major-like	(1, 2) 3	3	(5, 6)	3/4	*ABC*
9	Hijāz	1	1	6	4/4	*A(ab)*
10	Pentatonic?	3	1	7	free	*A(abc)B(d)*
12	Phrygian (GK.) (Bayāt)	5	1	7	3/4 & 2/4	*A(aa₁)B(cd)*

MODALITY: In four songs (Nos. 1, 3, 7, and 8) the melodies exhibit modal organization akin to or identical with the major mode; in four cases (Nos. 2, 4, 5, and 12) the organization is modally akin to that found in Greek modes; modal organization which might be termed "Oriental" and which includes augmented seconds is found in two cases (Nos. 6 and 9); and in one case (No. 10) the mode is perhaps pentatonic. Thus, in the eleven wedding songs which have been considered, modes similar to the modern major and the Greek modes are the most frequent.

BEGINNING OF MELODY: Most of the melodies (seven) begin on the first note of the mode; two begin on the third, one on the fourth, and one on the fifth.

END OF MELODY: Five melodies end on the first note of the mode, four melodies on the third, one on the sixth, and one on the second. Thus, the number of melodies ending on the first note (five) is smaller than the number beginning on the first note (seven).

COMPASS: Three melodies have a range of a fifth; one melody, of a sixth; five melodies, of a seventh; and two melodies, of an octave. Thus the over-all range is from a fifth to an octave.

RHYTHM: Three melodies have free rhythm, and in one the rhythm is ¾ and free. One melody has ¾ and ² time, three have ¾, and three have ⁴.

FORM: The forms are simple, with *AB* predominating.

Notes

1. Most of the ceremonies were described to me by the Yemenites themselves. Rabbi Qafaḥ, from San'a, Yemen, was gracious enough to let me consult his manuscripts on wedding ceremonies in San'a and helped me greatly in my work. I am also indebted to Professor S. D. Goitein of the Hebrew University, Jerusalem, who introduced me to Yemenite culture and gave generous advice and help in the field of Yemenite folklore.

2. Arrack is made of dried grapes and dates.

3. Any Sabbath of the year on which a wedding week begins is called "The Sabbath of the Beginning."

4. *Ghalāya*: the roomy wedding coat of golden brocade with wide sleeves. Usually rented or borrowed for the occasion.

5. *Tisbūk lūlū*: a diadem of pearls, usually rented.

6. *Mghannīya*: the woman musician. Musicians, dancers, and jesters belong to the lowest class in Yemen. Honorable women are not expected to sing or dance in public.

7. There was not a single newspaper in Yemen until a few years ago.

8. A bride is not permitted to leave the house for at least two weeks before the wedding.

9. Use of the plural pronoun is a form of modesty in Yemen.

10. Lamps are symbols of marriage; fire functions as a protection from evil spirits.

11. Meaning, "There is danger."

12. Erotic meaning.

13. "Us," "we": plurals, of modesty. (It is not always easy to interpret old texts, which are often sung by the people as handed down without any attempt at explanation. Raphael Patai has suggested that this particular passage is reminiscent of Canticles 2:7 and 3:5.)

14. In this paper, the term "finalis" is not used in the accepted sense, as a word meaning the final pitch which determines the mode of a melody. The term "finalis" here applies rather to the *initial note of the maqām*, which in most cases, but not always, is the initial note of the melody.

Determination of the mode is not always easy, since the Yemenites do not seem to have a defined concept of *maqāmāt* as do the Arabs or Turks. Since the "finalis," as this writer uses the term, is often neither the first nor the last pitch of the melody, the task becomes even more difficult. Whenever a melody fits into the *maqām* perfectly, as in No. 9, it is so identified. When the melody does not fit any of the *maqāmāt* known to the writer, but resembles either minor or major, this fact is indicated. In doubtful cases, like Nos. 5 or 8, different versions of the melody have been compared and a mode thus determined.

15. *Ghalfa*: the presents from the bridegroom.

16. *Kabīr*: the name of a certain type of fancy embroidery.

17. Again reminiscent of Canticles 1:7 and 3:1–3 (suggested by Raphael Patai).

18. Verbally: "who has turned into another being" (out of passion). Interpretation suggested by Dr. S. D. Goitein.

19. Ownership of a *farsh* (pillow) in the synagogue equals maturity for a male and ensures him a permanent seat.

20. Yosēf Qafaḥ.

21. The Yemenite Jews give their children in marriage before the onset of puberty, saying that it is wise if marriage takes place before erotic feelings awaken. One does not marry for sexual pleasure, and earthly love should not be too important. The goal of every Yemenite Jew is to be as learned as possible, in order to be worthy of the world to come and of the delivery from exile.

22. The importance of ample food becomes clear if one realizes how poor the Yemenite's daily diet is: flat bread, coffee (made of coffee-husks instead of coffee beans), and a few vegetables. Meat and fish are for Sabbath, and butter, eggs, and white flour are delicacies.

23. "Us": plural of modesty.

24. "Somebody": the singer himself. Suggested by Dr. S. D. Goitein.

25. "Where nobody can catch me" (S. D. Goitein).

26. For thirty days no bride, mature or immature, is permitted to step over her husband's threshold, since demons may get hold of her and harm her. This belief was quite common in Yemen and was fought by Rabbi Yihye Qafaḥ (grandfather of the informant referred to in n. 1).

5 | Jewish Folk Custom and Belief

Two Remedy

Books in Yiddish

from 1474

and 1508

MORDECAI BERNSTEIN   New York City

by Mordecai Bernstein

IN 1950 two codices were encountered amongst the Orientalia of the Württemberg National Library (formerly the Royal National Library) of Stuttgart. The codices were described in the catalogue as *Tuetsches Rezeptbuch mit rabbinischer Schrift, sacc. XVI–NN. H. B. XI/17; H. B. XI/18.* Although in the Bavarian National Library in Munich there was access to all sources where mention is made of Yiddish manuscripts and collections, whether private or in libraries, the *Teutsche Rezeptbücher* were never encountered.

During the war the *Rezeptbücher* were removed from the library in Stuttgart and transferred to a safer location along with other rare and valuable items. Some of the manuscripts were hidden in a monastery in the Schwarzwald while others were concealed in the basement of the University of Tübingen. Examination of the codices revealed that these remedy books are rarities, written in an antiquated Yiddish dating back approximately five hundred years. Both manuscripts bear seals attesting to their presence in the *Monasterii Weingartensis* in 1654, and both are bound, but it is obvious that they have been extensively used since some of the pages are missing and many are torn or faded. There are a great number of marginal commentaries, interpretations, explanations, and translations in Middle High German, apparently made by the monks. The bookbinder, evidently unable to read the script, jumbled a number of sections, binding many of the later pages before the earlier ones. The pages themselves have been numbered by a later hand, not by the Jewish authors, and consequently read from left to right.

Codex H. B. XI/17 contains 165 folios (308 numbered pages). The remedies are arranged according to Hebrew numeration, and the volume contains 1,252 items. Of these, the first 1,248 were written by the original author or copyist, the rest having been added later. In addition there are some ten-odd unnumbered items from a later date.

There is a special index of all the remedies. The early pages of the volume, however, are missing and the work commences with remedy 261. As has been said, the pages were not bound in order, and as a result the index, which should appear at the end, is in the middle of the volume between pages 31 and 65.

At the end of the original remedies there is a further addition:

> Dedicated to the honorable Reb Zeligman Nurberg, [copied] out of a *büchlein*.
>
> [At this point one and a half lines have been erased.]
>
> Finished the first day of Adar 5234, in the Holy Community of *mestre* in the house of Hashn'i [the Ashkenazi?]
> Reb Moses the son of our teacher and leader Reb Zeligman, blessed be his memory, from Ulm.

Here we have a location and an exact date, namely, the first of Adar, 5234 (in the year 1474).

The second codex, H. B. XI/18, contains 114 folios (228 numered pages—also reading from left to right). Here the parts are generally well-bound with the exception of a few reversed pages, but again, the early pages are missing. Of the numbered remedies (Hebrew numeration), ten are missing. The volume begins with No. 11, folio 114, and ends with No. 506, folio 2. It is not certain, however, that the volume actually terminated with remedy 506.

This second codex consists of a number of units written by

the same author. Thus, on folio 94 (reading from left to right), is found this addendum, following No. 137: "Finished the first book, began the second." Then the author commences with No. 138.

On folio 21 (reading from left to right) there is a further addition, following No. 441: "Finished the book of remedies, 268, 22nd day of Tamuz, on a Tuesday." In this case there is also an exact date for the writing of the volume, i.e., Tuesday, the 22nd day of Tamuz, 5268 (in the year 1508).

In the same handwriting there follows immediately: "Here begins a good book of herbs, and their efficacy." This passage, which continues the former numeration, beginning with No. 412, tells of various herbs and their strength. In short, the age of both codices is known: the first dates back to 5234 (1474) and the second to 5268 (1508). Obviously, the copyists used older manuscripts.

The question remains, How did these remedy books come into the possession of the monks of Weingarten? One must assume that the books were stolen from the Jewish community in the course of the persecution so common to that region during the latter part of the 16th and the beginning of the 17th centuries.

The remedy books must be examined from various angles. First of all, there is the question of the contents. For what diseases and infirmities are the remedies recommended? Of what do these remedies consist? Second, there is the question of language: What was the form of the Yiddish language some half a millenium ago?

Certainly these questions are matters of interest to scientists and to experts in the field of medicine generally, and, specifically, in the field of folk medicine. As will be shown later, every one of the 1,252 remedies in the first codex and of the 506 in the second presents its own problem. And the specialist, in addition to his analysis of a given remedy, will have to compare it with similar remedies found among Jews in other regions and in various parts of the Gentile world. A thorough study of the material contained in the codices could well become a lifetime project. In this paper, the intention is to present only a fragmentary portion of the contents, in order to bring the material to the attention of experts. These two books are excellent examples of an all-encompassing folk medicine. They give remedies for diseases of the body and soul and advice about such other misfortunes as fire and theft. There are countless "aids" to good luck, charm, and grace in the eyes of judges and instructions for getting revenge on enemies and for defeating the evil purposes of murderous individuals. These remedies apply not only to men, women, and children, but to animals as well (primarily horses). Finally, there is a mass of data relating, for the most part, to physio-chemical and metallurgical problems.

Maintaining the order of the first codex (from which all the remedies listed have been selected) we have remedies for: wounds, 5; nerve pains, 6; headache, 10; fever, 22 (various fevers—recurrent fever, third fever, fourth fever—are mentioned); pains in the left side, 58; pains in the right side, 59; dropsy, 91; cancer, 92; food poisoning, 107; dry breasts, 118; nosebleeds, 122; swollen bellies, 196; spitting of blood, 327; underdeveloped teeth, 353; swollen genitals, 381; watery eyes, 375; swollen or painful throat, 387; running ear, 393; pain in the lungs, 425; spleen, 431; pain in the side or ribs, 435; irregular menstruation, 439; excessive menstruation, 440; insomnia, 476; epilepsy, 477; bleeding, 479; all forms of skin diseases, 489; red spots in the eyes, 495; broken bones, 519; stanching the flow of blood, 521; hydrophobia, 526; difficulty in conception, 532; burns resulting from fire or boiling water, 560; hoarseness, 568; thirst, 686; snakebite, 746; bee sting, 747; spider bite, 801; kidney stones, 1,010.

A second group of remedies might be listed under "cosmetics." These include cures for facial blemishes, 713; falling hair, 347; gray hair, 346; sweaty hands and feet, 31; flushed face, 916; pendulous breasts, 949; suggestions for lightening a dark complexion, 620; whitening blackened or stained teeth, 697; bleaching hair, 854; and controlling the growth of a young girl's breasts, 1,229. There are also formulas for acquiring a pleasant voice, 918; curly hair, 856; white hands, 723; and facial beauty, 368.

The philters and potions prescribed for problems arising in sexual and marital relationships are also numerous; thus, for cohabitation, 408; love, 528; losing the love of one's wife, 547; preventing one's wife from desiring another man, 590; exciting the passions of a woman who is unyielding during coition, 593; deciding whether one should take a woman or die, 609; bewitching someone to prevent him from lying with a woman, 614; causing a woman to ascend naked from her bath, 675; insuring pursuit by one's beloved, 780; causing a marital rift, 836; inducing the effect of virginity in a woman, 951; causing one's destined to come to one's bed, 1,204.

In a broader category are the "remedies" for problems arising in man's relationship to his environment. These problems, predominantly of an interpersonal nature, include the following: speaking before judges and elders, 506; killing one's enemy, 507; causing a woman to answer from her sleep when interrogated, 525; winning at various games, 548; freeing prisoners, 553; traveling (good luck in), 559, and praying for safe traveling, 531; acquiring charm, 560; discovering a thief, 562, and detecting a criminal, 563; avoiding witchcraft, 601; protecting oneself from a murderer, 606; finding bargains, 685; calling down a fever upon one's enemies, 705; inducing sleep in a group sitting around a table, 1,038; causing enmity between two individuals, 1,040; discovering whether a sick person will live or die, 1,049; striking one's enemy blind, 1,081.

Still another category refers exclusively to the nonhuman environment and includes instructions for catching fish, 541; making a roan horse white, 689; snaring birds, 634; laming a horse, 710; inducing a nightingale to alight on one's hand, 719;

snaring doves, 753; exterminating vermin, 927; dealing with a stallion in heat, 561; relieving a horse that cannot pass water, 962; making a horse run, 1,227.

Among the problems of a more technical nature are: separating gold from silver, 512; skimming the film off silver, 513; softening ivory, 534; gilding objects, 535; reading the faded script on parchments, 542; softening hard stones, 543; blanching pearls, 545; coating copper or brass with silver, 619; writing with a plume so that the result looks as if it were written in gold, 623; making wine mouldy, 676, and making it clear, 923; making gold and silver heavier, 720; making iron malleable, 767, and hardening it, 769; causing writing to fade from parchment, 785; keeping roses fresh until Christmas, 960; making ink without water, 1,055; softening glass, 1,186; opening a lock without a key, 1,190 writing in a script legible only at night, 1,236.

From the sicknesses, ailments, plagues, and diseases listed we can derive some conclusions about the ills prevalent some five hundred years ago, and, more important, we can learn something of the Jewish socio-economic situation of that epoch. Thus we see, among other things, that Jews were involved in lawsuits; knew of, or underwent, imprisonment; travelled; caught fish and birds; and, presumably, bought and sold horses and traded in gold, silver, pearls, glassware, wine, and roses.

In the following pages various specific remedies (numbered as in the first codex) are given.

553 If you wish to free a man from prison, walk outside the city at night, where the open sky is above you, and recite Psalm 30, which begins: "A song at the dedication of the House of David."

660 In treating someone for a fourth fever take an apple and slice it in three parts. On the first day write the following on the first slice: "I shall not die, but live, and declare the works of the Lord" (Psalms 118:17). The next day write the following on the second slice: "The Lord hath chastened me sore; but He hath not given

me over unto death" (Psalms 118:18). On the third day, write on
the third slice: "Open to me the gates of righteousness; I will enter
into them, I will give thanks unto the Lord" (Psalms 118:10). Each
morning give the patient a slice to eat before allowing him to eat
anything else.

693 Before going on trial, say the following three times: "Terror
and dread falleth upon them; by the greatness of thine arm, they
are as still as a stone" (Exodus 15:16).

744 For love, divide an ounce of quicksilver into three parts and
cast one part into the fire every day for three days, while saying,
"As I burn this quicksilver, so should the heart of so-and-so, the
daughter of such-and-such, burn until she does my will and desire." When this has been said, recite the passage, "Fire shall be
kept burning upon the altar continually; it shall not go out" (Leviticus 6:6).

795 In order not to fear judges and elders and to avoid harm,
pick up a handful of earth and repeat the following three times:
"Terror and dread falleth upon them; by the greatness of thine
arm they are as still as a stone" (Exodus 15:16). Then say this backwards. Now take the earth, and throw it down on the ground in
front of two houses.

1001 For a woman in delivery whose child will not emerge, say
the following passage three times: "And all these thy servants shall
come down unto me, and bow unto me, saying 'Get thee out,' and
all the people that follow thee, and after that I will go out" (Exodus
11:8). This helps, with God's help.

1006 For a woman who cannot conceive, repeat the following
into her ear: "A psalm of David. The heavens declare the glory of
God, and the firmament showeth His handiwork; day unto day
uttereth speech, and night unto night revealeth knowledge; there
is no speech, there are no words, neither is their voice heard. Their
line is gone out through all the earth, and their words to the end
of the world. In them hath he set a tent for the son, which is as a
bridegroom coming out of his chamber, and rejoiceth as a strong
man to run his course" (Psalm 19). Say nothing thereafter. This
helps, with the will of God.

1042 To find grace in everyone's eyes, take the stomach of a
black rooster, and there you will find small white stones; carry these

same stones about with you. They are a charm against the Evil Eye, are good for lawsuits, and help you to sleep well. They will also serve against witchcraft, and if someone hates you, they will cause him to love you. If you tie the same stones to your right foot and say, "The Lord is a man of war" (Exodus 15:3), you will become stronger. Twist the same stone with each incantation, and say every incantation twice.

1069 In case of theft, if you wish to know who the thief is, take a spindle and place it in the Book of Psalms where the passage "But He, being full of compassion" (Psalms 78:38) begins. Close the book and say: "I cast lots to see if so-and-so is guilty of theft. If he is, let it be shown; if not, let not the guilt fall upon him." Repeat this three times, then say "Nathan the Prophet came unto him" (Psalms 51:2).

In the remedies just quoted Biblical chapters and passages are woven with various rituals. Following are remedies which depend upon the use of "shemes," Holy Names. In the "shemes" remedies, the names of the angels Gabriel, Michael, and Raphael appear repeatedly along with a variety of combinations of words stemming from acrostics formed by the initial letters of Biblical passages. There are also certain words that, generally speaking, cannot be interpreted and explained.

531 The following *shemes* are good when said on a journey: "Argiel, Sargiel, Nargiel." The words are derived from the passage in Genesis 42:4: "But Benjamin, Joseph's brother, Jacob sent not with his brethren; for he said, 'Lest, peradventure, harm (*ason*) befall him.' " Jacob, may he rest in peace, told this to his sons when they wished to journey to Egypt.

552 For love, take a thorn, place it in a kerchief, and say: "Tartie, Partie, Gurtie." She must then run after you without her undergarments.

559 If you are about to go on a journey and wish to know whether things will go well or not, draw your sword, gaze into it, and say: "I place my faith in thee, Angel, to show me a sign or miracle, if my way will be succesful or not." If you see your re-

flection reversed, things will go poorly, but if your face is properly reflected, then you may depart, for it is a sign that things will go well with you.

605 To stanch the flow of blood write "Agaf, Sagaf, Nagaf" on your forehead in your own blood or burn chicken feathers to a crisp and place the ashes on the bleeding spot.

657 To fend off witchcraft, hammer out a thin sheet of lead, and scratch the following words on it with a knife: "Thou shalt not suffer a sorceress to live (Exodus 22:17); a sorceress to live thou shalt not suffer; thou shalt not suffer to live a sorceress; thou shalt not a sorceress suffer to live; to live, a sorceress, thou shalt not suffer; to live thou shalt not suffer a sorceress. I charge you, Mchashpiel, Ktsasiel, and Sandriel, in the name of what I am and what I shall be, and in the name of the Lord God Jehovah, and in the name of the Lord of Hosts, who presides over the angels, that they shall nullify any sorcery committed against so-and-so, the son of such-and-such, from now until eternity, Amen, Selah."

685 To find a bargain write the following *shemes* on a parchment: "Sandalfon Gavriel Candri Sandriel." Place it at your head upon going to sleep, and the angels will come and tell you.

696 If you travel through the world and do not wish to tire, write "Ditsmiel, Tsfiel, Tarngiel" on your right leg, and you will not weary.

777 If you wish to win a lawsuit, remember the *shemes* "Chets, Pets, Chafets."

1047 If you wish a child to grow up to be a good pupil, write "Aime" on the mother's right breast and "Taime" on her left breast when she nurses the child, and he will grow up to be a scholar.

1073 To cause enmity take three stones, and throw them at a dog that has barked at you. Then pick up the stones and say "Af, af, af" three times and "chamo, chamo, chamo" three times, and throw the stones among friends; a great enmity will arise among them.

1197 To open a lock without a key, take the parchment of an aborted [kid] and write the following on it with the blood of a bat: "Ardak, ardak." Then place the parchment in the opening of the lock, and it will open.

1204 If you want to cause the woman who is destined for you to come to your bed, take a cabbage—it must be picked before sunrise—and take a shingle from the roof, or straw, and some earth from under the doorstep. When you go to sleep, place the cabbage under your head and the shingle on your body, and scatter the earth around your bed, and say the following: "Shingle that covers me, cabbage that wakes me, I charge you in the name of the Lord, God of Israel, to bring my love to me so that we may drink mead and wine. An angel should bring her and show me her form as she walks the earth." And when you wish to send her back, say "I charge you to go from me in the name of Michael, Raphael, and Gabriel." She will leave you.

The remedies quoted thus far function under the impetus of Biblical passages and *shemes*. Below, we give examples of characteristic remedies carrying the impress of folk superstition (frequently stemming from neighboring peoples). These remedies often border on magic.

555 A stone that is found in the stomach of a chicken and looks like a hailstone should be kept, since it helps in many things. It is even more effective if it has the appearance of a crystal.

591 If you take the tongue of a frog and place it under the breast of a sleeping woman, she will have to answer all that you ask. If you wish to do the same thing to a man, place the tongue on his heart.

598 Take the eye of a rooster, and tie it to your right side; then neither dog nor man will be able to harm you.

596 For love, cut out the heart of a rabbit while it is still alive, and pour boiling wax into the wound. Be careful, however, to place the heart on the ground. Then place the rabbit's heart over the woman's heart, and say: "As this rabbit ran in the forest between the trees and along the paths until she did the will and desire of the hare, so shall you find no rest until you do my will and desire." If you wish to arouse the love of a man, use the heart of a hare.

606 If you want to punish a murderer, take salt and place it on the wounds of his victim; the murderer will die within a year.

609 If you wish to know whether you are destined to take a wife or die before doing so, take an egg that has been laid on a

Thursday, and fry it. Cut the egg into two parts; eat one, and place the other part under your head when you go to sleep. Then the woman who is destined for you will come to you in your sleep. If you don't see a woman, but a coffin, you will know that no woman is destined for you and that you will die without taking a wife.

648 For love, take the milk of a kosher, first-born cow, and wash your face with her milk. On the same day an angel will come to you, and all your words will be heard, and all your wishes fulfilled.

705 If you have an enemy and want him to succumb to a fever, take a thread from his garment, or a hair of his body, and thread a needle with it. Stick the needle into a tree, and say "As this tree shivers, so shall so-and-so shiver all the time."

718 When you have to appear in court, take a bone from a corpse or a carcass, and say, "As this bone has been forgotten, so let them forget what they have said; let all those who have spoken evil of me lose their memories."

721 For a sick person who cannot sleep, take some earth that has been under the head of a corpse, wrap the dirt in a handkerchief, and place it under the head [of the sick person] without his knowledge.

779 To kill an enemy, take a white rooster, call it by your enemy's name, and feed it for a month. After a month's time has elapsed, kill the rooster, and say, "I kill my enemy so-and-so." Bury it before the gate of your enemy, and he will die immediately.

988 To discover whether a woman is pregnant, let her eat the meat of walnuts every morning on an empty stomach. If she is pregnant, the child will move in her body three days later.

998 If you wish to guard against a woman's becoming pregnant by you, carry around the heart of a mouse.

1037 If you have forgotten a dream, take your shirt and reverse it, and reverse it again, and once again; and your dream will return to you.

1038 To cause people sitting around a table to fall asleep, take a new needle and plunge it into the body of a corpse three times; then withdraw the needle and stick it into the table. Everyone sitting around the table will fall asleep.

1039 To keep someone from sleeping, take the head of a bat and place it under the person's head, and he will not be able to fall asleep. As soon as you remove the bat's head, the person will fall asleep.

1045 To get possession of someone's will, take a needle that has been used for sewing shrouds and pierce his clothes [with the needle] without his knowledge. He will be compelled to do whatever you wish.

1050 The tooth of a mad dog is good for three things: to be placed on the arm of someone who has been bitten by a dog; to be hung on your arm so that you will not be bitten by a dog; or to be hung around the neck of a child in order that his teeth will grow without causing him any pain.

1217 Whoever carries quicksilver around is protected against imprisonment.

These examples give some conception of the powers ascribed to animal heads, stomachs, eyes, tongues, and teeth, and of the qualities possessed by needles; we also learn for what purposes dogs, mice, frogs, bats, and the like can be employed. In addition, there is a wide assortment of remedies (constituting the bulk of the material) for specific diseases, disabilities, and accidents.

428 For congested lungs, take the lung from a suckling bear cub, and pound it into powder on a new pan. Pour the powder on to a slice of bread soaked in wine [and feed it to the patient].

430 For rotting lungs, take bay leaves, powder them well, and eat them with bread. This will heal the lungs.

473 For a congested heart or poor digestion, take walnuts, shell them like almonds, and grind them very fine. Mix the ground nuts with white flour, and boil in fat. The mixture should be eaten on an empty stomach.

533 For a person spitting blood, take the horn of a ram, burn it, and grind it down to a powder. Mix it with red wine or rainwater, and give it to the patient to drink. It helps.

569 For a woman who has lost her milk, take linseeds, grind

them well, and feed them to her with wine or water. Her milk will be restored.

572 For deafness, take the fat from chickens or geese, fresh and salted, and render it. Let it drip into the ears. It helps.

704 For a fourth fever, take a bone from a carcass, grind it down to a fine powder, and give it to the patient. If the patient is a man, the animal must be male; if the patient is a woman, the animal must be female.

740 For a weak stomach, take an apple and make a hole in it. Fill the hole with wax, bake the apple well, and eat it.

829 For cataracts, take ginger and bay leaves, and peel off the outside. Then take the inner parts [of the ginger and bay-leaves], and grind them together. Strain the mixture. Leave the powder soaking overnight in rose water. Cover it to preserve the essence. Put the same water into the eyes. It heals.

834 If a woman is pregnant and wishes to miscarry, feed her horseradish on an empty stomach. She will miscarry.

848 For epilepsy, mix pigeon dung with wine. Give the mixture to the patient to drink. The epilepsy will disappear, with God's help.

905 For bad teeth, take pepper, mustard, and salt; grind them and mix them together; and put the mixture into a linen kerchief. Press the kerchief to the bad teeth. This draws away the bad blood and cures the teeth.

983 If you have been bitten by a spider, catch a fly and press it over the wound; the fly will draw the poison into itself.

993 If a woman is having a difficult pregnancy, give her bitch's milk mixed with wine or honey, and she will give birth immediately.

996 To stop the flow of menstrual blood, take roses found amongst corn, grind them down, and feed them to the woman. The blood will stop flowing.

1010 For kidney stones, pain in the penis, or difficulty in passing water, use the small, white stones that you will find in the stomach of a year-old rooster. Grind them up, mix them with wine, give the mixture to the patient, and have him drink it from time to time. It helps.

1016 For all sorts of fever, grind four heads of garlic just before the fever is due. Give the garlic to the patient, and have him drink vinegar with it. On the day that the fever is due, have the patient fast.

1018 To cure an abscess or a boil, take a dough of fine flour and honey, and place it on the abscess [or boil]; or fry figs in butter, and place them on the abscess [or boil]. Both of these remedies will cause the abscess to burst.

1027 For someone who has been scalded or burned, take milk, and wash the burn. Then take horse manure, burn it to a powder, and spread it on the burn. It helps.

1029 For a swollen tooth, take a fig, and place it over the swelling.

1032 For a toothache, smear the aching tooth with onion juice, and the tooth will stop aching.

1035 To soften a hard abscess, take red wine, milk, and sour dough, and bake them into a cookie. Bind the cookie to the abscess, and it [the abscess] will become soft.

1037 For a cough, eat boiling garlic as hot as you can stand it.

We have tried to include a sample of the thousand or so remedies that apply to human diseases. Very often, of course, the same cure is repeated for a variety of diseases.

As we have said, the remedy book also contains cosmetic suggestions and suggestions for the handling of problems of a technical nature. Below, we offer a few examples of these categories as well as a number of remedies relating to animals.

480 For those who wish to be beautiful, take lily roots, butter, quicksilver, wine, honey, and fat. Boil them together, and wash with this mixture, and you will have a beautiful face.

534 To soften ivory, place it in strong vinegar, and let it lie there for three days and three nights. It will become soft.

629 To make a roan horse white, burn sulphur, and let the horse stand in the smoke. If you really want him to become white, he will become white.

643 For an unblemished face, catch rain water in a clean vessel during the last days of the month of Iyar (April) and the first four

days of Sivan (May), and pour it into a glass vessel so that it will keep. The water will become as bitter as violet water or rose water. It is also good for pain in the eyes.

720 To make gold or silver heavier, take thin chalk made of eggshells. To make this chalk, wash the eggshells well, and then let them dry. Place the shells in a newly fired pot, cover it, and place in the oven. The shells will become white and turn into egg chalk. Afterward, take two ounces of the chalk, powder it thoroughly, put it back in the same pot, cover it, and bury the vessel in warm dung so that the chalk will of itself become fluid. Then place the gold or silver in this fluid, and it will become heavier over night.

843 To whiten teeth, take a whole nutmeg, and grind it up; take a pearl of the same size, and grind that up. Then mix the two together, and rub your teeth with the mixture, and they will become white. Whoever does not have any pearls should take alum the size of a nutmeg. Also, whoever wishes to may take pumice and rub his teeth with that.

854 Whoever wishes to have yellow hair should take swallow dung and mix it with the bile of an ox and wash his hair with the mixture.

910 For a horse with a cataract, take a pound of butter and a plate of salt, make butterballs, and insert them in the horse's ear on the side where the sick eye is. Bandage the ear so that the horse cannot shake the butterballs out. Leave them there for an hour or two, until they melt. Do this three times.

921 To make hair grow, take garlic or onions, and rub the place where the hair is falling or has fallen out.

928 To kill lice, take quicksilver and butter, mix them together, and smear the spots where the lice are found.

949 For women with pendulous breasts, take eggshells, red pears, and butter, and rub them into the breasts. The breasts will stiffen.

962 For a horse that cannot pass water, take garlic and pepper, and rub them into his teeth.

979 For worms in a horse or a human, take the head of a pike, bones and all, place it on a brick, and burn it until the bones turn white. Pulverize the bones with a pestle, and scatter over the worms. They will die in three days.

1055 To make ink without water, take acorns and press them with an iron. The juice that comes out will be as black as ink.

1057 To make hair fall out, take the blood of a young sheep, and smear the [hairy] spot with it. It helps.

1093 For a florid face, take the blood of a tench, boil it in wine, strain well, and wash your face with the solution.

1185 To separate gold from copper, melt lead, get it red-hot, place the copper in the molten lead, and the gold will separate from it.

1189 To whiten black teeth, take barley meal, honey, and salt; mix them together; and rub the black teeth with the mixture. Do this in the morning and at night. It helps.

Of the 1,252 remedies of various types found in the first codex, we have given close to a hundred which are representative of all the categories mentioned. It becomes evident that neighboring peoples, chiefly the Germans, had a decided influence on the formulation of the remedies. We can see this in the use of the sword as an instrument of divination; in the mention of "keeping roses fresh until Christmas"; in the interest in and references to fishing and hunting—all extremely uncharacteristic of Jews of the period. It must be assumed that some of the remedies were derived from other than Germanic sources by the author and adapted by him to a Yiddish framework. We see this not only in the use of Biblical passages and *shemes* but also in the fact that the language itself is relatively far from its German source. It finds its expression most strongly in the wealth of Hebrew elements found in the manuscript. (Cf. my article—written in Yiddish—in *Davke* [Buenos Aires, 1953], No. 17, pp. 330-61.)

Finally, a few words about the unknown author. As has been mentioned, he certainly drew some of his material from non-Jewish sources, but without question he also had other Jewish works before him. Very often he remarks, "I found a manuscript" or "I found this in a book." In remedy 554, dealing with the avoidance of imprisonment, he writes, ". . . and

I heard that Rabbi Jacob Weil, may he rest in peace, so coun-
selled his sons. . . ." (Rabbi Jacob Weil was born in Württem-
burg at the end of the 14th century and died at Erfurt in 1456,
that is, some twenty-five years before the first remedy book
was written.)

From the foregoing sampling, it is clear that a treasury of
Jewish custom and folklore is contained in these remedy
books. Only one of the codices (the first) has been considered
in this paper (to present a full account of both would require
years of research), but there is no reason to doubt that the
second codex is of comparable interest and value.

Jewish Popular
Beliefs and Customs
in Los Angeles

WAYLAND D. HAND   University of California
at Los Angeles

by Wayland D. Hand

Although Los Angeles is one of the great Jewish centers in America,[1] little effort has been made to survey the resources of Jewish folklore in the California metropolis. In 1948, however, evidences of real interest in Jewish popular tradition and antiquities appeared. At this time a course in Jewish folklore—perhaps the first such course ever to be given in the United States—was offered in the summer session of the University of California at Los Angeles. The course was entitled "Yiddish 146: Yiddish Popular Literature and Folklore" and was taught by Dr. Max Weinreich of the Yiddish Scientific Institute on the invitation of UCLA's Department of Germanic Languages.[2] Approximately forty students, including a few from New York, elected the course. From their own family and community backgrounds many of these students contributed items of folklore to Professor Weinreich's class discussions. Another impetus to systematic field work in folklore came with the establishment in 1948-49 of a scholarship for the collection of Jewish folklore in Los Angeles. It is unfortunate that this generous grant in aid—provided by the local branch of the Yiddish Scientific Institute—was not renewed, because the first year's garnering included many choice items, particularly some fine old tales and folksongs. One of these songs, bearing the hallmarks of antiquity, deals with the selling of Joseph into Egypt.

About the time of this activity in Jewish folklore I began collecting folklore in earnest from my students with a view to

establishing a folklore archive at UCLA. A considerable number of Jewish students elected my courses in folklore and
often contributed items of Jewish lore to class discussions in
addition to communicating various other items gathered in
their own homes or in the communities in which they lived.
The popular beliefs and superstitions treated in this paper
were collected largely in this way, although the study does
contain material obtained directly from Jewish townspeople
and others.

Far too little work has been done, and too little material is
actually at hand to make possible any definitive treatment of
Jewish folklore in the Los Angeles area. The prospect is
scarcely better even in the field of my specialty, where Jewish
popular beliefs and superstitions are only gradually being
worked into my files for inclusion in a projected dictionary of
American popular beliefs and superstitions. From the sampling
of unpublished material presented here, however, it appears
that what is true of popular beliefs and superstitions in general
holds true also for Jewish material in these categories; namely,
besides the body of material that is distinctively Jewish, and
non-existent in other cultural *milieux*, there is a liberal sprin-
kling of popular beliefs that are part of a common store. Many
of these beliefs are well known in America, and some are
widely distributed throughout Europe.[3] Analysis of these, and
indeed of the whole body of American popular belief and
superstition in the light of their European background, must
await further collecting in this country before comparisons
can be made between this American material and its European,
and sometimes Asiatic and African, antecedents. When basic
studies in this field are made, the Jewish material will undoubtedly have the same crucial importance, culturally and
historically, that it has always had in folktale study and in
other branches of folkloristic research.

Little can be said about the evaluation of the lore itself by
its bearers that will throw light on the religious and cultural

patterns of the Jewish community in Los Angeles. For this, the material is too fragmentary, and there has been too little opportunity to question informants on their own background and outlook. Under such conditions it has been impossible even to sense attitudes, much less to venture interpretations of the data. Even so, it is safe to say that in most cases the beliefs have been reported objectively with something more than a mere in-one-ear-out-the-other type of interest. There is no way of knowing, of course, how many superstitions relating to the most religious customs and practices have been withheld by informants otherwise willing to talk freely about themselves and their people. Matters of this kind that bear upon ultimate religious and social attitudes must, it seems to us, enlist the interest not only of leaders of the Jewish community but of sociologists and psychologists as well.[4] Central to this whole problem, admittedly, are the sweeping changes in Jewish life in the United States and the modification and discarding of ancient beliefs and customs as assimilation increases.[5] When more studies in the field of Jewish folklore have been made, folklorists, like their confreres in the social sciences and the humanities, will be able to make signal contributions to an understanding of many of the vexing problems of Jewish acculturation in our midst. Los Angeles itself should offer a fertile field for such study, since the Jewish population is made up largely of people who have lived in other American Jewish centers before taking up residence in southern California. Social mobility of this sort, as is well known, predisposes to a modification of social patterns and contributes to a liberalized point of view in matters of religion. Stabilizing factors in the Jewish life of Los Angeles, on the other hand, are seen in the large Jewish community on the east side of the city, where many families have struck roots, as it were, tracing local patrimony back two, three, or more generations. A study of these subtle interactions between sedentary and migrant strains could be made with profit by workers in several of the social sciences from basic human data recorded in folklore. It is my hope that this modest study may stimulate more systematic work in what is still an uncharted field.[6]

Jewish popular beliefs and superstitions having to do with birth, infancy, and childhood inevitably loom large in the folk mind because of the importance of birth as the first and one of the most important *rites de passage* in the mortal span.[7] Fragmentary though the following treatment is, it will nevertheless afford some notion of the kinds of popular belief about the beginnings of life that have been preserved among Los Angeles Jews. Sterility, a bugaboo of marriage, and considered by many as a curse imposed by God for parental indiscretions and want of piety,[8] may be overcome if the husband and wife separate for a while, maintaining strict continence during the period. The fear of prenatal marking and disfigurement of the unborn child, and of other harm, including stillbirth, has found expression in such assorted notions as the following: If a pregnant woman steps over nails, she will lose her baby (Sephardic);[9] don't throw a rope at a pregnant woman because it will strangle the child;[10] don't look at anything frightening if you're pregnant, or you will scare the child and make him a half-wit;[11] if a pregnant woman sees a nut and doesn't eat it, but scratches herself, the baby will be marked at that spot (Sephardic). A related belief, involving the general concept of not denying a pregnant woman anything she desires,[12] particularly food,[13] is seen in the unusual belief, brought to Los Angeles by Russian Jews, that mice will eat up your clothes if you fail to grant a pregnant woman her wish. The sex of the unborn child may be determined in the following manner: send the pregnant woman out of the room and place a fork on one chair and a spoon on the other; cover them, and when she returns and chooses a chair, the chair chosen will determine the child's sex, with the fork indicating a boy and the spoon a girl.[14]

Folk obstetrical practice decrees that the newborn child shall be wrapped up in bandage-like cloth (swaddling clothes?) to keep it from becoming a cripple (Sephardic). If you step over a child, it will not grow,[15] and when a child sneezes, stunting of growth will result if you pull its right ear rather than its left. Teething will be impaired if a baby is allowed to see itself in a mirror;[16] and, according to one account, no teeth at all will develop. If a child is slow in learning to walk, draw a line in front of him, and that will speed him up.[17] If you slap a baby's face, you will stop him from talking at an early age.

The sanctity of names, and the identification of the soul itself with the name assigned to a child, has given rise to a series of beliefs attendant upon naming.[18] It is considered bad luck to name a child after a living person. This taboo has been extended to include naming a child after a person who has died young. From this discussion it follows that children are named after dead people; also there is some predilection for naming children after people who have attained a venerable age, since the longevity of the newborn child is thus assured.[19] Another curious belief about names has to do with the fear that prospective sons-in-law or daughters-in-law, with the same names as their parents-in-law, will in some mysterious way bring about the unseasonable demise of their acquired elders. From Biblical times forward a sick child's name has been changed so that the angel of death would pass him by, or be "fooled," as one informant has indicated. Perhaps the name most frequently given in such cases is Chayim, which by derivation means "long life."[20] In connection with the christening ceremonies, godparents are appointed to look after the spiritual welfare of the child. In a curious custom of this sort, the first-born son of a Jewish couple is "auctioned off" to the highest bidder, who thus gains the coveted honor of being a godparent.

Fear of the evil eye is still encountered among Jewish parents;[21] thus for a new baby to be given the evil eye, it may be sufficient for a Gentile to look at the child. (The more familiar phases of "overlooking," praise of the child's beauty, etc., are

not among the few items at my disposal; but the belief has been
noted that parents should not divulge intimate facts and
knowledge about the child—height, weight, and the like—lest
these secret data be used to put the child under fairy influence.) The newborn child, and its mother, too, may be protected from witches by decking the bed out in red ribbons,
or by placing a knife underneath the mother's pillow. An
adult may avert the evil eye by making a *Feige*[22] (thumb
gesture) or wearing red;[23] washing a child's face with urine
from its own diaper will have the same effect.

Two informants have noted the use of molten lead poured
onto water to divine the shape of things which have frightened
the child. Upon seeing such a representation of the creature
(or thing) that provoked fright, the child will lose all signs
of fright. The use of molten lead in other divinatory practices
is, of course, well known.[24]

Folk medical beliefs are poorly represented in the collection,
but there are enough to enable one to see the nature and possible extent of such medical practices among the Jewish folk
of Los Angeles. From items listed here it is clear that many beliefs have been appropriated from the common store. The
notes will indicate possible borrowings. Having one's ears
pierced will cause better eyesight;[25] and inflamed eyes in children may be cured by bathing them in the mother's urine.[26]
A sty may be cured by making a *Feige* with one's right hand
three times. Although onions are generally thought to prevent
disease, Sephardic Jews believe that leaving a cut onion in the
house will bring on sickness. Urinating on a bad cut or infec-
tion will cure it;[27] and a cold knife pressed to a swelling caused
by a bump on the head or elsewhere will allay the swelling.
Bleeding of the nose can be stanched by dropping keys down
the person's back.[28] To stop the spitting of blood, on the other
hand, one should cook cactus until it attains a jelly-like consistency and then swallow it. This will stop the bleeding. Three
informants, all girls, attest to the belief that when a girl first

begins to menstruate, her mother must either slap her face or pinch her cheeks. This little ritual, performed no doubt partly in jest, will assure the girl of rosy cheeks for the rest of her life. Boils, caused, it is thought, by impure blood, may be cured by using a poultice made from boiled onions.[29] The common headache is caused by leaving eggshells in the sink.[30] Hiccoughs may be caused by someone's talking about you, and may be cured by thinking of the guilty person. Piles may be cured in two ways: by sitting on a hard, hot board smeared with lamb's tallow; and by piercing cloves of garlic with holes and applying the cloves to the affected parts. This will cause the piles to dry up. A belief of Russian Jewish provenience prescribes the securing of a dead man's hand for the cure of goiter.[31] An instance is given of a young girl who obtained such a *membrum disjunctum* and applied it to the goiter, with the desired results.

Culinary and other domestic practices provide a fertile field for the imagination, and are sources of many beliefs. Here again there is only token representation from Jewish life in Los Angeles. Beliefs and practices connected with the kosher kitchen date from early Israelitish times and are more properly a part of religious observance than of folklore, but for convenience the few items in my files may be considered here. Notions deviating from standard practice may be accounted for by the fact that some of the information communicated has been supplied by non-Jewish informants. Pork, as is commonly known, is unclean as a food; likewise shellfish. In butchering, cows must not be struck over the head; cutting through the neck is the approved manner of slaughter.[32] Meat from the "waist down" cannot be eaten,[33] nor can the meat of cattle with lung blemishes of any kind.[34] Meat and dairy products cannot be consumed at the same time, a six-hour interval being prescribed between the consumption of foods of these two different categories. Fish and milk eaten together at the same meal are poisonous.[35] In a kosher kitchen, soap may not be used on the dishes or utensils; and if it is, or if defilement comes about in any other way, the object must be buried in the ground for a certain number of days, or, if it is a sharp instrument, thrust into the earth several times. Among old Jewish wives it is thought that if two glasses are broken during the course of a day, a third one must voluntarily be shattered; in this way an evil spell is broken.[36] During her menstrual period, a woman should not try to ferment wine or to make pickles of any kind.[37] There are prohibitions against using a broom to brush the crumbs from a table (this will cause poverty) and, among Sephardic Jews, against wiping a table with paper; and some Jews are careful not to sit on anything that does not have legs.

The staff of life is also the subject of certain beliefs.[38] Thus a blessing should be uttered on the cutting of the first slice of bread from a loaf. An even more primitive custom prescribes the baking of a little dab of dough in the oven as an offering. Failure to observe this gesture of gratitude will, if nothing worse, impair one's digestion. Among Jewish bakers, in Los Angeles, of Polish and Russian extraction, a portion of dough from a previous batch is saved out to qualify the new mixing. By observing this rule, they keep the bread from turning mouldy or otherwise coming to harm.

The pre-eminence of Jews as tailors and seamstresses explains the prevalence of beliefs involving sewing and the garment industry. Only a sampling of these have been recoverd in Los Angeles. One of the prevalent superstitions concerns the taboo against sewing on a garment while it is being worn, either mending it in any way or sewing on a button.[39] Failure of the person whose clothes are being mended to chew on a piece of thread will result in his brains' being sewed up. In the Talmud Jewish tailors are forbidden to thread needles on the Sabbath (but the proscription is evaded by threading the needles the day before). According to other beliefs pertaining to needles and sewing, you must not give a needle or pin directly to someone (put it down, and let him or her pick it up[40]); if you take a needle from someone, there will be a fight;[41] if you drop a hairpin, you must not pick it up, or you will lose a fight; if you put a garment on inside out, you will have bad luck all day;[42] shoes placed upside down will cause an argument (Sephardic); and never mend anything that a mouse has chewed up.[43]

The financial fortunes of a family or of its members is naturally of great interest, and a family is greatly honored if one of its sons becomes a rabbi, a doctor, a dentist, or a lawyer. Jewish mothers are delighted to have their daughters marry into one of these honored professions. If a person happens to be financially successful, he prefers not to have anyone mention his success, or praise him for it, since this open admission may bring on a reversal of fortune.[44] When giving a wallet as a gift, see that there is some money in it. If you give someone something sharp, be sure that you get a penny in exchange so that a curse may not be communicated to the recipient.[45] A dream of silver indicates good luck, and a dream of paper money foretells bad luck.

Moving into a new house, traveling from place to place, visits, and news and communications of all kinds are little documented. In moving into a new house, the first things to bring in are bread, salt, and sugar (or sweets in one form or another).[46] These same items are taken by guests into the home of a friend on the occasion of their first visit. In this way, good luck will result for the family. A kitten walking into the house also brings good luck.[47] "One brings sweets to a house of mourning to offset sadness, and one brings sweets to a new home so that life there will be happy." Visits are indicated by the falling to the floor of cutlery, a fork for a man and a spoon for a woman (Sephardic).[48] When you set an extra place at the table unintentionally, a hungry guest will arrive. Scratching the

anus indicates an impending visit of bad company. Itching of
the right eye betokens good news, and of the left, bad.[49] On
setting out, be sure to step on the right foot first.

Beliefs concerning love, courtship, and marriage offer in-
sight into what has been called the second of the three main
events of human life, namely the seeking out of a mate and the
founding of one's own home.[50] A number of such beliefs have
been collected. Thus when your eyebrow itches, your sweet-
heart is talking about you;[51] and if a particle of food drops
from your plate, your lover is hungry. Don't sweep the floor
and sing at the same time, or you will marry a stammering
husband; and while you are sweeping, be sure to pick up
everything—otherwise you will marry a bald-headed man.

There are also, of course, certain customs pertaining to the
marriage ceremony itself. Parents who have married off their
last child are placed in the center of a circle formed by the
wedding guests, who sing and dance around the parents and
place garlands of flowers on their heads. The groom is supposed to lower his bride's facial veil before the ceremony
begins, and he places the ring on her right forefinger because
this finger has the most direct connection with the heart.
(The ring must not be cut—engraved?—in any way, nor may
it contain precious stones.) The glass which is stepped on
and broken by the groom is explained as being the last thing
broken in his life and his bride's (thus being equivalent to the
marriage bond itself[52]) or is a means of propitiating evil spirits
or, finally, is symbolic of the destruction of the Temple[53] and
the ever-present threat of sorrow, even in the face of great
joy.[54] Also, in certain parts of Europe a dish was often broken
on the occasion of the announcement of the betrothal.

Some additional beliefs pertaining to the wedding day and
the marriage itself may be mentioned. Once you have left your
home on your wedding day, do not return, for bad luck
awaits you. If either of the parties to a marriage becomes unfaithful, or if either wavers, the complaining mate should go

to a rabbi, who will fire a brick to red-hot intensity and say a prayer over it. This will renew the mate's initial ardor and cause him to return.[55] It is thought to be unhealthy for a husband to sleep in the same bed with his wife during her menses, and, according to a stricter view of things, cohabitation should not occur until after fourteen days following menstruation. The wife is "unclean" during this period of time.

There are only a few popular beliefs dealing with death and mortuary practice in the Los Angeles collection, a number entirely disproportionate to the interest in the subject in Jewish folk belief.[56] A dream of death, for instance, will add years to your life. If a member of an orthodox Jewish family walks around the house in his slippers, or in his bare feet, he invites death for a member of his family.[57] By way of variation, walking around with only one foot slippered and the other in a stocking will cause the death of your father or mother. Furthermore, if you walk in through the front of a house and out the back, there will be a funeral. Dying on the Sabbath, or on any other holy day, indicates that the deceased person has lived a righteous life; only the very holiest people, however, die on Yom Kippur, the most sacred of all Jewish holidays.

At a time of death all mirrors are covered with cloth.[58] Some people say that the mirrors should be covered for at least a week. Members of the family are barred from working or from any form of entertainment for a week. If work must be done in the household, it is usually done by the wife of the youngest son. In the older practices of mourning, "sitting *shivah*," the family of the deceased mourns for a whole week, without washing or shaving and without wearing shoes. There is also the related practice of wearing sackcloth, and rending one's garments.[59] (Today, however, the mourners attach commercially manufactured ribbons to their clothing instead of tearing it into fragments.) When a man dies, his wife sits on a backless stool for seven days and seven nights, wailing the while and refusing all comfort. Men, women, and children must be segregated in cemeteries, or, as one Jewish informant has indicated—perhaps incorrectly—in different cemeteries.[60] An ancient Yiddish superstition has it that the dead come out of their graves periodically to enjoy themselves, but there are probably very few people today who take this seriously. Three items reveal a belief in the connection between the living and the dead and contain notions of contagious magic. When you talk about a dead person and you sneeze, pull up on your right ear to chase away the evil spirits. To cause someone to become deathly sick and die, take an image of the person and bury it, face down, three feet in the ground. The converse of this practice is to bury fingernail clippings so that an effigy cannot be made.

Animal and plant lore is poorly represented; likewise, beliefs attaching to animal and plant husbandry. The paucity of material may be explained in part by the fact that the Jewish people traditionally have not followed agricultural pursuits. Tillage and herding in modern Israel are of too recent occurrence to have produced much folklore, and the scene of this activity is too far removed from the area studied to have produced traditional material. Whether in jest or not, it is said that to make a cat kosher, one should cut off its tail. To dream of fish is good luck, but it is bad luck to dream of trout. In the only item of weather lore in the collection, we learn that stepping on an ant will bring rain. It is taboo for a menstruating woman to plant flowers, or anything else, since the flowers will not thrive. A bit of "Wandering Jew" (a type of vine) growing in a bowl of water in the house will bring bad luck. At harvest time, when the first crop is gathered, there should be a blessing, and thoughtful people will leave one little corner of the crop unharvested in the field as a gift to the poor.[61]

Jewish religious lore is well represented in the collection, but many informants have only a sketchy knowledge of the rituals and their symbolic import. This lack of familiarity with traditional usages would seem to indicate some breakdown in the religious observances themselves.[62] During the Sabbath, which begins at sundown on Friday and ends at sundown on Saturday, the devout abstain from work of all kinds, take care to light no fires, to carry no money, nor to ride in any vehicles, except to go to the synagogue to pray.[63]

In an orthodox Jewish home, the Hebrew scriptures are rolled on a scroll. According to one (non-Jewish) informant the scrolls are fixed not only to the entrances but to the doors between rooms and must be kissed by anyone who passes them. This custom very likely has reference to the mezuzah, a small scroll including verses from Deuteronomy, vi, 4–9, and xi, 13–21. From Russian Jewish immigrants comes a description of a sacrificial ritual occurring on Rosh Hashannah, wherein a man takes a rooster to prayer and his wife a hen. At the conclusion of the praying, the fowls are killed and later eaten in a religious feast.[64] At Passover, Jewish homes are marked with sheep's blood, to commemorate the passing over of Israelitish homes by the angel of death during the period of bondage in Egypt. Only new dishes are used at Passover;[65] and the door is always left ajar for the entrance of Elijah, and food and drink kept in readiness for him.[66] This custom is widely observed among Los Angeles Jews. During the holiday of the Ninth of Ab, Jews are supposed to stay out of the ocean (or water), or they will drown. From the first of Ab to the 9th of Ab (the period commemorating the destruction of the Temple), evil spirits are in the water, and one should not swim at this time. When "the Cohens" (a religious sect whose members claim Aaron as an ancestor) are pronouncing their benediction in front of the Ark, to look at them three times in succession will cause blindness.[67]

In Jewish lore, Tuesdays and Fridays are lucky days,[68] and it is especially lucky to begin a venture on Tuesday. Thirteen is reputed to be a lucky number.

Notes

1. No completely reliable figures for the present Jewish population of Los Angeles are available, but a conservative estimate places the number at somewhere between 325,000 and 340,000. This figure is based on a statistical survey made in 1951 by Fred Massarik, whose estimate was 323,000 (*A Preview of the Greater Los Angeles Community* [Los Angeles, 1951], p. 4). I do not know whether this figure included approximately 7,000 Sephardic Jews living in the city. In addition to the older Jewish communities on the east side of Los Angeles, in the so-called Boyle Heights area, there are strongly populated areas of Jewish folk in the La Brea and Fairfax sections that have been rapidly building up over the past two decades. Latterly there has been a large Jewish influx into the San Fernando Valley.

2. A brief account of the Yiddish program, including the graduate course in Yiddish Linguistics, is contained in *News from Yivo*, No. 28 (New York, September, 1948).

3. The whole problem of the assimilation of other ethnic materials into Jewish folklore and folkways is admirably treated in Theodor H. Gaster, *The Holy and the Profane: The Evolution of Jewish Folkways* (New York, 1955).

4. Leibush Lehrer has contributed two excellent studies bearing on the psychology of Jewish life in America: "The Jewish Elements in the Psychology of the Jewish Child in America," *Yivo Annual of Jewish Social Science*, I (New York, 1946), 195–216; "The Dynamic Role of Jewish Symbols in the Psychology of the Jewish Child in America," *ibid.*, VI (1951), 37–72.

5. A most illuminating study of the changes in Jewish life in America is Abraham G. Duker's article, "Emerging Culture Patterns in American Jewish Life," *Publications of the American Jewish Historical Society*, XXXIX (1950), 351–88. See also the same author's study, "On Religious Trends in American Jewish Life," *Yivo Annual of Jewish Social Science*, IV (1949), 51–63; and Henry Loeblowitz Lennard, "Jewish Youth Appraising Jews and Jewishness," *ibid.*, II-III (1947–48), 262–81. A more broadly based study, thought to be some years out of date, is Arthur Ruppin's *The Jews in the Modern World* (London, 1934).

6. Nathan Hurvitz' article, "Jews and Jewishness in the Street

Rhymes of American Children," *Jewish Social Studies*, XVI (1954), 135-50, is based in part on field work in folklore done in Los Angeles, where he is engaged in Jewish recreational work. Work in Jewish folklore in other parts of the United States is getting under way, particularly in New York City; but, as is indicated by Charles Haywood's *A Bibliography of North American Folklore and Folksong* (New York, 1951), pp. 578 f., *passim*, only the barest start has been made.

7. Gaster, pp. 3-77.

8. *Handwörterbuch des deutschen Aberglaubens* (10 vols., Berlin, 1927-42), IV, 1381. (Hereafter abbreviated *HDA*.)

9. Cf. *Mitteilungen der Gesellschaft für jüdische Volkskunde*, I (1898), 90, where the reference is specifically to fingernails or toenails.

10. This belief is related to a widespread American folk belief that a pregnant woman's hanging up clothes, or becoming entangled in any way in a rope, will cause the umbilical cord to wrap around the unborn child's neck and strangle it.

11. Cf. the author's edition of the popular beliefs and superstitions in *The Frank C. Brown Collection of North Carolina Folklore* (5 vols.; Durham, N. C., 1952-58—VI-VII forthcoming), Nos. 97 ff., where further American references are cited. Hereafter this collection will be cited simply as Brown, with appropriate numbers. Items appearing in Brown are generally well known; moreover, it may be assumed that the particular item in question is "American" in a broad sense rather than specifically "Jewish."

12. Brown, No. 83.

13. Brown, Nos. 84 ff.

14. Cf. *HDA*, III, 729 f.

15. Brown, Nos. 181, 638.

16. Brown, Nos. 352 f.

17. Somewhere in Jewish folkloristic literature I have read of the custom of standing a young child on the floor and cutting a line in the floor between its legs as a means of starting the child to walk.

18. Gaster, pp. 33-38.

19. For a full discussion of the beliefs and customs of naming, see Leah Rachel Yoffie, "Popular Beliefs and Customs of the Yiddish-Speaking Jews of St. Louis, Mo.," *Journal of American Folklore*, XXXVIII (1925), 383 ff., especially 384.

20. This practice of changing names dates from the 12th century, at the latest, and perhaps earlier. See Richard Andree, *Zur Volkskunde der Juden* (Bielefeld und Leipzig, 1881), p. 181; and Angelo S. Rappoport, *Folklore of the Jews* (London, 1937), pp. 87, 90.

21. Cf. Rappoport, pp. 7, 75 f., for Jewish beliefs in the evil eye. The standard work on the subject is S. Seligmann, *Der böse Blick und Verwandtes* (2 vols.; Berlin, 1910); students not using German will find Frederick Thomas Elworthy's *The Evil Eye* (London, 1895) more than adequate. See also Edward S. Gifford, *The Evil Eye: Studies in the Folklore of Vision* (New York, 1958). For a discussion not only of the evil influences which beset the newborn child, but of its mother before delivery, see Gaster, pp. 18–32.

22. Rappoport describes this gesture as "to fig him" (cf. German *Feige*, "fig"). The gesture is made by advancing the thumb between the index and middle fingers, and the thumb is sometimes snapped in defiance of the person to be jinxed. Sometimes both hands are involved in the gesture (p. 76).

23. Red is generally effectual against witchcraft and evil influences, and pieces of red silk, red silk ribbons, etc., are worn.

24. This use of molten lead, which the Germans call *Bleigiessen*, is usually limited to divinatory practices, and its use to allay fright is somewhat exceptional. Cf. *HDA*, I, 1389 ff.

25. Sailors wear earrings (hence have their ears pierced) to cure sore eyes. See Brown, Nos. 1384 f.

26. Cf. Brown, No. 1359.

27. For the use of urine in folk medical practice, see *HDA*, III, 1481 ff.

28. Brown, No. 1896 ff.

29. Cf. Brown, No. 934.

30. This curious item suggests a possible connection with the belief that witches delight in using unbroken eggshells as boats. Several items in the *Brown Collection* dealing with headaches impinge on witchcraft, and there are references to these matters also in *HDA*, V, 231 ff.

31. A dead man's hand, sometimes called the "hand of glory," is believed not only to be efficacious in folk medicine but also to act as a charm for criminals. For its use in the cure of goiter, see *HDA*, V, 604.

32. For a treatment of Jewish slaughtering customs, see Andree, pp. 173–75. For a general discussion of Jewish dietary laws, see Gaster, pp. 199–214.

33. Undoubtedly the hind quarters are meant here. For a discussion of this, see Andree, p. 175.

34. Andree, p. 175.

35. Cf. Brown, No. 2819.

36. Cf. Brown, No. 2891.

37. This belief, though not specifically contained in the *Brown Col-*

lection, is nevertheless commonly known in the United States as well as throughout Europe.

38. For various beliefs and customs associated with bread, see *HDA*, I, 1590 ff.

39. Brown, Nos. 3287 ff., 3296.

40. For various beliefs about pins, see Brown Nos. 3309 ff.

41. Pointed instruments of all kinds must be treated with care, since they sever friendship. Cf. Brown, Nos. 3576 ff.

42. Brown, Nos. 3184 ff.

43. Cf. Brown, No. 3291.

44. Kindred ideas underly notions connected with the evil eye; often, in this connection, praise and well-wishing are believed to produce opposite results.

45. Cf. n. 42, above.

46. Cf. Brown, No. 2949.

47. For various beliefs about cats, see Brown, Nos. 7150 ff., 7394 ff., 2955 f.

48. Brown, Nos. 4003 ff.

49. Cf. Brown, Nos. 4079 ff.

50. Gaster, pp. 81–133.

51. Cf. Brown, No. 4156.

52. Cf. Andree, pp. 244 f.

53. *Ibid.*

54. Rappoport, p. 100.

55. Cf. Brown, Nos. 4870 f.

56. Gaster, pp. 137–95.

57. Cf. Brown, Nos. 4959 f.

58. Brown, Nos. 5414 ff.

59. For various customs connected with the *shivah,* see *Mitteilungen der Gesellschaft für jüdische Volkskunde,* I, 95 f.; and Gaster, pp. 149–55, especially p. 154.

60. These beliefs are not borne out by Jewish mortuary practice in Los Angeles. They may arise from old European practices that forbade women to accompany the male deceased to the cemetery. Cf. the *Mitteilungen, ibid.,* pp. 93 f.

61. For a cartographic representation of the prevalence of this custom in Germany, see *Atlas der deutschen Volkskunde* (5 portfolios; Leipzig, 1937–39), V, map 89.

62. Cf. the two articles by Duker, mentioned in n. 5, preceding.

63. These customs are still observed. Thus, my secretary knows a rabbi who habitually walks to the synagogue for Sabbath services.

64. Andree mentions this custom, but connects it rather with Yom Kippur (pp. 179 f.).

65. Many families keep ceremonial dishes for use only on this day; in this sense they are "new."

66. Rappoport, p. 268.

67. The "Cohens" are mentioned by two different informants in widely different connections. The reference may be mildly opprobrious, even though the material came from Jewish rather than Gentile students.

68. For a discussion of lucky and unlucky days, see *HDA*, III, 899 ff. (lucky days); VIII, 1427 ff. (unlucky days).

The Americanization

of Passover

BEATRICE S. WEINREICH

New York City

by Beatrice S. Weinreich

IN 1949 THE Cahan Folklore Club of the (Yivo) Institute for
Jewish Research embarked on a project of gathering ethnographic descriptions of the celebration of various Jewish holidays. It was then that the author's interest in the topic under
study was first aroused. As chairman of the group that prepared the questionnaire on Passover, the author helped adapt
an old question list (geared only to East European material)
that had been used by Yivo in the thirties;[1] analyzed descriptions of the holiday in various published sources; and interviewed a number of experts. The aim of the group was to
compile a worksheet that would elicit comparable data on
Passover customs as practiced (1) in the East European
shtetl ("small towns") at the end of the last century and the
beginning of the present century; (2) in the ghettos and concentration camps during the holocaust of World War II; (3)
in America and other countries of emigration.[2] About seventy
written replies to the Passover questionnaire were received.
Ten additional oral interviews were recorded by the present
writer. This material (now in the Yivo archives awaiting analysis[3]) is of intense interest for Jewish culture study, and its
American section in particular offers a fine opportunity for
analyzing culture change in process. We have an example here
of an ongoing transformation of culture patterns which can
be observed in slow motion.

The present article[4] is limited to a description and discussion of some of the more striking aspects of culture change that have come about in the celebration of Passover in this country among East European Jews and their descendants. The purpose here is not to synthesize the entire process of culture change involved in the Americanization of the holiday. Rather it is proposed merely to point out a number of interesting trends in the changes that have taken place in the last few decades. These changes will be considered from two points of view: (1) in terms of the urbanization of *shtetl* culture and (2) as a phenomenon of acculturation involving all Jews in the United States. It is hoped that this preliminary study may (in addition to having obvious implications for Jewish culture history) also contribute to the general body of knowledge about the effects that urbanization and acculturation have on the religious practices of minority groups.[5]

In investigating the transformation of Passover in America, an initial difficulty arises from the paucity of authentic historical records covering the main incidents of change. On the other hand, the changes are so recent that it is possible to ascertain many of them from interviews. The data for this paper were derived from an analysis of the thirty-nine answers to the third (American) part of the questionnaire, from personal observations of many Passover celebrations in the homes of descendants of East European Jews, and from oral interviews, newspaper reports, and several additional sources.[6]

Correct procedure in describing any type of culture change is, of course, to begin with a statement of the "pre-contact," or "pre-change," situation. In our case, this would involve a description of the dogma which goes into the Orthodox Haggada[7] and of the preparatory rites, as well as those of the Seder night, performed by an East European Jewish family of the late nineteenth century and early twentieth. The first of these tasks may be dispensed with because dogma is very well treated in standard sources.[8] The ritual aspect, on the other hand, has not fared so well at the hands of the describers. Thus, in describing Passover customs in Europe, Schauss— see note 6(b)—and Zborowski and Herzog—note 6(f)—do not cover the entire body of ritual to the satisfaction of the ethnographer. On the other hand, books like Gaster's—note 6(c) —in the field of comparative religion are even less complete, since their main concern is to trace similarities and differences between Jewish and non-Jewish customs and to hypothesize about origins, rather than to present an ethnographic description in full.

It might be argued that regional variation precludes any over-all description, but a review of the thirty-two elaborate answers to the questionnaire (Part I) on old-country customs and of various printed sources shows that geographic variation was a minor factor. Hence the general picture will hardly be distorted if from among the thirty-two answers one set is selected as the pre-contact statement. Of course, not every last detail of the case described is universal, but in general the elaborate character of the celebration and the great majority of details are entirely typical. The question of regional and individual variation, though it is, of course, a problem in its own right, lies beyond the scope of this paper.

Many of the changes in Jewish culture which are indicated in Part II (for Jewish emigrants) were paralleled at the same time among those who remained in Europe. The trends of urbanization and acculturation were causing such profound changes even in East European Jewish culture and society that, by 1939, the concept of *shtetl* culture[9] was hardly more than a historical abstraction based on a telescoping of a century of profound upheavals. On the other hand, there was probably enough uniformity in the culture left behind by at least the oldest emigrants to make the *shtetl* concept workable as a starting point for a study of cultural Americanization.

It is for a sample of *shtetl* culture in this limited sense and as an orientation point that we now proceed to a description of Passover in an East European town.

2. PASSOVER IN THE OLD COUNTRY

The Passover description that follows has never been published. As will readily be seen, it is much more than a mere repetition of *Shulkhon Orukh* prescriptions, or a listing of "exotic" customs. The application of the laws and the practice of the customs are shown in a real-life setting, reproducing the perspective in which they were seen by those who lived them. In this sense the description is more accurate than many previously published descriptions of the holiday.

The complete text of the original Yiddish manuscript (including several items for which there are no equivalents in the American material discussed in Sec. 3, "Passover in America," of this paper) has been translated in the informal style of the informant. It was felt that to publish the material in its entirety would demonstrate an important point, viz., the high degree of integration of the elements of the holiday with one another and with the patterns of year-round living in the old-country form of Passover, as contrasted with its American versions. This detailed description may, in addition, help others to find further changes in the American material which have escaped the present writer's attention.

Place: Síslevitsh (Russian Svisloč), a town in Grodno Province, containing (1897) a population of 3,099 persons, of whom 2,086 (about 400 families) were Jews.

Time: From about 1893 to 1921.

Informant: Abraham Ain,[10] born in Síslevitsh in 1888, left for the United States in 1921. (According to the Yivo Passover Questionnaire, Mr. Ain's information was recorded in June, 1949.)

2.1. Preparations for Passover

The first signs of preparation for Passover appeared as early as *Khanuke* [December], the season of fat geese, when many housewives stocked up on goose fat for Passover. Some prepared fat not only for themselves but also for sale—my mother, for example, who had a small food store. Around *Khanuke* my mother would order a *pood* [40 lbs.] of goose skins to be brought by stagecoach from Bialystok. When they arrived, she would bring down from the attic a large iron pot, the Passover salting board, and a Passover knife and spoon and begin to prepare the fat for frying. She would make the large tripod stove kosher by heating it. During these preparations, she would caution the children not to approach the fat with any *khomets* [leaven]. "Children, take care," she would say, "don't touch these Passover things with your *khomets* hands." Of an evening, as she worked on the fat, a Passover mood prevailed in the house. After the fat had been fried and strained, it was poured into glazed earthen jars, and my mother would sell it to her steady customers, who trusted her *kashres* [i.e., relied on her thoroughness in keeping her kitchen ritually clean].

After *Khanuke*, the flour traders began sending for flour, which was brought from Volhynia Province. The owners of matse* factories ordered wood, usually alder wood because it gives a hot flame but no sparks. In the month of *Shvat* [January–February] the owners of the matse factories began hiring workmen. There were five, and sometimes six, such factories in town. The seasonal employment rise created a festive mood in many families.

Before Purim the owners of the *podrádn* [matzoth factories] prepared the halls where the matse would be baked. All furniture was removed, and the walls were whitewashed. The boards on which the dough would be rolled were brought down from the attic and freshly planed. One table was fitted with a metal sheet for perforating the matse. All tools were made ready.

Baking began right after Purim. The flour dealer brought the flour to the *podrád*. Matse would be ordered by the *pood*, and the

* See note 7.

podrád owner would also pay the workers by the *pood*. Under an alternate arrangement, some wealthy customers would pay the *podrád* owner only for the use of his oven and would remunerate the workers for their labor directly.

Water for the matse dough was obtained on the previous night; and the mixture was strained and left overnight, covered with a white linen cloth. The baking itself began at four or five o'clock in the morning. The *mélshiter* [flour pourer], usually an adolescent, would put into a copper vessel enough flour for a *meyre* [measure] of ten *teyglekh* [pellets]. The kneader [*knéterke*] would knead the dough in this vessel, telling the water pourer [*váser-giser*], usually a child, how much water to add. When the *meyre* [measure] had been kneaded, it was given to the rollers [*vélgerins*], who would cut it into ten or more pellets, according to the number of rollers. If the dough were ready but the rollers were not, it would be given a preliminary rolling (so that it would not begin to ferment while waiting) until the rollers could cut it into pellets. Each pellet was rolled flat and put on the table of the *redler* [perforator], who made lines of perforations in each cake. Then the *shiber* [pusher] placed the matse in the oven. Care was taken to see that the dough never waited, but that it passed from hand to hand until it reached the oven.

After the kneading of each measure, the rollers had to inspect the boards and rolling pins to make sure that no dough had gotten stuck anywhere. Pieces of glass were used to scrape the wooden tools, and a steel brush was applied to the perforating wheel [*redl*]. A supervisor [*mashgiakh*] appointed by the rabbi went from *podrád* to *podrád*, checking to see that the procedures were kosher.

Baking continued from the early morning until ten or eleven at night. Several times a day the work was interrupted in order that the oven might be reheated. During these breaks the workers rested and ate their meals. The *podrád* workers were all Jewish, the rollers young women from the town's poor families. Although the work was hard and often lasted seventeen hours a day, the atmosphere in the *podrád* was always gay, and singing was frequent, except when the supervisor approached.

Most housewives wanted their matse baked early in the morning, at the first, or perhaps the second, heating of the oven. They felt that the workers were more rested in the morning and produced thinner matse. But since everybody could not be accommodated early in the morning, the privilege was extended only to the richer or more aristocratic customers. The richer customers used to tip the workers, five or ten kopeks to each roller and a little more to the perforator, the kneader, and the pusher. The workers knew which customers would tip them and made a special effort to produce thin matse for them. The baked matse would be placed by the pusher in a large basket and would then be carried in this basket, or in white sheets, to the customer's home, where it was put away in a closed box in the pantry or in a side room. During the baking the whole family of the customer was usually present: the women and the girls helped with the rolling, while the husband helped the perforator and kept an eye on "purity." Even the grown children tried to make themselves useful.

In addition to the private bakeries, there was also a community *podrád* where matse was baked for the poor families. The workers there worked almost entirely as volunteers. The organizer of the community *podrád* was Yoshke Grodzeynkes, a *klál-tuer* [community leader] active in the *Khevre Line* [Society to Provide Lodgings for Transients], the *Khevre Kadishe* [Society for Burials], *Hakhnosas Orkhim* [Society for Hospitality to Strangers], *Ezras Yesoymim* [Society to Aid Orphans], etc. Before Passover, Yoshke would rent a hall that had an oven, hire a kneader and a pusher, and organize the young men and women of the well-to-do families who had time to devote to the community *podrád*. Flour was bought with community council funds, and the *moes khitin* ["wheat money"] was donated by all the families. Some wood was purchased, and the rest donated. A cart was sent around from house to house, and every housewife contributed some wood; no one would have refused. The community baking lasted for about two weeks. When Yoshke asked a girl to come to the *podrád*, she would refuse only if she were ill.

This same Yoshke also saw to it that the poor had meat, wine, and the proper vegetables for Passover. These were given to the so-called "professional poor." For the newly impoverished (*yordim*) cash was provided (with a minimum of embarrassment) for whatever was needed.

On the day before Passover the baking was completed. House-wives used to say that if the matse is in the house, half of Passover is in the house, because fat and potatoes would have been prepared ahead of time.

Right after Purim some families pickled beets for the holiday. My grandmother used to pickle beets, and her daughter and daughters-in-law used to get some brine from her for borsht. If a poor neighbor asked for some brine, she also would get it.

2.2. Getting the house ready for Passover

Soon after Purim, the cleaning and whitewashing of houses be-gan. While some houses had papered walls, most of them had plaster walls and ceilings, which were freshly whitewashed before Passover. The double windows were removed with the coming of spring, and all the furniture was taken out of doors. Every house-hold had some books (at least a Bible, a set of prayer books, a *Khayey Odom* book of ritual, in Yiddish, and a Mishna); these were put on boards outdoors and opened to be aired in the wind. All clothing was also aired. Lime was bought at the store, and a whitewasher was hired. Some people would add a little blue paint to the lime and some glue to make it stick better, but the more pious said that glue was *khomets* and could not be added.

The furniture was washed and wiped before being taken back into the house. The women decorated the houses for Passover. Flowers and other ornaments were cut out of colored paper, or else paper flowers were bought at the store. The ornaments were placed on the shelves and lamps. Fresh curtains went up on the windows; the floors were scraped and washed, and all *khomets* food was kept in one corner of the house.

Everyone tried to have new clothes or shoes for the holiday. Thus, several weeks before Purim, one would go to the dry-goods store with one's tailor or seamstress. There the tailor would take one's measurements and explain how much material was needed, and of what kind. The ladies' tailors had journals which displayed a selection of dress styles from which one could make a choice. The tailor would be visited for several fittings. The shoemaker also took measurements, but he would furnish the leather himself.

For several weeks before Passover, the artisans (tailors, shoemakers), with their assistants and apprentices, worked up to seventeen or eighteen hours a day. Everything had to be ready before the holiday. The finished work would be delivered by an apprentice, who would get a tip.

On the day before Passover, copperware, metal cutlery, and also unpainted tables and chairs were made kosher. The metalware was put into a kettle of boiling water and two or three heated stones were thrown in to make the water boil even harder. Then the utensils were rinsed in cold water. Some people gave all their metal things to a coppersmith to be whitened.

Wooden objects were washed, scraped, scalded with boiling water, and then gone over with a glowing iron or hot stone and rinsed with cold water. New plates and glasses were put into a bucket and dipped in the well. This was called *tvile* [ritual submersion].

2.3. The day before Passover

On the evening before Passover, after the return from evening prayers at the synagogue, the search for leaven [*bdikas khomets*] was begun. Crumbs of bread were placed on window sills and in other visible parts of the house. The father, or the oldest member of a fatherless family, took a spoon (in which to collect the crumbs) and several large goose or hen feathers and went to look for the leaven with a candle in his hand, usually knowing in advance where the leaven had been placed. After the search was over, the spoon with the crumbs and the feathers were wrapped in a rag and put aside until the next morning, when they would be burned.

On the morning before Passover people arose very early. The women started to make the oven kosher, the stove was heated by spreading burning wood over it, the fowl was taken to the slaughterer to be killed, and the men went to pray.

Officially, the oldest son of the family had to fast, but there was an equally official way of avoiding this. Upon completing the study of one chapter of the Talmud, one is supposed to celebrate [*siyem*]. The learned son could arrange to finish studying a chapter on the day before Passover. Thus he had to celebrate with refreshments and was free of the commandment to fast. Another way of evading the commandment was to give something to charity.

At about eight o'clock in the morning breakfast was eaten— bread or a roll with milk and cheese. Breakfast was eaten in a corner, near a trough in which lay the bread, rolls, and other leavened foods that were left over. After the meal, the trough was taken out, and the house was completely ready for Passover. The men then went to sell the leavened food to the rabbi.

The boys took the spoons used in the leaven search of the previous evening to be burned. A bonfire was made in a garden, and the spoons and the crumbs, were burned there. The boys would shout in the streets: "Go and burn your leaven!" Care was taken not to let the fire die before everyone had burned his *khomets*.

[The leftover leaven was formally sold to the rabbi, and the rabbi would then formally sell the whole town's leftover *khomets* to a Gentile. After Passover everything would be "bought" back.]

After the leaven had been sold or burned, the Passover dishes and cooking utensils were taken down from the attic. The women washed everything and put things in place. The men attended to the crushing of matse for matse meal and *farfl* [larger crumbs]. This was done in a special wooden mortar. Only the most settled households had such mortars, and those that did not would borrow them from neighbors. The crushed matse was sifted; thus the meal was separated from the *farfl*.

Then the men went to the wine dealer to buy wine and mead. He would add some *kharoyses* [crushed nuts with wine]. Some housewives made their own mead for Passover. My grandmother told me that in the olden days people would make their own wine out of raisins, but this was no longer done in our day.

On the day before Passover, the father took his boys to the capmaker to buy new caps. The women were busy preparing the Passover meal and decorating the house. No matse was eaten before Passover. If a child were hungry, he would get a piece of potato pudding or some mashed potatoes with prunes. In the afternoon, everything was festive. When Shaye the Beadle was heard chanting in his baritone voice, "In shul arayn!" ("To the synagogue"), the stores were closed, the women blessed the candles, and the men, dressed in their new clothes, went to pray.

The coming of the holiday (which began in the synagogue at
evening prayers) was enjoyed most by the children, who would
show off their new things to one another. Even the poorest child
had at least one new thing—if not a suit, at least a cap.

2.4. The Passover meal

When the men and children returned from the synagogue, the
table was ready for the *Seyder*.* In the customary order, there
stood the plates of *karpas* [onion], *zroya* [chicken bone], *beytsim*
[hard boiled eggs], salt water, and *kharoyses*. Near each place stood
a glass. In the center of the table stood the cup of the Prophet
Elijah. Three matses covered with napkins, or placed in a special
mátsetash [matzoth bag] with three pockets, lay near the father's
place. The father's seat was the *hésebet*, consisting of several pillows on an armchair. In our house, during the *Seyder*, my father
sat in his ordinary attire, but my grandfather sat in a white *kitl*
[gown]. At a signal from my father, one of the boys who was already going to school said *kadish* [memorial prayer for the dead];
then *kidesh* [the festive blessing over wine] was said by my father
and all the men. The boy then asked the four questions, my father
answered, and the *hagode* [Passover service] was said up to the
point where one washes one's hands. The blessings were said over
the ceremonial dishes. Then the table was set for the meal itself.
The first dish was hard boiled eggs in fish sauce or salt water; then
came soup with matse *farfl* and maste balls. This was followed by
meat. It was our custom not to eat horseradish with meat until after
the *sdorim* [Passover festive meals], because horseradish, though
pleasant to eat with meat, was *moroyr* [i.e., symbolic of bitterness]
at the *sdorim*. Then we ate compote, and finally the *afikoymen*,
which had been kept under the pillows on father's seat. Sometimes
a child would "steal" the *afikoymen* in order to have it redeemed
for a present. After the *afikoymen* had been eaten, the blessing was
said, and the second part of the *hagode* was recited. At the point
of *shfoykh khamoskho* ["Pour Out Thy Wrath"], the mother or
one of the older children would open the door, to admit the
Prophet Elijah. The children would watch Elijah's cup to see if

* See note 7.

the amount of wine did not diminish by the prophet's sipping. The *Seyder* usually ended at about ten in the evening.

The Second *Seyder* on the following night, was celebrated in the same way, but it began and ended later, because during the holiday one is not permitted to cook from one day to the next. The soup and matse balls for the second *Seyder* were therefore not cooked until after the evening prayers.

2.5. Passover foods

On the first two and last two days of the holiday, one ate two meals a day: at eleven in the morning, after prayers, and in the evening after prayers. The meals consisted of fish or chopped liver (sometimes chopped onion with eggs and fat), soup with matse *farfl* and matse balls, meat, and *tsimes* [stewed vegetables or fruit]. In the intervening four days, a meat meal was eaten once a day; the other meals consisted of potatoes, potato pudding, borsht made of beet brine, matse *farfl* with milk (or matse balls), and hard-boiled or fried eggs. As a sweet dish, we made matse pancakes, which were called *pámpushkes*. Although the rabbis permitted the eating of herrings (provided they came from a newly opened barrel and were rinsed in water several times), few people ate them during the holiday.

2.6. Matse for Christians

Many Jews who had Gentile friends, neighbors, or business associates gave them matse. Some Christians (for example, village peasants) would simply come and ask for matse. To those in town, matse together with a bottle of wine or mead was sent as a gift. I had many occasions to take matse and wine or mead to our Christian friends or steady customers. I was always given a return gift of half a dozen or more eggs; this was called *hóstinets*.

2.7. The Middle Days

On the Middle Days of the holiday the shops of the tailors, carpenters, and shoemakers were closed, but the other stores remained open, and small traders did business with peasants in the market.

Normally, the butchers worked on the Middle Days because meat was needed for the holiday.

Since the weather was almost invariably good during Passover, people spent more time out of doors than at home. The streets were as noisy as they were during a fair. Teachers went from one family to the next to enroll children for the next term. Well-to-do house-wives engaged maids for the coming year while artisans made agreements with journeymen and apprentices. Matchmakers made matches, and prospective brides and grooms came to get acquainted. There were also many visitors from out of town. Since no one was working, people had time for visits. Our town was larger than the surrounding ones, and because of its leather factories there were many young men there. Girls from the surrounding towns would come in to meet them.

2.8. Customs and games

It was customary to give children walnuts and colored boiled eggs, which were called *valétshovnes*. These were given by parents and close relatives. The eggs were not to be colored with paint, because paint is *treyf* [ritually impure], and/or leaven; but they could be boiled with hay or onion skins and colored green or yel-low-brown, respectively. Incidentally, the pots used for cooking eggs—whether *valétshovnes* or any others—were not to be used for cooking anything else.

There were many nut games. One of them was *bretl*. A board [*bretl*] was leaned against the wall. At the bottom of the board was a heap of as many nuts as there were players. The nuts were heaped in the form of one of the *nekudes* [Hebrew vowel points]. The players would roll an iron ball down the board at the nuts. If the ball missed the nuts, the next player would try. If one hit the nuts, they were his. There were also such other games as *restl*, *eygl*, and *teler*.

3. PASSOVER IN AMERICA

Before turning to the analysis of the preceding Passover description, a few words ought to be said about the general framework of the culture-contact situation with which we are dealing in this paper. East European *shtetl* culture—literally, a "small-town" development—was rural in many respects. Thus the transportation of *shtetl* Jews into urban America involved the replacement of many rural traits by urban ones. On the other hand, ours is also a situation of what has been termed cross-cultural acculturation, in which "groups of individuals having different cultures come into continuous first-hand contact."[11] We shall be dealing then with *both* rural-urban and cross-cultural acculturation.[12]

In general, culture change has been classified into two categories: (a) change resulting from innovations which originate within a society, and (b) change stemming from without.[13] Whatever the type of change—be it the loss of an element, the substitution of a borrowed element for an older one, or the addition of a new, internally invented element—it will, of course, be taken for granted here that significant processes of *selection* and *reintegration* have been involved.

In studying the Americanization[14] of Passover, we have found it convenient to divide the material on culture change as follows:

3.1. External Change

3.11. Caused by mechanization and urbanization (rural-urban acculturation);

3.12. Resulting from adaptation to non-Jewish American holidays and themes (cross-cultural acculturation);

3.2. Internal Change (adaptations to internal historical events—e.g., the murder of six million Jews in World War II; the establishment of the State of Israel in 1948; a general trend toward secularization).

Students of culture change have found that "new traits are accepted primarily on the basis of two qualities, utility and compatibility. . . . Very often the advantages and disadvantages [of a new trait] . . . may seem desirable to certain members of the society and undesirable to others."[15] This is perhaps especially true in the case of stratified immigrant groups faced with complex urban cultures. Thus, the changes in the Passover celebration which were noted in the course of this study are not necessarily manifested by all East European Jews and their descendants. The degree of observance ranges widely from the extreme Orthodox (who continue their religious observance almost to the letter as they practiced it in the old country), to the fully "assimilated" (who practice no overt form of Judaism). It is with the large numbers who are somewhere between the extremes that we are mainly concerned here. Despite the differentiation noted, all of these are subject to similar tendencies toward change. For certain families, some of the changes mentioned will be in the "alternative"[16] stage, or still in active competition with older elements or groups of elements; for others, the innovations have been completely integrated into their new way of observing the holiday; still others may have decided a given innovation is not compatible with the spirit and the letter of the holiday and have rejected it.

3.11. External Change Caused by Mechanization and Urbanization

A. *Pre-Passover preparations*

It would seem that there is a tendency to replace by more "modern devices," or to drop completely, many of the preparatory customs that did not have symbolic meaning attached to them in the pre-contact stage, i.e. which were not explicitly related to dogma.[17]

1. In the *search for leaven*, or *bdikas khomets* (cf. sec. 2.3), which was traditionally carried out with candle and quill, a flashlight and brush (Questionnaire Reports 38, 43) are some-

times substituted. The tradition of the search is an ancient
one, and has a symbolic meaning, but the candle and quill
(the means by which the search is conducted) do not, and so
the substitution of more modern equipment is easily made.[18]

2. As shown in Sec. 2.2, it was customary in the old country
for a mother to take her childen to the tailor to be measuerd
for *new clothes* timed expressly for Passover. The preparations
would begin several weeks before Purim.[19] Urbanization,
coupled with the fact that tailored (as distinguished from
ready-made) clothes had no particular symbolic meaning,
have made it easy to replace the custom of visiting the tailor
with the practice of shopping (at a time much closer to the
date of Passover) in the stores of the city or town. It is interesting to note that of all the preparatory customs related to
Passover, this one seems to be the most universally practiced
in America. Among the thirty-nine persons who answered the
"American" part of the questionnaire, the custom of visiting
the tailor was the only one on which well-nigh all agreed. A
typical answer is the following (Questionnaire Report 30):
"I remember, as a child, that most of the Jewish boys in my
neighborhood would turn up in the street during Passover
dressed in their new finery. My mother would always buy me
a new suit." (Cf. this with the statement in Sec. 2.3 about the
children's pride in their new Passover clothes.) One of the
reasons for the tenacity of this custom is probably the indirect
reinforcement which it receives from the near-coincidence
of Passover with Easter, when Americans generally are in the
habit of buying new bonnets and clothes. An additional factor
helping to explain the persistence of this feature of Passover
is undoubtedly the coincident change of seasons from winter
to spring.

3. The ritual *scouring* of dishes, pots, and pans in order to
purify them for the holiday after year-round use was a major
preparatory ritual for the many households which possessed

no extra set of Passover dishes. In America, the higher standard of living, including the effects of mass production, make it possible for many more families to own special dishes and thus to dispense with the scouring. On the other hand, less observant Jews and the Reform Jews have often dispensed with the scouring even of their single sets of dishes, preferring to wash them thoroughly in hot sink water,[20] since they view the method of scouring prescribed by the *Shulkhon Orukh* as outmoded. It should be noted, in this connection, that the details of the cleansing process have no particular symbolic reference.

4. The custom of *whitewashing* houses before the holiday has, of course, disappeared in the cities. Replacing this is the custom of a thorough spring cleaning just before the holiday, often accompanied by a "paint job at least in the kitchen," as one informant has put it.

5. In the East European *shtetl* the collection of *moes-khitin* by door-to-door soliciting was part of the pre-Passover ritual. In American cities the tradition has been continued in radically new forms which utilize the newspapers and the radio. For example, the Yiddish press in the week preceding Passover in 1953 was full of appeals for contributions to various *moes-khitin* campaigns. Several New York *yeshives* (rabbinical schools) conducted their own advertising campaigns (see *Der Tog–Morgn-Zhurnal* for March 13, 17, 26, etc.). The newspapers appealed in their own names for contributions to the United Jewish Appeal. Contrary to general old-country practice, the funds are distributed far beyond, and indeed mostly beyond, the community in which they are collected. An example of a newspaper request follows:

In hundreds of communities this year, special *moes-khitin* committees were created which enrolled leading rabbis, presidents of congregations, and public leaders generally who cherish the tradition of *moes-khitin*. . . . The balance of the funds must be collected urgently if we want to prevent tens of thousands of Jews overseas and in the State of Israel from being left this Passover without matzoth.

Alarming requests have arrived this week from Jewish centers in Europe and North Africa to increase the quotas of the *moes-khitin* funds allocated to them. The leaders of these communities stress the fact that the number of needy Jews has recently increased considerably, so that more people will have to be provided with matzoth and other holiday foods this Passover. . . .[21]

As a matter of fact, the function of "matzoth for the poor" often recedes into the background, with many organizations using the term "moes-khitin campaign" merely to signify a general fund-raising campaign held during the month of Nisan (March-April). Since East European Jews were traditionally accustomed to give at this time of year, the month of Nisan is one of the best for soliciting funds for any purpose whatsoever. The term *moes-khitin* has thus come to have a new meaning in America.

B. *Production of Passover foods*

In Eastern Europe, as we have seen, part of the festival ritual was the preparation by the housewife of most of the foods necessary for the Seder and the holiday week. The preparation of some products (goose fat, borsht, etc.) was begun weeks in advance of the holiday. In American cities, on the other hand, dependence on the food industry (i.e., on out-of-the-home preparations) is so great that much of this part of the home ritual is gone; but the food industry itself makes allowances for Passover. This then is an example of the "reciprocal character of contact situations;"[22] the general American culture here makes certain adaptations to the holiday.

r. For most industries catering to Jews, the adaptation is

just a matter of getting rabbinical supervision and approval. Running through the advertisements in the Yiddish press of March 27 ff, 1953, we found that producers of such holiday favorites as gefilte fish, borsht, and wine, as well as of such everyday foods as salt, vegetable fat, milk, coffee, and frozen vegetables, used this method of assuring sales during the holiday season.

2. For some industries, Passover involves the production of a special food. This is the case for the entire matzoth and matzoth-product industry, as well as for the newly born Passover chocolate industry. In these industries the whole manufacturing process must be seasonally converted.

The process of baking matzoth was revolutionized with the invention of the matzoth machine, which came about a century ago.[23] "At first there was a great controversy about the *kashres* (ritual purity) of matzoth made with a machine. But technical progress scored a victory here as everywhere else."[24] In an advertisement in *Der Tog—Morgn-Zhurnal* of March 25, 1953 (p. 8), one matzoth company described the installation of a brand new matzoth machine and the celebration in its honor. It is of special interest that the matzoth manufacturers try to appeal to the most Orthodox by having on hand, during the baking process or for the installation of new machinery, some leaders of undisputed piety to participate with songs and chants, as they might have in the old country when baking matzoth.[25]

An indirect result of the mechanization of matzoth production was the coming into fashion of the square-shaped matzoth. In Eastern Europe the shape was generally round, since this was the natural form resulting from the rolling of spherical pellets of dough. In view of the fact that there was no symbolic meaning attached to the shape of the matzoth,[26] there has been little objection to the square shape, which "proved [to be] most convenient for machine-baked matzoth and

which is the predominant form in the United States."[27] (In
1942 "special V-shaped matzoth were baked as part of the
V-for-Victory movement."[28])

A new Passover-chocolate industry has arisen in America.
Previously only marmalade candy was permitted during the
holiday. The point is amplified in a note that appeared in *Der
Tog—Morgn-Zhurnal* for March 25, 1952:

In the Old Country candy producers were unable to keep the
whole process under control and to supervise the *kashres* of the
ingredients that went into the candy, since these were obtained
from various countries. . . . In America, however, the producer
finds all the necessary ingredients within the country, which enables him to produce chocolate candy kosher for Passover. . . .
Milk . . . is purchased from farms that produce kosher-for-Passover
dairy products. . . . The sugar that is used has the rabbinical stamp
of approval for Passover use. . . . Synthetic flavors to replace alcoholic fluids have been created by chemists working for the candy
company. The machinery used in the production of the chocolates
is scoured with hot steam in the manner prescribed by ritual under
the supervision of a group of rabbis. This combination of careful
supervision of the purchase of ingredients with the invention of
new synthetic ingredients and with absolute ritual cleanliness . . .
has enabled the producers to come out with a new Passover chocolate candy.[29]

3. Some industries stop the sale of their food to Jews in the
Passover week. Many bakeries in Jewish neighborhoods close
down for the holiday. One large food company (Heinz) that
ordinarily advertises in the Jewish press placed an advertisement during the pre-Passover week wishing its Jewish customers a happy holiday and advising them to put all products
of this company away under lock and key for the duration of
the holiday, since "our products are *not* for Passover use."
This was an effective way of gaining the public's trust in the
year-round *kashres* of the company's products.

Retailers as well as manufacturers make adaptations to Passover trade. Grocers in predominantly Jewish neighborhoods store away all non-Passover stocks and display only seasonal products. A large supermarket of the Grand Union type advertised (in *Der Tog–Morgn-Zhurnal*, March 19, 1953) that it was opening special "Passover departments."

C. Consumption of Passover food

From the point of view of the celebrants as consumers of Passover food, the changes wrought by urbanization and mechanization have also been substantial. In Eastern Europe, the baking of matzoth had been a family and community event (see Sec. 2.1). City conditions have put an end to this aspect of the celebration. On the other hand, in spite of the individualization that comes with urban life, some new quasi-customs have arisen around the purchase of food for the Passover celebration.

1. Placing the complete "Peysakh order" at one time with a particular Jewish grocer in the neighborhood is looked upon almost as a rite (Questionnaire Report 69).

2. Patronizing *particular* brands of matzoth and matzoth products has become traditional in many families (Questionnaire Report 58, 3a).

3. Purchasing Palestinian (now Israeli) wine, or special brands of American "Jewish" sweet wines, has achieved tradition status in some families (Questionnaire Report 63).

4. The variety of foods in use has been greatly increased. One of the results of urbanization is that people are more anxious for variety. This is reflected in Jewish cookbooks, which are generally potpourris of Jewish dishes from many regions, and which enable the housewife of East European background to add many West European Passover specialties to her repertory, and vice versa.[30]

5. Apparently as a result of the higher standard of living,

kharoyses is no longer as rare a delicacy as it once was. Whereas in the old country the wine dealer, the rabbi, or a generous rich man would distribute this nut-and-wine mixture in minute doses, almost anyone in America can afford to produce it at home.

6. Urbanization has generally loosened the mechanisms which make people custom-abiding and has weakened community sanctions. As a result, some Jews who in the old country would not have thought of breaking, or dared to break, tradition do not, in this country, stay on a leaven-free diet for the entire holiday week. They see fellow workers at their jobs eating the taboo foods, and these foods also stare at them from shops and restaurant windows. The "closed community" of the *shtetl* has been broken.

D. The Seder

There is little in the performance of the Seder in America that can be attributed to urbanization or mechanization (but see Sec. 3.23, following, on internal changes). Three minor points will be mentioned here.

1. *Dress.* In some families it has become customary to dress formally (tuxedo) on this occasion.[31]

2. *Photographing the Seder.* A custom unheard of in the old country is the photographing of the Seder ceremony. To the extent that it is practiced in America, it would seem to be a borrowing from the general urban banquet-custom of taking group pictures.

3. *Records, Radio, and Television.* After the Seder ceremony is over, it is customary in some homes to play records (appropriate Yiddish and Hebrew songs), to listen to the radio, or to watch television until bedtime (cf. Questionnaire Reports 30, 52, 58, *et al.*).

How widespread these three new customs are remains to be tested.

4. *Hotel Sedarim.* An interesting development of the urban custom of leaving town on a holiday is the country-hotel Seder. A brief review of *Der Tog–Morgn-Zhurnal* during the pre-holiday week (1953) reveals that scores of hotels in the Catskill Mountains and in Atlantic City, N. J., compete for this type of public, promising their clients a traditional Seder to be led by a renowned cantor. One advertisement ran as follows:

Our hotel is run on a strictly kosher basis. Everything has been ritually scoured [*gekashert*], so that even those of our guests who are extremely pious will be able to spend the Passover week here with a clear conscience. . . . We have obtained the services of the well-known cantor, X, who will conduct the Sedarim for us.[32]

A study of this type of communal (i.e., non-family) Seder is also needed.

3.12 External Change Caused by Adaptation of Non-Jewish American Holidays and Themes

a. Flowers and Gifts for the Housewife. Many East European Jews who did not present gifts to the housewife at home have adopted the general American (and, incidentally, West European) custom on Passover eve (e.g., Questionnaire Reports 9, 50, 55, 61, 62, 64).

b. Public Display of the Celebration. The development of Passover and other institutions should be viewed in the light of the acceptance atmosphere of the various minority groups in this country. Just as the non-Jewish American uses all the media of communication for the public display of festivals, so, too, does the Jew. In 1953 for the first time, there was a televised broadcast depicting the Seder ceremony (March 29, three P.M., Channel 11). On March 27, 1953, there was a special program of Passover chants (4:00 P.M., Channel 4). As for the radio, there have been special broadcasts in honor of Passover for years (e.g.,"The Eternal Light," the Sunday program of the Jewish Theological Seminary, etc.).

Also in line with this inclination toward public display are the Passover celebrations in the armed forces and in institutions such as hospitals, prisons, and the like. One of the informants (No. 54) has had extensive experience in conducting institutional Sedarim and furnishes a fairly good description. More information, however, is necessary for a full study of this American phenomenon.

c. Association of Passover with Easter. There is a vague tendency to associate Passover with Easter. In the words of Abraham G. Duker:[33]

[There is] a recent practice of joint celebrations of Passover and Easter in the schools. Featured as the observance of the festivals of freedom, the origin of the custom seems to date back to the present decade. . . . The use among [some] Jews of the term "Jewish Easter" for Passover is another example of Christian influence on the religious area.

d. Association of Passover With Freedom Ideals. Theodor Gaster has discussed the tendency to make the Passover festival "a celebration of freedom *tout court.*"

[There is a] current tendency to transmute the particular into terms of the general . . . , [of] propounding approximate equations. The Covenant of Sinai, for example, . . . is [called by] certain overzealous enthusiasts . . . a Hebrew Declaration of Independence . . . , Moses an Israelitic Lincoln.[34]

Sermons, radio broadcasts, magazine and newspaper articles, and schoolroom lectures have of late been emphasizing the theme that Passover celebrates a kind of freedom that is similar to, if not identical with, what all Americans celebrate on the

Fourth of July. Thus there seems to be a trend away from the Jewish holiday toward the universal elements, and, more specifically, a tendency to identify certain components of the dogma with American tradition.

e. *Change of Language.* Many of the Haggadoth printed in the United States are in both Hebrew and English, ranging from the Orthodox to the Reform Haggadoth. In some homes, even where the leader of the Seder recites the service in Hebrew, many participants read the Haggada in English. As for songs, it is interesting to list here as examples of English songs sung during and at the close of the Seder those that go into the *Revised* Reform Haggada: "America" (My country, 'tis of thee," p. 120), "The Springtide of the Year," "To Thee Above," and others. The Negro spiritual "Go Down, Moses" is considered by many an American Jewish child a Passover favorite.

f. *Invitation of Non-Jewish Friends to the Seder.* In Eastern Europe, though matzoth and other Passover foods were often given to non-Jewish neighbors, they were never invited to participate in the Seder ceremonies, which were considered a strictly religious and familial affair. In America (as might be expected from the identification of the holiday with American ideals of liberty) it is not uncommon among less observant Jews to invite non-Jewish friends to witness and participate in the "freedom celebration" (e.g., Questionnaire Reports 55, 64).

g. *New Passover Games.* It would make a fascinating study to record the various nut games that have appeared in America. A Philadelphia informant (Questionnaire Report 30) described two street games that combine elements of Passover old-country games (use of nuts) plus American formal elements. In one, "a nut is pitched at a coin—a penny or a nickel. If you hit the coin you get a point." This would seem to be an adaptation of the popular American street game of aiming a ball at a coin. The second was described as follows:

In another game we made use of an empty egg box. In each of the compartments we wrote a number from o to 10. Most of the compartments contained zeros and the lower numbers; only a very small portion had nines and tens. The owner of the box placed it against a wall, and all of the players stood about five paces away. One at a time each would try his luck at pitching a nut into a numbered compartment. All the nuts that did not get into any compartment, or went into zero partitions, were kept by the owner of the box. If, on the other hand, a nut fell into a numbered compartment, the owner of the box would "pay" the player that amount of nuts. The game lasted as long as the players and the owner had nuts to play with.

3.2. Internal Change

A. New Memorial Function of Passover

Ever since the murder of six million Jews in World II, a need has been felt by many Jews to amend the various Haggadoth to include a passage about this catastrophe, thus giving Passover an additional memorial function.

Monday evening, when we sit down to the first Seder night, we shall have two historic dates to remember. We shall remember that Pharoah, the King of the Egyptians, who wanted to destroy all Jewish men so that the Jewish people would not be able to survive; and we shall remember that Pharoah of our times, Hitler, "King of Germany," who sought to destroy Jews—men, women and children —so that not a remnant remain of them. . . . We have an entire Haggada about the trials and tribulations that Jews were subject to under the first Pharoah. Rufus Lazarus, the American-Jewish historian, has composed an addendum to the traditional Haggada in regard to the second Pharoah. This should become incorporated into the Seder ceremony and be said by every Jew before the passage, "Pour out thy wrath." . . . This year (1953) a committee of rabbis, learned men, and public leaders was organized to see to it that the new passage be brought into as many homes as possible.[35]

Changes are rarely made in the traditional Orthodox Haggada, but it seems that this addition may become a permanent feature of the Haggada in the future.

B. *The State of Israel and Passover*

It is perhaps too early to say what effects the establishment of the State of Israel has had on Passover customs in America, but its influence can be seen in the development of the Third Seder in Zionist circles [see below]. Also of interest in this connection are the new "Passover Tours to Israel," a type of secular pilgrimage which capitalizes on the fact that Passover was one of the three annual pilgrimage holidays.

C. *The Birth of a New Tradition: The Third Seder*

A new type of Passover celebration has developed in the United States during the past few decades—that of the Third Seder. A brief statement about its background is necessary since, unfortunately, there has been no study of this new phenomenon to date. The following is the author's own historical reconstruction, based on direct observation and interviews.[36]

That sector of East European immigrants which wanted to renounce the religious content of Judaism while retaining affiliation with Jewry on an ethnic-cultural basis (*véltlekhe yídishkayt*, "secular Judaism") was faced with the problem of what to retain and what to reject in Passover customs (as well as in other holidays). Many chose to continue the observance of Passover by staying home from work on these days, by recounting the historical parts of the Passover story, and finally by recalling (but without themselves practicing) the elaborate Passover celebration of the "less enlightened generations." Many also liked to partake of Passover foods, but as an addition to, rather than as a replacement of, the year-round diet. The Seder from this point of view appeared as a religious ritual difficult to secularize.

Many members of this group had had traditional religious upbringings in childhood, and it could probably be shown that some of them eventually missed experiences of a more religious type. After several decades of secularization, they sensed a desire for dogma which, under the pressure of world events in the 1930's and 1940's, turned into a strong wish to re-identify themselves in some measure with traditional Judaism. The wish to give their children a sense of belonging to the Jewish people was perhaps uppermost in their minds. It was extremely difficult, however, to force oneself to believe and practice what had already been renounced. The solution which many adopted was to re-institute part of the ritual. This modified ritual was to reflect the experiences of the secular period as well and therefore included, for example, the writings of modern Yiddish and Hebrew poets.

One feature of the movement toward a new ritual is that it evolved on an *organizational* rather than on an individual or familial basis. Thus it became possible to consider one's increased participation in the holiday as part of the general social and cultural activities to which one's particular organization was devoted. This, of course, fits in with the general urban trend in which the importance of organizational affiliation increases at the expense of familial ties.[37]

In connection with Passover, the manifestation of this urban trend was the institution of a Third Seder. Competition with the traditional two Sedarim (of familial provenience) is avoided, although there is no doubt that for some the Third Seder is the only Seder of the holiday. This Third Seder may be held in a school, a home, or the banquet hall of a hotel and may be celebrated during or immediately after the eight-day period of Passover celebration. Each organization sets its own ritual for conducting the Third Seder, and there is no attempt at standardization across organizational lines.

Thus, the historian of the Third Seder would have to describe the origin and evolution of this phenomenon separately for each of the organizations that practices it. In a sense, any attempt to work on the problem at this time would be a little premature. The documents pertaining to the Third Seder are still in the "live files" of the organizations in question, and the researcher, unless he has the good fortune to be an insider, is rarely allowed to look into them. (Also, these organizations have only a scant awareness of the historical interest of their activities). On the other hand, the very initiators of the Third Seder can still be interviewed (at least theoretically) by the researcher. After weeks of almost futile attempts to pursue the latter course, the author succeeded in obtaining a few basic facts relating to the development of the Third Seder of the Histadrut Campaign and of the Workmen's Circle. These findings are, of course, tentative and in need of confirmation and elaboration.[38]

In 1922 the Workmen's Circle had its first Third Seder in Clinton Hall, New York.[39] It was a small affair (its purpose almost entirely educational) consisting of a Passover celebration for the children attending the Workmen's Circle Jewish afternoon schools. As the number of people attending the Third Seder grew, the affair moved to Manhattan Center and finally to the Grand Ballroom of the Waldorf Astoria. It is no longer a celebration for children only; Jewish writers and cultural leaders, as well as students, teachers, and parents of students of the Workmen's Circle schools comprise the participants. In 1953 more than a thousand people attended. (The sheer number of people who participate in the organizational Third Seder is staggering when it is recalled that Passover was until fairly recently a *family* celebration.) The Third Seder has now assumed revenue and social functions, in addition to

the original educational function (although the latter ostensibly remains in the foreground, since the students of the
Workmen's Circle *Mitlshul*—supplementary high school—have
a large hand in the Seder ceremonies.)

The Workmen's Circle has been developing its own "New
Haggada,"[40] the latest edition of which was published in 1952.
The songs incorporated into it are the favorites of this particular fraternal order, as are the Yiddish poems recited by the
students. Some of the traditional Haggada material remains
intact, but in Yiddish translation (the four questions, for example). However, much has been discarded.[41]

The program of the Workmen's Circle Third Seder has
gradually begun to take the form of a set ritual, containing
many fixed ingredients. In addition to the reading of the "New
Haggada," there is usually an address by an educational official of the Workmen's Circle, and the guest artists—singers,
dancers, and an orchestra from the Jewish stage—perform
numbers appropriate to the holiday.

The Histadrut Third Seder has followed its own separate
line of development. The idea of celebrating a "Third" Seder
is said to have originated with Mr. Alter Boyman, an active
member of the labor Zionist movement. The first celebration
took place in his home town of Providence, Rhode Island, in
1927.[42] Five years later, a Histadrut Third Seder was held for
the first time in New York City (in Trotsky's Restaurant on
40th Street), mainly on the initiative of Hersh Ehrenreich.
According to one informant,[43] about two hundred people including members of the Labor Zionist movement and some
Jewish theater notables (Maurice Schwartz, Zvi Skuler, etc.)
were present. Although the meal served was of the traditional
Seder type, only portions of the traditional Haggada were
read. The program consisted of recitations and songs by the
guest artists and also of political addresses. Unlike the early
Workmen's Circle Seder, this Histadrut Seder was an experi-
ment in extending financial, cultural, and political activities,

rather than an educational affair. Similar sentiments for a return (in one degree or another) to tradition were certainly involved, but it was actually the adult members of the Labor Zionist movement (not the children of the Farband-Labor Zionist schools) who were in the limelight.

After 1948, when the State of Israel was established, the Third Seder celebrations developed great momentum in this Zionist movement. The Third Seder of the Histadrut was envisaged as a celebration of the "New Liberation" (*zman kheyruseynu*) and has since grown by leaps and bounds. In 1953 some four thousand people attended the celebration in New York City alone.[44] There was no ballroom large enough to accommodate the group, so two celebrations had to be carried on simultaneously, one in the Commodore Hotel and one in the Astor.

The programs of the Histadrut Third Seder have not taken any fixed form, but the following components are almost always present: the singing of the American national anthem and "Hatikva"; speeches (often by some prominent non-Jew such as James McDonald or Joseph Chapman); a play, performed by the school children of the Farband schools; and songs and recitations by noted Jewish artists.

In 1953 a special Haggada was published for the Histadrut and used at the Seder.[45] Whether or not this will become the fixed form for all future Third Sedarim of the Histadrut remains to be seen. It would be an interesting study to compare the Haggada of the Workmen's Circle with this Haggada, since each is a mixture of elements from the *true* Haggada, on the one hand, and poems and songs by modern writers, on the other.

In addition to the foregoing, smaller Third Sedarim have mushroomed in recent years and spread to such cities as Miami, Los Angeles, and Baltimore. The smaller celebration, adapted from the larger by schools and branches of the Workmen's Circle, the Farband, and the Sholom Aleichem Institute, is

closer to that of the family Seder. (Food, for example, is prepared not by a caterer but by the female members of the
group.) Of even greater interest, however, is the fact that the
Third Seder, a phenomenon born and nutured in the United
States, has spread to Mexico City and Havana and indeed to
most Latin American countries.[46]

4. CONCLUSION

It has often been shown by students of culture that religious
festivals change and develop in accordance with various modes
of life and periods of history. The late Hayim Schauss[47] has
thus given a concise view of the evolution of Passover:

1) a spring festival of shepherds
2) an agricultural festival
3) a historic holiday commemorating the Exodus
4) a national holiday (before the destruction of the first
Temple)
5) the greatest Jewish holiday (last century of the second
Temple)
6) the festival of Messianic hope (post second Temple)
7) the festival of fear (Middle Ages)
8) the family festival (the last few centuries)

In each historic period Schauss delineates changes in ritual and
dogma.

Passover has thus undergone many changes in its history. It
is questionable, however, whether this holiday has ever undergone so many changes in so short a time as it has in the hands
of immigrants and their descendants in this country during
the last half century.

The study of American Jewish religious customs is made
rather complicated by the highly stratified nature of both
groups in contact and by the uneven pre-contact background
of the members of the Jewish group. We must therefore recall

the limitations and qualifications set forth earlier in this paper.

The Americanization of Passover should eventually be studied in the context of the breakdown of a relatively self-sufficient Jewish society into a number of subgroups of American society, which nevertheless are associated by certain bonds, tenuous though they be. In the case of Passover, this process is manifested at present in the atomization of the holiday—as of other elements of the religion and culture—into an indeterminate variety of celebration forms. On the other hand, one also finds that the Jewish immigrants and their descendants, regardless of their subgroup allegiance, make use of American institutions (e.g., industry and mass media) to serve the celebration of Passover in new ways.

To a cultural anthropologist the following observations suggest themselves on the relation of dogma to ritual in a situation of intense culture change. First, elements of religious ritual are highly tangible and therefore quite subject to culture change, despite the generally assumed conservatism of religion in culture-contact situations. Furthermore, in our study, we have seen that it might be important to distinguish, among the elements of ritual, between those that have explicit symbolic meaning and those that do not. For example, the horseradish eaten during the First Seder symbolizes the bitterness of the Hebrews' enslavement in Egypt, and the unleavened matzoth is a symbol of the hurried exit from Egypt. On the other hand, there is no symbolic reference to dogma in the nut games or in the purchase of new clothes or in the use of borsht during the Second Seder. As far as our evidence goes, it seems that, other things being equal, the ritual items endowed with symbolic reference change less easily than others.

Dogma and ritual may change independently and at different rates of speed. We have seen that in some cases (e.g. language change or the introduction of the custom of having flowers at the Seder table) ritual may change while the dogma remains unaffected. The reverse has also been observed, as in the association of the Passover myth with the anachronistic theme of political liberty.

The development of the Third Seder is an interesting illustration of the "de-dogmatizing" of a religious holiday, plus the selection of certain formal elements of traditional ritual (the use of *a* Haggada) coupled with the invention of new ritual. In this development we see very clearly reflected the situation of those Jews who, though continuing to renounce the intellectual and practical (or instrumental) aspects of the Jewish religion, seem to feel a need for some of its emotional content.

Notes

1. *Etnografishe Anketes* (Ethnographic Questionnaires), Yiddish Scientific Institute—Yivo (Vilna, 1928); especially No. 1, *Yontoyvim* (Holidays), pp. 10–13.

2. Mr. Abraham G. Duker, who has frequently written about Jewish customs in America, was extremely helpful in setting up this part of the questionnaire.

3. A preliminary report on the replies to the questionnaire was published in *News of the Yivo*, No. 34, Sept., 1949, pp. 6, 6*.

4. This paper was originally written in 1953 in connection with a course given at Columbia University. In a number of notes to section 3.23, material from more recent newspaper sources has been added.

5. Anthropologists have been showing increasing concern with ethnic minorities in urban centers. Thus, Ralph Beals in "Urbanism, Urbanization and Acculturation," *American Anthropologist*, LIII (1951), 6, has called attention to the fact that "within urban areas . . ., characterized by rapid growth produced mainly by immigration and including a wide variety of ethnic minorities, we . . . [can] find abundant material for studies which . . . relate to acculturation."

6. For example: (a) Albert I. Gordon, *Jews in Transition* (Minneapolis, 1949), pp. 106–10; (b) Hayim Schauss, *The Jewish Festivals* (Cincinnati, 1938), chapters v–ix; (c) Theodor Herzl Gaster, *Passover, Its History and Traditions* (New York, 1949); (d) T. H. Gaster,

"What Does The Seder Celebrate?" *Commentary* (April, 1951), pp. 312–18; (e) Avish Dworkin, "Matsa A La Mode," *Furrows*, IX (April–May, 1952), pp. 22–25; (f) Mark Zborowski and Elizabeth Herzog, *Life Is with People* (New York, 1952), pp. 382–90.

7. Generally all Yiddish and Hebrew terms will be rendered according to their Yiddish rather than their Hebrew pronunciation, in conformity with the widely accepted Yivo rules for transliteration. Exceptions to this have been made for words like Haggada, Seder, Hanukka, and matzoth, which have been rendered in their usual English spelling, but in Sec. 2, for the purposes of ethnographic exactness, the Yiddish forms have been retained for all terms, including these. The accent falls on the penultimate syllable unless otherwise marked.

8. For example, "Seder," in *The Universal Jewish Encyclopedia* (New York, 1942), IX, 453 ff.

9. Familiarized recently by the anthropologists Zborowski and Herzog, *op. cit.*

10. The same informant is the author of "Swislocz: Portrait of a Jewish Community in Eastern Europe," *Yivo Annual of Jewish Social Science*, IV (1949), 86–114; originally published in Yiddish in *Yivo Bleter*, XXIV (1944) and XXV (1945). This article, as well as other contributions to the Yivo collections of primary source materials, have established Mr. Ain's excellence as an informant.

11. This is part of the traditional anthropological definition of acculturation by Redfield, Linton, and Herskovits in "Memorandum on the Study of Acculturation," *American Anthropologist*, XXXVIII (1936), 149.

12. Beals has advanced the hypothesis that rural-urban acculturation and cross-cultural acculturation differ only in degree and do not represent substantially different processes of change. It is noteworthy that in the case under study simultaneous processes of both types of acculturation are involved. (See Beals, *op cit.*, p. 6.)

13. Melville J. Herskovits, *Man and His Works* (New York, 1951), p. 492.

14. By "Americanization" is meant culture change that occurred *in* America—whether this be borrowing from the American culture, loss of old traits, or new inventions from within the Jewish community itself.

15. Ralph Linton, *The Study of Man* (New York, 1936), p. 341.

16. *Loc. cit.*

17. Although this hypothesis is suggested by some of the material, its complete proof awaits further investigation.

18. Reform Judaism has dropped this ritual completely. See p. 142 of the *Union Haggada*, rev. (Central Conference of American Rabbis, Cincinnati, 1923).

19. See also Zborowski and Herzog, *op. cit.*, p. 382, for a description of the importance of this custom.

20. "Reform Judaism does not consider this practise essential to the proper observance of Passover"—*Union Haggada*, p. 142.

21. Translated from the Yiddish, *Der Tog—Morgn-Zhurnal* (March 13, 1953).

22. Ralph Beals, "Acculturation," in *Anthropology Today*, A. L. Kroeber, ed. (Chicago, 1953), p. 628.

23. See Hyman B. Grinstein, *The Rise of the Jewish Community of New York, 1654–1860* (Philadelphia, 1945), pp. 306–12.

24. Schauss, *op. cit.*, p. 78.

25. See, for example, *Der Tog—Morgn-Zhurnal* (April 1, 1954), p. 8.

26. The shapes of some Jewish foods do have symbolic meaning. On Rosh Hashona, for example, round loaves of khale are eaten to symbolize happiness for "all the year round" (Yiddish: *a káylekhdik yor*).

27. *Universal Jewish Encyclopedia*, VII, 414.

28. *Loc. cit.*

29. P. Rubenstein, "Far vos me kon itst krign a groysn oysval fun peysakhdike kendis" ["Why It Is Now Possible to Obtain a Wide Variety of Passover Candies"], *Der Tog—Morgn-Zhurnal* (March 25, 1952), p. 9; translated from the Yiddish.

30. See, for example, Mildred Grosberg Bellin, *The Jewish Cookbook* (New York, 1948), pp. 360–82; or Betty D. Greenberg and Althea O. Silverman, *The Jewish Home Beautiful* (New York, 1941), pp. 109–17.

31. See the photograph in the *Universal Jewish Encyclopedia*, IX, 455; also Questionnaire Report 50.

32. *Der Tog—Morgn-Zhurnal* (March 19, 1953).

33. Abraham G. Duker, "On Religious Trends in American Jewish Life," *Yivo Annual of Jewish Social Science*, IV (1949), 55.

34. T. H. Gaster, "What Does the Seder Celebrate?" *Commentary* (April, 1951), p. 314.

35. S. Dingol, "Di vokh in yidishn lebn" [This Week in Jewish Life], *Der Tog—Morgn-Zhurnal*, (March 28, 1953), p. 7; translated from the Yiddish.

36. This section on the Third Seder, as well as the remainder of the article, was written in 1953 (see n. 4). In the spring of 1954 Jacob

Glatshteyn, who writes a column entitled "Prost un Poshet" for *Der Tog—Morgn-Zhurnal*, devoted portions of four of his columns (April 18, 30; May 14, 28) to the Third Seder and particularly to letters which he received from persons claiming to have originated the institution. These were written in reply to a provocative column in which he invited readers to help clear up its history. The material presents some good leads, but the history of the institution is still to be written.

37. Cf. Louis Wirth, "The Urban Society and Civilization," *American Journal of Sociology*, XLV (1939-40), 753: "[In urban society] . . . instead of kinship and tradition, interest and ideology come to serve as cement that binds human individuals into effectively working groups. Relationships between men tend to be depersonalized so that no one literally counts in the city except as his voice speaks for an organized group." On p. 752 he writes: "The anomalous situation symbolic of urban life consists in the presence of close physical proximity coupled with vast social distances of men. This has profoundly altered the basis of human association and has subjected the traits of human nature as molded by simpler social organizations to severe strain."

38. Some of the letters received by Glatshteyn (n. 36) were from people interviewed by the present writer in 1953; Glatshteyn's findings regarding the Histadrut Third Seder completely corroborated our own. In addition, he learned of a few more apparently independent "first" Third Sedarim which occurred in: (a) the Volhynia Branch of the Farband-Labor Zionist Order in Philadelphia in 1919; (b) the Arbeter-Ring-Klub (ARK) in Boston in 1923. He also reports that a special Seder was organized by the Central Committee of the Labor Zionist Organization for Jewish legionnaires en route to Palestine in 1917. Finally, a letter to the editor published in the column "A tribune farn folk" in *Der Tog—Morgn-Zhurnal* (May 27, 1954), advises that in 1930 the National Fund Council of Cleveland celebrated a "first" Third Seder (of the fund-raising type) on one of the Middle Days of Passover. All of this new information leads one to the conclusion that a very definite *need* for this type of celebration was in the air and that such celebrations occurred quite independently in different cities at different times. I believe, however, that it was only after the central bodies of the Histadrut and the Workmen's Circle in New York adopted this form of celebration that it began to spread like wildfire to the smaller branches of these organizations and became an enduring custom.

39. The following information has been offered by Mr. Mendl Elkin, Yivo librarian, who was kind enough to get in touch with some of the

leaders of the Workmen's Circle. All attempts on my own part to confirm and elaborate this information by direct contact with the educational director of the Workmen's Circle have thus far proved fruitless.

40. *A naye hagode shel peysakh* ["A New Passover Haggada"], Education Committee of the Workmen's Circle (New York, 1952).

41. It is interesting to note that now and then protests are raised in the Yiddish press that the "New Haggada" has already become too rigid. It is felt that it should be changed "a little" from year to year and constantly regeared to new circumstances. See, for example, F. Vayn's article on the Workmen's Circle Third Seder in the April 25, 1954, issue of *Der Tog—Morgn-Zhurnal*, p. 3. It is characteristic of *véltlekhe yidishkayt* that rigidity is suspect.

42. This information was given to me in May, 1953, by Mr. M. Kochansky, a public-relations officer of the Histadrut. In a letter to J. Glatshteyn in *Der Tog—Morgn-Zhurnal* (May 14, 1954), p. 4, Mr. Henry Burt is also credited with the idea of celebrating a "Third" Seder.

43. Mr. Samuel Bonchik, of the Labor Zionist Organization of America, also attended this "first" Third Seder. The information quoted was given to me by him in a telephone conversation in May, 1953. It was later confirmed in a letter that I received on November 24, 1953, from the secretary to Mr. Isaac Hamlin, National Secretary of the Israel Histadrut Campaign.

44. Mr. Kochansky (see n. 42) was the source of this information.

45. *Hagode shel peysakh farn dritn seyder* ["Passover Haggada for the Third Seder"], New York Histadrut Campaign (New York, n.d.).

46. Mr. Kochansky (see n. 42) informed me that the Histadrut Campaign has had Third Sedarim in Mexico, Cuba, Venezuela, and other South American countries.

47. Schauss, *op. cit.*, pp. 38–76.

Index